PRAISE FOR GLENN GREENWALD AND

Great American Hypocrites

"Glenn Greenwald has done it again. . . . Another great book.
From the myth that John Wayne was a great American hero (he
was a WWII draft dodger), to how the media perpetuates false
images of right-wingers (so much for the "liberal media"), to the
so-called "wholesome, family men" who tried to push Bill Clinton from office while they were courting their own mistresses
and divorcing their first and second wives for the younger
women they were boinking, to the falsehood that Republicans
bring us smaller government, Glenn lays it out beautifully."

> —Alan Colmes, *Hannity & Colmes*

"Glenn Greenwald is an angry blogger. Fortunately for us, he's
also intelligent, insightful, and on our side. . . . Glenn must have
donned an asbestos suit for this one. . . . [His] argument is
strongest and sharpest in his dissection of our political press
and how they are played, time and time again, to collude with
this myth-making to draw false contrasts between opposing
candidates."

> —Daily Kos

"Glenn Greenwald is ᵃ ꞏ   ɔt love a book
like *Great Ameri*   e by decimat-
ing the myth of ⌐   ? Greenwald
doesn't try to be d   ...ıı steaming as he
pens his columns,   ...ırough clearly in this book
of new ammunition.

> —BuzzFlash

"Those who ignore what Greenwald has to say act at our collective peril."

> —John W. Dean, former Nixon White House
> counsel and author of *Conservatives Without Conscience*

"Fast-paced and unapologetically biased, *Hypocrites* previews some progressive talking points we just may be hearing in the months ahead." —*Campaigns & Elections' Politics* magazine

"I rely on Glenn Greenwald, above all, for understanding the assaults on the Constitution by this administration, and for pointing the way toward regaining a republic. There's no one whose work has impressed me more."

—Daniel Ellsberg, author of
The Pentagon Papers

"This book is written with such vicious joy that it is just really fun to read. . . . I'm always amazed by the clarity of [Greenwald's] writing and his ability to indict the conservative mindset with well-articulated factual patterns."

—Matt Stoller, cofounder of OpenLeft

"The peerless Glenn Greenwald."

—Josh Marshall, founder of
Talking Points Memo

"One of the best political commentators out there . . . Unlike most other bloggers, Greenwald practices journalism. . . . Few others are better than Greenwald at sussing out the accidental propaganda inflicted on us by the mainstream press."

—*Village Voice*

"Perhaps the most influential civil-liberties writer on the Web."
—*The American Prospect*

"Blogosphere superstar." —*Mother Jones*

"Among the most intelligent and widely read practitioners of blogging."

—*GQ*

"It's not the hypocrisy, stupid—it's the reason behind the hypocrisy of right-wing moral rectitude that's the focus of *New York Times* bestselling author Glenn Greenwald. . . . A most timely book. Right-wing leaders are inflated into heroic cultural icons, while Democrats are demonized as weak and hapless losers. These personality-based myths overwhelm substantive discussions and consideration of the issues. That's [Greenwald's] case in a nutshell, and the rest of his book is devoted to proving it, in agonizing and often embarrassing detail."

—Random Lengths

GREAT AMERICAN HYPOCRITES

GREAT AMERICAN HYPOCRITES

TOPPLING THE BIG MYTHS OF REPUBLICAN POLITICS

GLENN GREENWALD

THREE RIVERS PRESS
NEW YORK

Copyright © 2008 by DMDM Enterprises, LLC

All rights reserved.

Published in the United States by Three Rivers Press, an imprint of the Crown
Publishing Group, a division of Random House, Inc., New York.

www.crownpublishing.com

Three Rivers Press and the Tugboat design are registered trademarks
of Random House, Inc.

Originally published in hardcover in the United States by Crown Publishers,
an imprint of the Crown Publishing Group, a division of Random House, Inc.,
New York, in 2008.

Library of Congress Cataloging-in-Publication Data
Greenwald, Glenn.
Great American hypocrites : toppling the big myths of
Republican politics / Glenn Greenwald.—1st ed.
p. cm.
Includes index.
1. Republican Party (U.S. : 1854–)   2. United States—Politics
and government—2001–   I. Title

JK2356.G73 2008
324.2734—dc22   2008009179

ISBN 978-0-307-40866-2

Printed in the United States of America

Design by Leonard W. Henderson

10 9 8 7 6 5 4 3 2

First Paperback Edition

CONTENTS

GREAT AMERICAN HYPOCRITES

PREFACE

For the past three decades, American politics has been driven by a bizarre anomaly. Polls continuously show that on almost every issue, Americans vastly prefer the policies of the Democratic Party to those of the Republican Party. Yet during that time, the Republicans have won the majority of elections. This book examines how and why that has happened.

The most important factor, by far, is that the Republican Party employs the same set of personality smears and mythical, psychological, and cultural images to win elections. These myths and smears are amplified by the right-wing noise machine and mindlessly adopted and recited by the establishment media. Right-wing leaders are inflated into heroic cultural icons, while Democrats are demonized as weak and hapless losers. These personality-based myths overwhelm substantive discussions and consideration of the issues.

Time and again, Americans vote Republican due to their perceptions that right-wing leaders exude such admirable personality traits as courage, conviction, strength, wholesome family morality, identification with the "regular guy," an affection for the military, fiscal restraint, and a belief in the supremacy of the individual over the government. Ronald Reagan, the wholesome "Everyman" rancher, and George W. Bush, the swaggering, conquering cowboy, rode to victory on the basis of the cartoon imagery and marketing themes that defined them.

Liberals and Democrats generally are relentlessly depicted as the opposite. Liberals are weak, irresolute, anti-military, elitist, effete, amoral, sexually deviant, profligate, and antagonistic to the values of "Real Americans." Democratic males specifically are soft, sissified, effeminate losers ("faggots," in the formulation of wildly popular right-wing author Ann Coulter), while liberal women are threatening, emasculating, icy, frigid, gender-confused, dyke-ish shrews (Rush Limbaugh: "I mean, where are the real men in the Democratic Party? Where are the real men? Hillary Clinton's one of them, but where are the others?").

It would be bad enough if these cultural themes were actually true. The argument would still be compelling that such themes are petty and manipulative and engender a corrupted and shallow political process. But if such imagery were real, it could at least be said that Americans decide their elections based on rational assessments of personality attributes rather than issues.

But these GOP marketing packages are complete fabrications. They bear no relationship to reality. Across the board, the leading heroes of the right wing who trumpet courageous masculine values and traditional morality exude exactly the opposite in reality. From Fred Thompson, Rudy Giuliani, Mitt Romney, to Newt Gingrich, Rush Limbaugh, Bill Kristol, Sean Hannity, and the rest of the right-wing noise machine—to say nothing of the likes of George Bush and Dick Cheney—those who playact as powerful Tough Guys and anti-Terrorist Warriors and Crusaders for the Values Voters have lives filled with weakness, fear, unbridled hedonism, unearned privilege, sheltered insulation, and none of the "Traditional Masculine Virtues" they endlessly tout.

Yet the myth of the plainspoken, honor-bound, courageous Republican man of the people persists. Throughout 2007, these themes were aggressively applied in order to dress up the most likely GOP presidential nominees into fictitious archetypes of the Strong, Courageous, and Moral Warrior even though those individuals practically never displayed any of those virtues in their actual lives. But these deceitful caricatures have worked, and it is long past the time to expose and stop them.

This rank mythmaking and exploitation of cultural, gender, and psychological themes had its roots in the transformation of actor Ronald Reagan into a John Wayne–archetype cowboy who alone had the courage to stand tall against the Soviet Empire. Combat-avoiding George Bush—who spent his entire life wallowing in privileged, sheltered hedonism—became the swaggering, brush-clearing, fighter-pilot warrior whose courage and masculine toughness we needed to protect us from the Terrorists.

Both of Bush's opponents in the past two presidential elections—Al Gore and John Kerry—volunteered to go to Vietnam; yet each lost the election because they were portrayed as effeminate, soft, elitist cowards. In 2000, Gore was controlled by the emasculating feminist Naomi Wolf and, in Maureen Dowd's formulation, he was "practically lactating," whereas in 2004, Kerry was dominated by his rich foreign wife and was an effete, windsurfing French pansy.

That Bush's and Cheney's lives were completely devoid of any acts of authentic courage or toughness or the traditional masculine and moral virtues mattered not at all. These manipulative psychological and cultural marketing tactics of the Republican slime machine rolled over reality and infected the entire media narrative, as it has continuously for years. Millions of Americans who oppose the defining Republican beliefs nonetheless voted for Bush and Cheney because the character mythology that was created of the Upstanding Tough Guy versus the Sniveling Loser—drawn directly from American entertainment and marketing methods—easily overwhelmed issues of substance.

Most infuriating is that GOP leaders who dress up in the costumes of the heroic icons are engaged in pure deceit. In fact, the playacting is *more important,* more valued, than the reality. The handful of political figures who actually do have lives that exhibit these qualities of warrior courage—John McCain and Chuck Hagel and Jack Murtha and Wes Clark and John Kerry—end up being rejected and despised by the hard-right base. Democratic politicians such as Nancy Pelosi who have been married to the same person their entire lives and have raised large and healthy families are demonized for having "decadent San Francisco values." And those accusations are voiced by right-wing moralists sitting next to their third wives obtained during an adulterous affair or on their way home from a Viagra-fueled weekend jaunt to Carribean islands.

The sheer pervasiveness of this political deceit is somewhat new, but the deceit itself goes back decades. As examined in **Chapter One,** one of the earliest pioneers of this manipulative right-wing marketing was John Wayne. Wayne was a draft dodger during World War II, staying at home in Hollywood, getting rich by playacting as a war hero in one film after the next while his acting peers were off fighting in combat. Wayne then spent the rest of his life preening around as a swaggering, über-patriotic tough guy—cheering for one war after another and viciously castigating war opponents as cowards and subversives.

With the enormous gap between his self-righteous moralizing rhetoric and the way he actually lived his life, John Wayne proved himself to be one of the first right-wing Great American Hypocrites. He tirelessly crusaded for wholesome American morals and publicly condemned any perceived deviations. Yet Wayne's personal life was a never-ending carousel of adultery, divorces, new wives, shattered families, pills, booze, and unrestrained hedonism.

Wayne was the true precursor to the Republican Party of Rush Limbaugh, Newt Gingrich, George W. Bush, Dick Cheney, and all the various and sundry leaders of the Clinton sex witch hunts of the 1990s. The more acts of cowardice in Wayne's life, the greater his compulsion to cheer on wars to show his masculine courage. And the more unbridled hedonism he wallowed in, the more self-righteous became his public moralizing. John Wayne is often held up as the model of the right-wing male leader, and he is—though not for the reasons they would like to believe. In the realm of reality, rather than image, today's Republican Party is, in every respect, the party of John Wayne.

These manipulative fictions could never succeed without the active help of the establishment media. And as demonstrated in **Chapter Two,** the media does far more than merely help to perpetuate these images. Far beyond that, its political coverage is dominated by the personality-based attacks cooked up by the right-wing noise machine during election time.

Discussions of political candidates in the establishment press are driven primarily by these personality caricatures. These vapid depictions completely drown out any examination of substantive issues, the candidates' positions, or even the truth of their claims. In Establishment Media Land, Ronald Reagan was the wholesome cowboy; Michael Dukakis, the limp and nerdy loser; Al Gore, the stiff and overly earnest bore; John Kerry, the effete, elitist windsurfer; and George W. Bush, the swaggering tough guy, fighter pilot, and amiable rancher.

Throughout 2007, this pattern continued and even escalated. The GOP presidential candidates were almost uniformly described by our media stars as masculine, strong, and tough, while Democratic males were mocked as weak and even effeminate, and Hillary Clinton was invariably castigated as "icy," controlling, and domineering.

As was candidly acknowledged by two of the nation's most establishment political journalists—Mark Halperin and John Harris—our entire political press has become Drudge-ified, taking its reporting cues from the lowly, dirtmongering right-wing gossip who was launched into stardom by Rush Limbaugh and helped fuel the most scurrilous aspects of the Clinton witch hunts of the 1990s. Our media now obsesses on what Harris and Halperin call the "Freak Show," dominated by "personality-based attacks." Ever since Halperin and Harris proclaimed Matt Drudge the "Walter Cronkite of our era," numerous other establishment journalists have stepped forward to acknowledge his supremacy in shaping our media's political coverage. The fact that our political press— by its own acknowledgment—is now shaped by the bottom-scraping methods pioneered by Matt Drudge has received relatively little attention, yet it is of incomparable importance in understanding how the media works hand-in-hand with right-wing smear artists to determine our elections.

The most important right-wing marketing method, as examined in **Chapter Three,** is the relentless effort to depict GOP male leaders as tough guys, real men of courage, and swaggering warriors. Conversely, Democrats and liberals are gender-confused freaks—their males are effeminate, soft weaklings, and their women are emasculating, controlling, threatening dykes.

Thus, virtually all Republican political leaders endlessly prance around as Real Men in the John Wayne mold. Yet just like Wayne, virtually none has anything in his life that remotely demonstrates any of these attributes. Despite many being of draft age during Vietnam, they ran away from combat. Instead, cheerleading for wars from a great and safe distance—sending other people to risk their lives in combat—has become the time-tested way in American politics for individuals to demonstrate their masculinity, strength, and courage.

This twisted template has now become rooted in American political discourse. Those who favor starting wars and sending others off to fight in them are somehow strong, tough, and courageous. Those who oppose sending their fellow citizens off to wars are weak and cowardly. The United States goes to war far more than any other country in large part because our political culture now demands pro-war (though always *risk-free*) advocacy as proof of one's manhood and courage. This ludicrous equation has produced an entire generation of right-wing male leaders who excel at acting the role of tough-guy warrior without having an ounce of real strength or toughness.

Chapter Four examines how the same methodology of deceit is applied by Republicans who parade around as wholesome, moral family men when the reality is exactly the opposite. While the right wing endlessly exploits claims of moral superiority and dresses up as the moral Everyman, virtually its entire top leadership have lives characterized by the most decadent, hedonistic, and morally unrestrained behavior imaginable—not merely once or in isolated instances, but chronically—as their defining behavior.

Leaders such as Limbaugh, Giuliani, O'Reilly, Gingrich, and scores of others have had a string of shattered marriages, divorces, active out-of-wedlock sex lives, and highly "untraditional" and "un-Christian" personal lives. Precisely because of the messy and often ugly reality of their own personal lives, demonizing others as abnormal becomes the only way they can parade around as moral and normal and righteous. *That* is the central psychological and cultural mythmaking tactic on which the entire right-wing GOP electoral edifice rests—crusading under the banner of personality attributes they so plainly lack.

Indeed, the vast majority of the leaders of the Clinton sex witch hunts in the 1990s have since been revealed to have been engaging in behavior, *even at the time when they were leading the impeachment crusade,* that was (at least) as sleazy and morally "untraditional" as any of the improprieties of which they so righteously accused Bill Clinton. And countless leaders of the "Values Voters" movement over the last several years—from Larry Craig and David Vitter to Ted Haggard and Mark Foley—have been caught in the most scurrilous scandals as a result of their oozing, chronic hypocrisy.

These right-wingers not only refuse to adhere to their alleged moral principles, but worse still, they apply those principles in the most exploitative way possible, *only* when doing so generates political advantage and demands no sacrifice or restraint from their own followers. Self-proclaimed "traditional marriage" advocates harp continuously on the need to ban same-sex marriages while not only endorsing but often *engaging in* the equally "untraditional" practice of shedding one's wife when the mood strikes and finding a new one (often from a pool of current mistresses).

They enforce moral dictates only as applied to small minorities (such as gay people) because doing so is politically popular, whereas enforcing those same dictates in a way that would re-quire sacrifice and restraint from their own supporters (such as opposing easy divorces and remarriages) would entail a political cost. This moral agenda is thus a hollow hypocrisy.

Despite all of that, the establishment press continues hungrily to eat up these manipulative themes, digest them, and mindlessly spew them back out. Hence, GOP leaders are "cultural conserva-tives" and wholesome, regular men, while Democrats reek of elit-ist "San Francisco values." This deceit of salt-of-the-earth, mainstream moralism from our right-wing leaders thus continues to thrive and plays a large role in determining the outcome of our elections.

Chapter Five examines what has perhaps become the most transparent Republican myth of all: that it is the party of small government, limited federal power, and individual liberty. When Bill Clinton was president, right-wing pundits and leaders never ceased warning of the dangers of expansive government power. Of particular concern, they claimed, was expanding police pow-ers and the ability of the government to spy on and control the lives of individual Americans. Republican leaders love to claim that they stand in support of regular Americans against incur-sions by power-hungry, controlling Washington politicians.

Yet once in power, these supposed limited-government mavens reversed course completely. They cheered on virtually every one of George Bush's unprecedented increases in presi-dential power, from how the government detains us, to how they interrogate us, to how they listen in on our telephone con-versations and read our e-mails. Whatever government power under the Bush presidency has been, it has been the opposite of "limited," yet the conservative movement has enthusiastically embraced every one of these radical measures and, even now, advocates still further expansions of such powers.

These power grabs are by no means limited to federal police powers. In virtually every realm, Republicans seek to use the force and power of government to control the lives of American citizens. To secure this control, they spend recklessly and with abandon, and propose one law after another designed to criminalize the private choices of citizens. They are the party of government power and control over the individual. And, as they do in every other realm, they disguise themselves as exactly the opposite when it comes time to win elections.

Chapter Six focuses exclusively on John McCain as the GOP nominee and examines how these manipulative personality themes are already being wielded by him in order to disguise himself to the American people. As is always true, McCain parades around as the paragon of exactly those virtues he most lacks: the apolitical, independent-minded, moderate maverick who rejects elitist values and is an honor-bound, truth-telling man of the people, pursuing his principles even when doing so comes at a great political cost. Even more so than any other politician in memory, the establishment press corps is giddily enamored of McCain and is gearing up, as always, to bolster the Cult of Personality that surrounds the Republican candidate.

The Republican Party of Karl Rove and Lee Atwater will use these same personality-based themes in the 2008 election, because it is all they know and, more important, because nothing has stopped it yet. Their actual platform of more Middle East militarism and domestic policies designed to further widen America's rich-poor gap is, as every poll shows, deeply unpopular. A mid-2007 Rasmussen Reports Poll revealed just how disadvantaged Republicans are when it comes to actual issues and substance, rather than personality smears:

> Democrats are currently trusted more than Republicans on all ten issues measured in Rasmussen Reports tracking surveys. Democrats even have slight advantages on National Security and Taxes, two issues "owned" by Republicans during the generation since Ronald Reagan took office. . . .
>
> Rasmussen Reports monthly surveys have shown a

sharp decline in the number of Americans considering themselves Republicans over the past eight months.

A *New York Times*/CBS poll released in mid-December 2007, as the primary presidential season intensified, revealed that Americans have an overwhelmingly unfavorable opinion of the Republican Party (33–59 percent), while their opinion of Democrats is favorable (48–44 percent)—a bulging 15-point advantage for Democrats. In early 2008, this mountain of anti-GOP polling data led conservative David Brooks, in the *New York Times*, to conclude: "**The Republican Party is more unpopular than at any point in the past 40 years.*** Democrats have a 50 to 36 party identification advantage, the widest in a generation. The general public prefers Democratic approaches on health care, corruption, the economy, and Iraq by double-digit margins."

Worse still for Republicans, they are burdened with the record and reputation of one of the most widely despised presidents in American history and by the country's most disastrous war. Trying to win this election with cultural, psychological, sexual, and gender-based smears and John Wayne mythology is their only option, and they will pursue it vigorously and with glee. They always do.

With the aid of the establishment media, which reflexively views the political landscape within this vapid framework, these already became the dominant themes during the primary season. Hence, John Edwards was an effeminate, elitist, hair-obsessed "faggot" and Hillary Clinton was a pants-wearing, emasculating dyke. Conversely, Fred Thompson was hailed as a down-home Regular Tough Guy and Southern Cultural Conservative by our media stars—*because he has played one on TV!* Contrary to his television and film persona, in which he's played the role of wise

---

*Boldface that appears in quoted text throughout was added by the author for emphasis.

prosecutor and military commander and CIA officer, in real life Thompson ran away from Vietnam and spent years as a rich Beltway lobbyist. His current wife—whom he married after years of short-term relationships with Hollywood actresses and New York socialites—is four years younger than his own daughter.

Two things are urgently needed to prevent deceitful electoral tactics from working again:

1. exposing the tactics the right-wing noise machine uses to drown out both reality and consideration of actual issues, thus ensuring that elections are decided based on manipulative cultural, psychological, and gender-exploiting marketing imagery;
2. demonstrating the Grand Canyon–wide gap between the Attributes and Virtues that these marketing campaigns tout and the actual lives of the GOP leaders.

These themes are all grounded in myth and propaganda. Across the board, the lives of the right-wing standard-bearers exhibit exactly the traits that are the opposite of those that they claim they represent. And the policies these party leaders advocate are designed to achieve exactly the opposite goals.

But the reason why this has worked is that there are almost never any attacks on these myths, no aggressive examination of the real lives of these leaders. Critics of Republicans shy away from these themes. There is a squeamishness to use their own weapons against them. To the extent Democrats address these themes at all, it is always in a defensive posture ("we love America, too"; "we're not unpatriotic"; "we also believe in God"; "we support the troops, too"; "I also love my family").

It needs to be shoved into the media's faces and into our public discourse how false and deceitful and artificial are these "Republican Values" and personality attributes that they concoct for themselves. To do that, the most prominent right-wing political leaders need to be put under a microscope—their actual lives and beliefs—to show how lacking they really are in the virtues they claim to exude and revere. Addressing these psychological and gender-based smears head-on—by subjecting the right-wing leaders to their own standards—can cause the whole edifice to crumble. It can't be refuted by defensive explanations or self-justifications or overly analytical critiques, but only by speaking plainly about what these right-wing leaders really embody and represent. And more than mere "hypocrisy" accusations are required; the GOP leaders need to be indicted with their own accusations, attacked with their own weapons, in order to make it impossible for them to use these tactics further.

By exposing the Republican Party's real playbook—by deciphering these cultural and psychological themes—they can be neutralized, even turned against those who resort to such tactics. This method can refute in advance the standard GOP smear machine that will be employed throughout 2008—not with overly rational discussions of why the themes are invalid or with petulant protests that the tactics are unfair, but instead, with highly visceral and personalized critiques that show that the GOP leaders are in no position to stake claim to virtuous behavior.

Allowing the results of these tactics to fester and letting these innuendos lurk have given us the "brave and upstanding" George Bush, "the sober and responsible" Dick Cheney, the "Christian conservatives" Newt Gingrich, Rush Limbaugh, Tom DeLay, and a country left in ruins. As the country decides who will succeed George W. Bush, there simply is no more important priority than ensuring that we topple the big myths of Republican politics and the Great American Hypocrites who feed off them.

CHAPTER ONE

The John Wayne Syndrome

THE DUKE AS PIONEER OF THE GREAT AMERICAN HYPOCRITE

The Great American Hypocrites of the right wing have a long and storied history. One of the earliest trailblazers of this specific course of deceit was John Wayne, whose life provides a vivid guide for how today's right-wing political movement parades around as everything that it is not.

Beyond his acting career, John Wayne has long been famous as a symbol of the ideal, supermasculine American right-wing male. From his all-American name to his cowboy swagger, from his numerous film roles as a war hero to his hard-core right-wing politics and steadfast support for American wars, the image of the Duke has remained the model of masculine American strength and wholesomeness.

Yet the gap between Wayne's image and the reality of his life is enormous. While Wayne adopted über-patriotic political positions and held himself out as a right-wing tough guy, he did everything he could to avoid fighting for his country during World War II.

Although he spent the 1950s enthusiastically promoting Joseph McCarthy and the 1960s excoriating war opponents as traitors and cowards, when his country needed him most, Wayne preferred that other Americans fight and die—including the country's wealthiest and most famous actors—so that he could remain in Hollywood and, as one of the only leading men not to fight, become very rich making one war film after another.

And in this critical regard, Wayne was a true trailblazer of the modern American right-wing movement. He was one of the first Americans to pretend that he possessed the "warrior virtues"— strength, courage, resoluteness, spine, a fanatical devotion to fighting for America—not by virtue of his own conduct but by virtue of how frequently and loudly he urged that other Americans be sent off to fight in wars.

Wayne scornfully condemned films that he claimed deviated from wholesome American values. Yet in his own life, Wayne was not only married to three different women but engaged in multiple affairs with a whole array of Hollywood actresses and socialites. While he loudly denounced those whom he deemed to be morally impure, Wayne indulged an alcohol addiction and a barbiturate and amphetamine habit for years.

John Wayne flamboyantly paraded around as the embodiment of courage, masculinity, patriotism, wholesomeness, and the warrior virtues. He adopted right-wing political positions that he claimed demonstrated his thorough, tough, and resolute patriotism. This man who ran away from war then spent the rest of his life loudly cheering for every American war he could find. And as he left a series of broken marriages characterized by ugly divorces involving allegations of abuse, and as he further entered multiple adulterous relationships, he insisted—with increasing shrillness—that he was devoted to wholesome, American, Christian values.

It is true, then, that John Wayne indeed epitomizes the American right-wing male—though not quite in the way that conservative ideologues have, for decades, suggested. The ideals that

Wayne endlessly claimed to stand for are the same as those that the modern right wing and its Republican Party endlessly exploit.

Yet, just as was true of John Wayne, the leaders of today's right-wing movement could not be any further removed from these values in their actual lives. They talk tough and prance around as wholesome warriors, yet their conduct in their personal lives reveals—time and again—that they are the exact opposite.

Almost invariably, it is those modern right-wing leaders with the filthiest, most untraditional, and most decadent personal lives—from Rush Limbaugh and Ann Coulter to Fred Thompson and Newt Gingrich—who become the most boisterous advocates for so-called traditional marriage and family values. And even more so, it is those with a history of cowardly avoidance of combat and wars, including wars they claim to have supported—such as Rudy Giuliani, Mitt Romney, Bill Kristol, and Limbaugh and Gingrich again, to say nothing of Dick Cheney and George W. Bush—who become the most aggressive and bellicose, endlessly questioning the courage and manliness of those who oppose them.

And so it was with the original model of this right-wing strain of manly virtue, John Wayne. Two of his most notable features—his all-American, masculinity-exuding name and thick head of hair—were pure artifice. Wayne, born Marion Morrison, wore a toupee for most of his career to conceal his baldness. Although he stood 6′4″, he frequently wore large lifts in his shoes to appear taller still. Like the right-wing warriors who would idolize him and follow in his path, Wayne excelled at playacting the masculine virtues but failed miserably at adhering to them in his life.

The more Wayne was confronted with his failure to conform to these virtues, the more desperate he became to use political extremism to compensate. Endlessly cheering on new wars became his path to assuaging feelings of weakness and cowardliness for having avoided World War II. Joining in McCarthyite

crusades and attacking Vietnam War opponents as traitors became his way of proving his patriotism. And proclaiming himself
a steadfast adherent of American Morality gave cover to the
decadent and amoral personal life he led.

To this day, Wayne is held up as an icon of right-wing
courage, American virtue, and conservative manliness. On his
hundredth birthday in 2007, the right-wing *Orange County Reg-
ister* published an article glorifying his "legacy," which quoted a
local leader as saying: "When they say 'John Wayne: American,'
they described him well. He was one of a kind." The same
week, the *Orange County Weekly* published an article that satir-
ically though accurately captures Wayne's image, even today:

> John Wayne is not about gray areas.
>
> John Wayne is not about faggy fogs of war.
>
> John Wayne IS America, the greatest country ever created by
> God, forever and ever, amen.

In 1980, Ronald Reagan delivered his first speech after receiving the GOP nomination at the Neshoba County Fair in Mis-
sissippi. Neshoba County is the place where civil rights workers
James Chaney, Andrew Goodman, and Michael Schwerner were
murdered in 1964. As the *Boston Globe* noted in 2004, "The
county fair was legendary for segregationist speeches and Dixie
ditties." Reagan, however, did not mention Chaney, Goodman,
and Schwerner at all in his remarks, but did, according to the
Globe, "effusively praise John Wayne," saying,

> God rest his soul. I don't know whether John Wayne had
> this experience or not, but I wish he had, because I don't
> know of anyone who would have loved it more or been
> more at home here than the Duke would have been,
> right here.

Wayne's popularity among many Americans as the Ultimate American Male is hard to overstate. The *Los Angeles Times* reported in 1995—eighteen years after Wayne's death—that "Wayne has long been—and remains—one of the nation's most popular film stars. He ranked first in a 1995 Harris poll that included Clint Eastwood, Mel Gibson and Denzel Washington."

As the same article noted, "Wayne's image is still used in a beer commercial to exemplify the ideal American fighting man." When he died, Congress commemorated his life with a medal that simply read "John Wayne, American." Then-president Jimmy Carter said upon his death, "John Wayne was bigger than life. In an age of few heroes, he was the genuine article."

Wayne's status as a supreme icon of American patriotism and manly warrior virtues was expressed vividly by Ron Kovic, the Vietnam veteran and author of *Born on the Fourth of July.* Kovic described how he and a war comrade had watched Wayne in *Sands of Iwo Jima,* in which Wayne—as he so frequently did—played the role of a battle-hardened marine:

> We sat glued to our seats . . . watching Sergeant Stryker, played by John Wayne, charge up the hill and get killed just before he reached the top. And then they showed the men raising the flag on Iwo Jima with the marines' hymn still playing, and Castiglia and I cried in our seats . . . and every time I heard it I would think of John Wayne and the brave men who raised the flag on Iwo Jima that day.

Kovic goes on to describe how, after volunteering for the marines during the Vietnam War, he returned home paralyzed:

> Nobody ever told me I was going to come back from this war without a penis . . . Oh God oh God I want it back! I gave it for the whole country . . . I gave [it] for John Wayne . . .

In 1969, *Time* magazine published a lengthy cover story profiling Wayne, titled "John Wayne as the Last Hero." The article declared that Wayne "has become the essential American soul that D. H. Lawrence once characterized as 'harsh, isolate, stoic and a killer.'" Regarding his politics, *Time* wrote: "If Wayne stands to the right in sex, he is an unabashed reactionary in politics. A rapping Republican and flapping hawk, he has made the Viet Nam war his personal crusade."

Most revealingly, *Time* celebrated Wayne as the ultimate man's man: "In a field where male stars are constantly rumored to be epicene, Wayne's masculinity is incontestable." In his film roles, which quickly spilled over into how he was perceived and how he perceived himself, he was the "essential western man, fearin' God but no one else. Tough to men and kind to wimmin, slow to anger but duck behind the bar when he got mad, for he had a gun and a word that never failed."

As is true of most of our country's right-wing leaders today, however, Wayne's showy manliness and warrior courage masked an opposite reality. Yet Wayne's case is even more striking. Whereas large numbers of the top Republican leadership today evaded combat during the Vietnam War, Wayne did so during World War II, when combat-avoidance was exceedingly rare.

Indeed, the 1941 Japanese attack on Pearl Harbor generated a unity among the American citizenry rarely seen before or since. Americans from across the political spectrum supported U.S. involvement in the war and lined up behind the liberal Democratic president, Franklin Roosevelt, as he led the nation. Roosevelt had expressly campaigned in 1940 on a platform of reinstating the draft and was reelected easily. Among American males, there was a widespread desire to fight for their country.

For the past several decades, by contrast, only a tiny fraction of the U.S. population has actually fought in the numerous wars we've waged. And beginning in earnest with the Vietnam War, the children of our nation's wealthiest and most powerful individuals virtually never risked their lives in combat.

Today, the sons of our nation's wealthiest and most power-ful families frequently cheer on any war that our political class proposes. The most politically powerful right-wing families have an almost perfect record of advocating numerous wars while en-suring that their own sons and daughters do not risk their lives to fight in them. Now it is commonplace, even perfectly accept-able, for those who want the nation to fight in one war after an-other—who want us to remain in a state of Permanent War—to bear no personal risk or sacrifice whatsoever for the wars they spawn.

The vast, vast majority of our nation's most vocal war sup-porters—those who support not only current wars but new ones as well—find no contradiction in their warmongering while re-fusing to fight. Indeed, on television and in our nation's newspa-pers, one commonly observes young, able-bodied, right-wing American conservatives in their twenties and thirties boldly pro-claiming that America is involved in an existential War of Civi-lizations on which the fate of our country depends. They viciously attack those who oppose war as cowards and weak-lings. Yet they never appear to contemplate any duty to fight. They can playact as warriors, feign toughness and courage, but only by sending other people off to risk their lives.

This change in the approach Americans—especially Ameri-can males—take toward war is reflected in the behavior of pro-war political leaders. Whereas President Roosevelt advocated a draft even before the United States was attacked at Pearl Harbor, virtually every American politician today—and especially those who are fond of wrapping themselves in tough-guy pro-war rhetoric—considers calling for the draft to be the most toxic po-litical poison there is.

Even as the Bush administration started wars and threatened new ones—and even as the American military became stretched far too thin due to too many commitments and not enough vol-unteers—Bush officials emphatically insisted that they would never consider a draft. Suggesting the possibility of a draft is the death knell for any politician in a country that could aptly be called a John Wayne Nation—filled with people who want to cheer on wars but do not want to fight in them.

In today's America, war advocacy is a means of feeling tough and strong without having actually to be either. Huge numbers of Americans want to reserve the right to demand that the country fight wars without having to sacrifice or risk in any way for them. And the right-wing political movement is teeming with people who imply that their support for war renders them tough and powerful even though they themselves do everything possible to avoid combat service.

Such behavior, however, was virtually unheard of in America during World War II, particularly among the nation's able-bodied men. With the United States fighting a war that most Americans actually believed in, the nation's men overwhelmingly displayed the courage of their convictions. The war supporters of the 1940s were a breed much different than America's loudmouthed pro-war chest-beaters of today.

According to a study in the December 2004 issue of *Population Bulletin,* more than 9 percent of the American population served in the U.S. military during World War II—more than double the percentage that served during any foreign war in U.S. history. By contrast, less than 2 percent of the American population served in the Vietnam War, and less than 1 percent during the 1991 Gulf War.

As of 2006—even with President Bush and most of the right wing unceasingly pounding the claim that we are engaged in an existential, permanent war, requiring endless fighting in Iraq as well as new wars in Iran and beyond—*fewer than one-third of 1 percent of the American population serve in the armed forces.* Thus, the percentage of American citizens serving in the armed forces was twenty-seven times greater during World War II than it is today.

Today, the very idea of our nation's top movie stars volunteering to fight in Iraq is simply unthinkable. One cannot imagine, say, Brad Pitt, Matt Damon, Bruce Willis, or Tom Cruise anywhere near a marine platoon or a tank in Anbar Province.

But the male American movie stars of the World War II era—from the most politically conservative to the most liberal—went off to fight for their country in droves. Virtually every one of the top male box-office draws of that time enlisted, among them William Holden, James Stewart, Clark Gable, Tyrone Power, and Henry Fonda.

But *not* John Wayne, the Ultimate Icon of right-wing Male Courage. At the time of the Pearl Harbor attack, Wayne was already a major star due to his lead role in the 1939 hit Western *Stagecoach*. Yet once the war began, Wayne told friends and associates he feared that leaving Hollywood for an extended period to fight would harm his career. Later in life, Wayne claimed that he was unable to fight in the war because of his age and the need to support his three children.

But at the time of the Pearl Harbor attacks, Jimmy Stewart was thirty-three—just a year younger than Wayne—and he flew more than twenty combat missions. When Clark Gable volunteered for World War II combat duty, he was forty. The liberal Henry Fonda could easily have avoided combat had he wanted to. When the Japanese struck at Pearl Harbor, he was thirty-seven years old—three years older than Wayne—with three children. Yet Fonda, like many of his wealthiest and most powerful peers in the film business, went off and fought for his country.

Wayne simply refused. Throughout World War II, he turned to a series of increasingly extreme measures to protect himself from being drafted. According to Garry Wills's *John Wayne's America,* the Duke did not even reply to letters from the Selective Service System and applied for numerous deferments.

Initially, Wayne obtained 3-A status, "deferred for [family] dependency reasons," and assured numerous friends that he would enlist as soon as he made one or two more films that would provide his family more financial comfort than they already enjoyed. Yet Wayne never fulfilled this promise.

With virtually all of his competition overseas fighting, Wayne's acting career soared during the war. Wayne made one successful film after another for enormous and ever-increasing fees. During World War II alone, he starred in thirteen films. Ironically, he often played courageous war heroes even as his peers were away doing the real thing. As the 1969 *Time* profile put it,

> During World War II, the western dwindled in popularity, but the hero could pull more than one trigger. Wayne switched from Colt to M-1 and became a screen soldier. He was a bit unsteady out of the saddle, but there was conviction behind his "Let's get the Nips!" rallying cry.

In 1944, Wayne actually invoked his astoundingly successful movie career not as a justification for finally enlisting (as he promised ultimately to do), but instead as an excuse for not being sent to fight. Based on the argument that his war films provided value to the country, Wayne received a 2-A classification, "deferred in support of [the] national . . . interest." A month later, however, the Selective Service—with the U.S. armed forces increasingly in need of fresh American fighters as the war dragged on—decided to revoke many previous deferments. It thus reclassified Wayne as 1-A, which would have led to his being drafted. But Wayne implored his film studio to appeal on his behalf, which it did successfully, and his 2-A "national interest" status was reinstated until after the war ended.

John Wayne thus spent the entire war *pretending* to be a tough guy while doing everything in his power to avoid the real fight. He became an extremely rich man while his peers served their country. And the more success, fame, and money he garnered, the more selfishly and desperately he sought to preserve his comforts and avoid fighting. He thereby created the mold of the Great American Hypocrite of today's right wing.

Despite (or because of) his fanatical combat avoidance during World War II, John Wayne would spend the next forty years of his life strutting around as though he were some sort of über-patriotic war hero. He became as well-known for his far-right, pro-war political views as he was for his acting career. In 1944, he helped found the right-wing Motion Picture Alliance for the Preservation of American Ideals, eventually becoming its president.

Not only in films, but particularly in politics, he deliberately held himself out as a symbol of manly courage and resolute strength. And perhaps most reprehensibly of all—given his own history—he was often found leading the demonization of those Americans who opposed war, and especially those who did not want to fight in combat.

Luis I. Reyes and Ed Rampell, coauthors of *Made in Paradise: Hollywood's Films of Hawaii and the South Seas,* reported that Wayne's third wife, Pilar, drew a clear connection between Wayne's selfish and war-avoiding behavior during World War II and the hard-core, right-wing, pro-war viewpoints he espoused for the remainder of his life. The authors drew the obvious parallel to today's right-wing war cheerleaders:

> According to Pilar Wayne, her husband "would become a 'superpatriot' for the rest of his life trying to atone for staying home" during WWII. Like Wayne, the current crop of GOP chicken hawks are great actors, overcompensating for their previous patriotic failings (draft dodging, etc.) by sounding the jingoistic battle cry for a new generation of working-class sons and daughters to go to war.

Wayne himself frequently and expressly claimed to be the very epitome of the virile fighting male, making swaggering, chest-beating pronouncements like the following at various stages of his life:

"God-damn, I'm the stuff men are made of!"

"Courage is being scared to death—and saddling up anyway."

"I am an old-fashioned, honest-to-goodness, flag-waving patriot."

In one interview, Wayne explained that he single-handedly innovated the concept of the Real Cowboy:

> I made up my mind that I was going to play a real man to the best of my ability. I felt many of the Western stars of the twenties and thirties were too goddamn perfect. They never drank or smoked. They never wanted to go to bed with a beautiful girl. They never had a fight. A heavy might throw a chair at them, and they just looked surprised and didn't fight in this spirit. They were too goddamn sweet and pure to be dirty fighters. Well, I wanted to be a dirty fighter if that was the only way to fight back.
>
> If someone throws a chair at you, hell, you pick up a chair and belt him right back. I was trying to play a man who gets dirty, who sweats sometimes, who enjoys kissing a gal he likes, who gets angry, who fights clean whenever possible but will fight dirty if he has to. You could say I made the Western hero a roughneck.

In the 1969 *Time* profile, Wayne similarly boasted: "When I came in, the western man never lost his white hat and always rode the white horse and waited for the man to get up again in the fight. Following my Dad's advice, if a guy hit me with a vase, I'd hit him with a chair. That's the way we played it. I changed the saintly Boy Scout of the original cowboy hero into a more normal kind of fella."

So the actor who in reality hid from the opportunity—and the duty—to "belt right back" when his country was attacked by the Japanese and threatened by the Nazis spent the rest of his life loudly claiming to be the Real Man, the one who Fights Back.

Worse still, after World War II, Wayne repeatedly and viciously attacked various films for being allegedly anti-American or insufficiently reverent of America. In one interview, he complained: "*High Noon* was the most un-American thing I have ever seen in my whole life. The last thing in the picture is ol' Coop [Gary Cooper] putting the United States Marshal's badge under his foot and stepping on it. I'll never regret having run [screenwriter and accused Communist] Carl Foreman out of this country."

Wayne's boast that he ran Foreman "out of this country" referenced the fact that, in the 1950s, Wayne became a fervent and paranoid anti-Communist McCarthyite. He actively assisted the House Un-American Activities Committee in its effort to ferret out suspected Communist sympathizers in Hollywood. He made a practice of accusing Hollywood figures of being Communists based on the flimsiest of evidence, proclaiming in one interview:

> The only guy that ever fooled me was the director Edward Dmytryk. I made a picture with him called *Back to Bataan.*
>
> He started talking about the masses, and as soon as he started using that word—which is from their book, not ours—I knew he was a Commie.

In 1960, Frank Sinatra—at the request of his political ally, then-senator and presidential candidate John Kennedy—hired a Hollywood writer, Albert Maltz, one of the "Hollywood Ten" who had been blacklisted during the height of the anti-Communist hysteria. Wayne led the charge in attacking Sinatra: "I wonder how Sinatra's crony Senator John Kennedy feels about him hiring such a man."

Wayne became even more extremist later in life, and his delusions of grandeur as a Warrior for Freedom grew steadily. He told a *Time* reporter in 1969: "I think those blacklisted people should have been sent over to Russia. They'd have been taken care of over there, and if the Commies ever won over here, why hell, those guys would be the first ones they'd take care of—after me."

As the 1950s came to a close, Wayne's domestic Communist-hunting began to transform into fanatical support for the American war in Vietnam. In 1960, he produced and directed the film *The Alamo,* in which he starred as Davy Crockett. Historians across the board condemned the film for its litany of historical inaccuracies, all designed to glorify the battle for Texas. When confronted with such criticisms, Wayne issued this solemn lecture to Americans on the cost of "liberty and freedom":

> This picture is America. I hope that seeing the battle of the Alamo **will remind Americans that liberty and freedom don't come cheap.** This picture, well, I guess making it has made me feel useful to my country.

After evading service during World War II, Wayne proclaimed that producing a film in which he pretended to be yet another war hero "made him feel useful to his country." He made *The Alamo,* he said, "to remind people not only in America but everywhere that there were once men and women who **had the guts to stand up for the things they believed.**"

Throughout the 1960s, Wayne was situated at the epicenter of the pro-war, right-wing American political faction. He spent the 1960s campaigning in California for Ronald Reagan—who, while at least enlisting in the military during World War II, also avoided combat by being classified "for limited service only" due to eyesight difficulties, then spent much of the war safely ensconced in the so-called 1st Motion Picture Unit in Culver City, California.

In 1965, Wayne wrote a letter to President Lyndon Johnson explaining why he wanted to make the pro–Vietnam War propaganda film *The Green Berets*. In his letter, Wayne intoned: It is "extremely important that not only the people of the United States but those all over the world should know why it is necessary for us to be there." He stressed that he wanted to "tell the story of our fighting men in Vietnam . . . in a manner that will inspire a patriotic attitude on the part of fellow-Americans—a feeling which we have always had in this country in the past during times of stress and trouble."

According to his 1979 *Newsweek* obituary, Wayne's initial script for *The Green Berets* was such a transparent and inaccurate piece of pro-war propaganda that even the U.S. military was uncomfortable with it: "The Army rejected the initial script because Wayne's Green Berets were too gung-ho in their anti-Communist enthusiasm."

After much controversy, *The Green Berets* was finally made, one of the very few films about the Vietnam War that Hollywood produced during the time the war lasted. The film glorified the war in every way. Wayne played a swaggering, courageous colonel assigned to the dangerous mission of kidnapping a North Vietnamese general, and uttered tough-guy lines such as "Out here, due process is a bullet." The film was almost universally panned by critics, yet it was so popular among American war supporters that it became the second-most-profitable film of Wayne's career.

In a 2003 issue of the *Journal of Film and Video,* Brian Woodman reviewed just some of the jingoistic fiction pervading Wayne's film:

In *The Green Berets,* the Vietcong are almost always seen in long shots or in shadows. They commit dastardly acts, such as stabbing an American soldier in the back, and they often use primitive weapons such as knives and swords, as if to underscore their barbaric nature. The film's racist depiction of Vietnamese communists is reflected in the opinion of the film's lead actor, conservative cold warrior John Wayne, who stated in a 1971 *Playboy* interview that the Vietcong were treacherous and "that the dirty sons of bitches are raping, torturing gorillas."

The Green Berets was so wildly propagandistic that at the time of its release, New York congressman Benjamin Rosenthal accused Wayne and the army of producing the film in cahoots. According to Congressman Rosenthal, the film "became a useful and skilled device employed by the Pentagon to present a view of the war which was disputed in 1967 and is largely repudiated today."

During the Vietnam War, the draft-dodging Wayne vocally condemned teenagers who went to Europe or Canada in order to avoid the draft, calling them "cowards," "traitors," and "Communists." He was fond of issuing similar chest-beating attacks on Hollywood activists who opposed the war, such as Jane Fonda and Donald Sutherland.

Like so many of our current right-wing political leaders and pundits who playact at being a warrior for so long that they come to believe it is their reality, Wayne spent his last several decades convinced that "war hero" was not merely a fictional role he played, but was what he in fact was.

And it is no surprise that Wayne came to view himself as a genuine war hero, since that is how the country—more enamored of the image of warrior courage than the reality—continuously treated him. According to the 1969 *Time* profile: "Nobody took a dim view of Wayne for staying out [of World War II]. In the '50s, General Douglas MacArthur told him, 'Young man, you represent the cavalry officer better than any man who wears a uniform.'"

The gap between Wayne's tough-guy image and his fear of

combat was perhaps matched only by the gap between Wayne's public moralizing and the decadent, adulterous, and hedonistic personal life he led for decades. Almost as much as he paraded around as a tough warrior, Wayne held himself out as a defender of traditional moral values and the beacon of the wholesome American man.

Long before it was fashionable as a political weapon, Wayne attacked anything that had any whiff of homosexuality to it. Upon the 1959 release of *Suddenly, Last Summer,* he denounced Tennessee Williams's vaguely homoerotic film as "too disgusting even for discussion" while making clear he would never see it. Wayne sermonized: "It is too distasteful to be put on a screen designed to entertain a family, or any member of a decent family."

A decade earlier, in 1949, producer Robert Rossen had offered Wayne the role of Willie Stark in *All the King's Men.* After reading the script, Wayne refused to have anything to do with the film, sending his agent an angry letter claiming that the film "smears the machinery of government for no purpose of humor or enlightenment"; "degrades all relationships"; and is suffused with "drunken mothers; conniving fathers; double-crossing sweethearts; bad, bad, rich people; and bad, bad poor people if they want to get ahead." The film, wrote Wayne, degraded "the American way of life," and he concluded by telling his agent that "you can take this script and shove it up Robert Rossen's derrière."

Yet again, like so many of our current right-wing moralizers, Wayne's actual life could not have been any less faithful to the moral standards he loved using to attack others publicly. And it was not merely a sinful act here and there that Wayne committed. To begin with, Wayne—like much of the leadership of the right-wing political faction today—was incapable of adhering to any of the basic oaths of so-called traditional marriage. He vowed on three different occasions, with three different women, that he would remain in holy matrimony till death do us part, yet failed to do so even once.

Wayne, after twelve years of marriage, divorced his first wife, Josephine, after he became a successful film star. While married to Josephine, with whom he had three children, he had a series of affairs with various actresses he met on the sets of his films, while his wife and children were at home. Wayne divorced Josephine in order to marry his then-mistress, Esperanza Baur. His marriage to Esperanza occurred literally weeks after his divorce from Josephine was finalized.

But Wayne's second marriage fared no better than his first. Plagued by reports of chronic adultery, Wayne divorced Esperanza after seven years of childless marriage. Once again, Wayne did not wait long to take on his next wife, this time marrying Pilar—a Peruvian woman he met while filming a movie in her homeland—*on the very day his second divorce was finalized.*

The marriage with Pilar also did not last. Although he never formally divorced Pilar, with whom he had four more children, they separated in 1973 so that Wayne could live with his new mistress—his secretary, Pat Stacy, with whom he remained, while still married to Pilar, until his death in 1979.

The numerous broken families Wayne created could not have been any more antithetical to the traditional moral values he endlessly claimed to espouse. His confirmed adulterous relationships are too numerous to chronicle, including a lengthy affair with Marlene Dietrich during his first marriage. His multiple divorces and split-ups were anything but amicable. As entertainment journalist Emanuel Levy reported concerning Wayne's breakup with his second wife,

> There were indeed charges and counter-charges of unfaithfulness, drunken violence, emotional cruelty, and "clobbering." Wayne described his wife as a "drunken partygoer who would fall down and then accuse him of pushing her." He deplored the publicity his divorce pro-

ceedings received in the press, though they did not hurt his career or popularity.

The 1969 *Time* profile gives a small glimpse into the enormous disparity between the Moral Crusader Wayne and the reality of how he lived his life:

> Aging and raging, he began to take on all enemies in the same spirit: Commies, Injuns, wrongos, Mexicans—and his wife Esperanza. "Our marriage was like shaking two volatile chemicals in a jar," he said. She recalled the night he dragged her around by her hair. He countered with a claim that when he was on location she had a house guest named Nicky Hilton. During the divorce proceedings, Wayne uttered an aside that could have come from one of his early oaters: "I deeply regret that I'll hafta sling mud."

The moral mess in Wayne's private life was not confined to draft dodging and serial broken marriages. And in that regard, his life was an almost exact precursor of one of the current leaders of our nation's Values Voters movement—superpatriot and war lover Rush Limbaugh. Like draft evader Limbaugh, the law-and-order moralizer Wayne, in the midst of his serial marriages and divorces, developed a rather nasty addiction to drugs.

Throughout the 1960s, Wayne regularly took amphetamines during the day in order to work and barbiturates at night in order to sleep. On one occasion, Wayne actually confused his habits. During a taping of a guest appearance on *The Dean Martin Show* in 1969, Wayne accidentally took a downer rather than the speed he used in order to work, and arrived announcing: "I can't do our skit. I'm too doped up. Goddamn, I look half smashed."

In the midst of the initiation of the now-infamous Republican "Southern strategy" led by Richard Nixon, whereby the

Republican Party would seek to exploit racial tensions in order to recruit white Southerners to the GOP, John Wayne gave a 1971 interview to *Playboy* magazine filled with one reprehensible comment after the next. The most enduring one was his explicit embrace of "white supremacy" as his governing ideology:

> We can't all of a sudden get down on our knees and turn everything over to the leadership of the blacks. I believe in white supremacy until the blacks are educated to a point of responsibility. I don't believe in giving authority and positions of leadership to irresponsible people.

The *Playboy* interview was one of the few truthful and candid moments of Wayne's sad and deceitful life. Just like George W. Bush on his Texas ranch, even the recreational activities Wayne pretended to enjoy, in order to cast an image of a macho tough guy, were the opposite of how he actually lived. As Reyes and Rampell wrote,

> Although the star of countless Westerns such as John Ford's 1939 *Stagecoach* and 1953's *Hondo* owned a ranch, the Duke "didn't particularly like horses and preferred suits and tuxedos to chaps, jeans and boots," according to his son, Michael Wayne.

The more he demonstrated in his own life that he lacked particular virtues, the more loudly and flamboyantly he claimed to embody them. The more guilt he experienced over his draft dodging, the more loudly he cheered on new wars and attacked war opponents. The more adulterous affairs he carried on and the more broken and hedonistic his personal life became, the more publicly and boisterously he crusaded for America's traditional moral values.

And thus John Wayne is indeed the pure and perfect model of today's right-wing political movement and the Great American Hypocrites who lead it. He was one of the first of the seemingly endless stream of right-wing polemicists who tout the very values and virtues that, in their own lives, they repeatedly prove themselves to be most lacking.

The principal sins of moralizing tough guys like John Wayne and his heirs in today's right-wing movement are not mere deceit and hypocrisy—pretending to be something that they plainly are not, or insisting that they believe in values that they repeatedly and deliberately refuse to live by in their own lives. To be sure, those are sins, and reprehensible ones at that.

But the sinister character represented by John Wayne is worse than merely hypocritical and deceitful. Those who wallow in feelings of inadequate masculinity become quite destructive, incomparably dangerous. Those who lack in their private lives any evidence of warrior courage—from Bill Kristol and Rush Limbaugh to Dick Cheney, Rudy Giuliani, and Mitt Romney—are far more likely to cheer on unnecessary wars and other acts of pointless brutality in order to feel the vicarious sensations of courage and masculine strength that they actually lack in their real lives. And those whose private lives are filled with moral disgraces and wrecked marriages, yet who want to impose "Traditional Morality" on others—the likes of Limbaugh, Newt Gingrich, Ann Coulter, and John Wayne, and a seemingly endless slew of "Values Voters" leaders—become the most invasive, the most authoritarian of moralizers. Public moralizing against others becomes the only tool available to obscure the profound, grotesque moral failures in their own lives.

In an astoundingly revealing *Wall Street Journal* column in October 2001, Peggy Noonan proclaimed that the 9/11 attacks had ushered in the return of the Real Man—of John Wayne manliness:

> Men are back. A certain style of manliness is once again being honored and celebrated in our country since

Sept. 11. You might say it suddenly emerged from the rubble of the past quarter century, and emerged when a certain kind of man came forth to get our great country out of the fix it was in.

I am speaking of masculine men, men who push things and pull things and haul things and build things, men who charge up the stairs in a hundred pounds of gear and tell everyone else where to go to be safe.

Describing a man who once punched a shark to death after it attacked his wife, Noonan gushed further:

I don't know what the guy did for a living, but he had a very old-fashioned sense of what it is to be a man, and I think that sense is coming back into style because of who saved us on Sept. 11, and that is very good for our country.

Why? Well, manliness wins wars. Strength and guts plus brains and spirit wins wars. . . .

I was there in America, as a child, when John Wayne was a hero, and a symbol of American manliness. He was strong, and silent. And I was there in America when they killed John Wayne by a thousand cuts. A lot of people killed him—not only feminists but peaceniks, leftists, intellectuals, others. . . .

I missed John Wayne. But now I think . . . he's back. I think he returned on Sept. 11. I think he ran up the stairs, threw the kid over his back like a sack of potatoes, came back down and shoveled rubble. I think he's in Afghanistan now, saying, with his slow swagger and simmering silence, "Yer in a whole lotta trouble now, Osama-boy."

I think he's back in style. And none too soon.
Welcome back, Duke.

Truer words have never been spoken. The 9/11 attacks did indeed render once again dominant—especially among the war-crazed Right—the John Wayne version of "manlihood": those who masquerade as tough guys and warriors, cheerleading for wars and sending others off to fight them; the type who swagger around saying things like "Yer in a whole lotta trouble now, Osama-boy" while doing nothing to back up those words, and who pose as wholesome defenders of American morality while living deeply decadent and depraved private lives.

John Wayne has long been considered the epitome of the American right-wing male. And he is—but not because of the wholesome, tough-guy virtues that he has long been thought to embody. The opposite is true. He is the perfect symbol of the political right-wing movement in the United States because—just as is true of that movement's leaders today—his actual life was in every respect the precise opposite of what he claimed to be. And the larger his failings were, the more he lacked those virtues in his life, the greater was his need to present himself in public as the symbol of those virtues. As Noonan suggested, it is impossible to imagine a more perfect hypocrite and model for America's right-wing movement than the sadly conflicted and profoundly deceitful John Wayne.

CHAPTER TWO

How Great American Hypocrites

Feed Off One Another

RIGHT-WING SMEARS AND THE ESTABLISHMENT PRESS

Since at least the 1980 election of the combat-avoiding, divorced, and playacting cowboy Ronald Reagan, the Republican Party has relied on, and increasingly perfected, the same deceitful tactics John Wayne used to create his mirage of a wholesome tough guy. In all subsequent campaigns, personality and cultural images have far outweighed substantive policy positions in importance and emphasis. Republican campaigning since the Reagan era has been rooted far more in manipulation of candidate imagery than in debates over policy.

Throughout 2007, virtually the entire top tier of Republican leaders, both political and media figures, were little John Waynes—the very opposite of the virtues the conservative movement claims to embody. From Fred Thompson, Rudy Giuliani, Mitt Romney, and Newt Gingrich to Rush Limbaugh, Sean Hannity, Bill Kristol, and the rest of the right-wing noise machine, including our brave neoconservative warmongers—to say nothing of the likes of George Bush and Dick Cheney—it is nearly impossible to locate genuine acts of strength, bravery, regular-guy wholesomeness, or any of the warrior attributes and virtues of traditional masculinity they claim to revere.

But a gullible, hungry press digests and spews the Republicans' cultivated Wayneseque themes religiously, and this illusion thus persists and dominates our political process. At the center of this tactic is the packaged depiction of the right-wing Male Leader as a strong, courageous, and tough warrior, exuding in equal measure the traditional American masculine virtues and Family Values wholesomeness, along with a regular-guy anti-elitism. Virtually every right-wing Male Leader playacts as an all-American mix of John Wayne and Ward Cleaver—a tough, swaggering warrior by day, a wholesome family man by night.

The flip side of this equation is an equally indispensable weapon in the GOP arsenal: Democratic and liberal males are demonized as effeminate, effete elitists, and liberal women as emasculating dykes. Every national Democratic male leader over the past two decades—and especially those who have fought in combat and who remained married to their first wives—has been ridiculed as a weak and effeminate, gender-confused freak.

These manipulative personality-based tactics do not merely obscure real debate over issues and degrade our political discourse. Far worse, these GOP marketing packages are complete fabrications. They bear no relationship to reality.

This rank mythmaking and exploitation of cultural, gender, and psychological themes had its roots in the transformation of actor Ronald Reagan into a John Wayne–archetype cowboy who alone had the courage to stand tall against the Soviet Empire. Combat-avoiding George W. Bush—who spent much of his adult life wallowing in privileged, sheltered hedonism—became the swaggering, brush-clearing, fighter-pilot warrior whose courage and masculine toughness were needed to protect us from the Terrorists.

Both of Bush's opponents in the past two presidential elections—Al Gore and John Kerry—volunteered to go to Vietnam;

yet they lost those elections because they were portrayed as effeminate, soft, elitist cowards. In 2000, it was repeatedly suggested that Gore was controlled by the emasculating feminist Naomi Wolf and, in Maureen Dowd's formulation, he was "practically lactating." In 2004, Kerry was dominated by his rich foreign wife and was an effete, windsurfing French pansy.

That Bush's and Cheney's lives were completely devoid of any acts of authentic courage or toughness or the traditional masculine and moral virtues mattered not at all. The Republicans' manipulative psychological and cultural slime machine rolled over reality and infected the entire media narrative, as it has for years. Millions of Americans who oppose the defining Republican beliefs nonetheless voted for Reagan and Bush 41 and Bush 43 and admired Dick Cheney because the contrived character mythology of the Upstanding Tough Guy versus the Sniveling Loser—drawn directly from Hollywood and Madison Avenue marketing methods—simply overwhelmed issues of substance.

The GOP—aided by a vapid, easily manipulated, and often sympathetic media—has reverted to this manipulative playbook over and over, for decades now. As psychology professor Stephen J. Ducat documented in his superb book *The Wimp Factor: Gender Gaps, Holy Wars, and the Politics of Anxious Masculinity,*

> Since the U.S. national elections of 1980, right-wing political propagandists have relentlessly, and with great success, linked liberalism to weakness, dependency and helplessness—qualities seen by most male-dominated societies as feminine.

Perhaps the most vivid early example of this tactic—the election where it really began to take root—was the total humiliation of Massachusetts governor Michael Dukakis by the burgeoning right-wing noise machine built by Lee Atwater and

Roger Ailes during the 1988 presidential election campaign. Ask most Americans today about Dukakis and few would likely be able to recall anything specific about the policies he advocated. Instead, numerous GOP attacks shaped Americans' perception of Dukakis, and these endure today—endless ridicule over his awkward attempt to wear an ill-fitting combat helmet while riding in a tank; his insufficiently impassioned response to CNN's Bernard Shaw about whether he would favor the death penalty for someone who raped and killed his wife; his "card-carrying" membership in the ACLU; and the weekend furlough granted to Willie Horton, the menacing-looking African American murderer who raped and killed helpless white victims during his state-sanctioned time away from prison.

Leading into the 1988 election, it appeared that after eight years of rule by Ronald Reagan the Republicans were in deep trouble. For most of the race, Dukakis maintained a huge polling lead on George H. W. Bush. And ironically, much of Bush's unpopularity was due to the widespread perception that, after years of remaining meekly in the background loyally supporting Reagan, *he* was an effeminate wimp.

From the outset of the campaign, Bush's primary liability was the perception that he—unlike the cowboy-dressing Reagan—lacked true manly attributes. He was regarded as a Connecticut patrician, scion of a wealthy and politically connected family, son of an aristocratic senator who preferred holidays in Maine and on Cape Cod. One of the most damaging "controversies" occurred during the primaries when it was widely reported that Bush visited a New Hampshire diner and, surrounded by blue-collar male voters, asked for a "splash more coffee." That event merely confirmed the damaging perception that had long been dogging Bush, a perception that led *Newsweek,* upon Bush's 1987 announcement of his intention to run for president, to proclaim on its cover that Bush was "Fighting the Wimp Factor."

Professor Ducat, in his book named after that cover story, comprehensively chronicles the "wimp" and "effeteness" problems that plagued the first George Bush and threatened his political future:

> "There you go with that fucking hand again. You look like a fucking pansy!" media advisor Roger Ailes bellowed at his client, the Republican presidential aspirant in 1988.
>
> Unfortunately for then vice president George Herbert Walker Bush, political pundits and other opinion makers of the 1980s, like those of the 1880s, did not take kindly to aristocratic manners, generally seeing them as feminine. . . .
>
> This was a perception held as much—if not more—by Republicans as by Democrats. Alexander Haig, Ronald Reagan's close friend Senator Paul Laxalt, and even Reagan himself regarded Bush as effete and unmanly. Newspaper articles appeared describing his life as one devoted to pleasing others. Conservative columnist George Will dismissed Bush as "lap dog" with a "thin tinny arf."

There are multiple levels of irony here, beginning with the fact that Ronald Reagan, depicted as the epitome of salt-of-the-earth, manly courage, avoided combat during World War II, remaining instead in Hollywood as a coddled actor, while George H. W. Bush, by all accounts, heroically served his country during that war as a fighter pilot. Yet, as has been proven true so many times since then, the ability to playact as a tough guy is far more important in American political contests than reality, and Bush's brave military service did not shield him at all from being cast as a soft and unmanly weakling, just as Reagan's combat avoidance did not preclude his being hailed as a warrior-defender of Freedom.

Faced, then, with a losing candidate whose very manhood

was in question, Bush 41's campaign handlers launched a two-pronged strategy: (1) they expertly staged multiple events designed to make Bush look like a tough guy and, more important, (2) they launched attack after attack against Dukakis intended to depict *him* as the wimp.

One of the first orders of business in "masculinizing" Bush and converting him into a "regular, normal guy" was to highlight his connections to Texas while downplaying his real roots in aristocratic Connecticut. The campaign frequently staged events where Bush would don a cowboy hat, attend rodeos, and incorporate Texas colloquialisms into his speech.

Atwater and Ailes understood that central to their prospects for victory was ensuring that their candidate was perceived as a swaggering tough guy, someone who exuded what were perceived to be the virtues of traditional American masculinity and, when necessary, was capable of striking a warrior pose. And even in light of how little they had to work with in George H. W. Bush, they proceeded to pioneer many of the tactics employed to this day by the right-wing electoral machine to convert their leaders into John Wayne avatars.

In 1988, Bush was scheduled to be interviewed by Dan Rather, and the campaign learned in advance from a CBS mole that Rather intended to question Bush very aggressively about his role in the Iran-Contra scandal. The Atwater-Ailes team recognized this as a key opportunity to remake the image of their candidate.

Bush was angrily defiant—uncharacteristically aggressive—throughout the interview, famously telling Rather, "It's not fair to judge my whole career by a rehash on Iran. How would you like it if I judged your whole career by those seven minutes when you walked off the set in New York?" Afterward, Bush boasted to his campaign aides, into a live microphone: "The bastard didn't lay a glove on me," a comment widely reported by newspapers. As Ducat wrote:

It was the display of the manly attitude—angry defiance, in particular—that made this contest politically useful for Bush. . . .

Lee Atwater summed up the significance of Bush's performance: "I think it was the most important event of the entire primary campaign. It was stronger than grits in the South . . . It solidified our base."

Just as Bush's campaign was bolstered by the calculated re-creation of him as a swaggering Real Man, Dukakis's was contin-uously undermined by the depiction of him as an unmanly loser. And Dukakis himself, guided by disastrous advice from his inept campaign manager, Susan Estrich, seemingly did everything in his power to reinforce this imagery.

Initially, under withering attacks from the Bush campaign di-rected at his "liberalism," Dukakis—rather than stand and fight for the term—ran away from it, insisting that he was no liberal at all, but rather was actually conservative, stressing his enthusi-asm for Reagan's policies of militarism and various weapons sys-tems. Scampering far and fast from his own ideology made Dukakis look weak and unwilling to fight, and Ronald Reagan himself mocked Dukakis's fear of his own positions this way: "We haven't seen such a radical transformation since Dustin Hoffman played 'Tootsie.'"

It was Dukakis's efforts to prove his manliness—not by standing firm for his beliefs, but instead by embracing a mili-tarism that was plainly not his own—that led him to his now-infamous visit to a General Dynamics tank factory, where he donned an ill-fitting helmet and uniform and awkwardly rode around in an M1 tank. It was the Dukakis campaign which in-sisted that his visit be filmed, ensuring the Bush campaign a po-tent weapon to mock Dukakis's masculinity.

Dukakis's perceived manliness deficiency was exacerbated severely when, after being asked in a debate by CNN's Shaw whether he would favor the death penalty for someone who raped and murdered his wife, Dukakis replied with a stoic and technocratic explanation as to why the death penalty was flawed, citing statistics and studies in an answer almost entirely devoid of any rage at the image of his own wife being raped and killed. As Ducat wrote: "After the debate, he was savaged by Republicans and most reporters for failing to summon manly emotions."

The coup de grâce in Dukakis's fall from manhood was the series of Willie Horton ads, produced by the Bush campaign, that accused Dukakis of furloughing into the community a menacing black male who proceeded to rape white women and kill their husbands. Dukakis was thus the soft male too weak to protect America's women from being raped and too effete to protect America's males from suffering that humiliation.

As Ducat documents, Bush surrogates devoted enormous resources to depicting Dukakis as effeminate and unmanly. Jerry Falwell urged his followers to disseminate a comic book depicting Dukakis as "Sheriff Pansy," a cross-dressing, limp-wristed liberal. In an interview, Orrin Hatch said that Dukakis's Democrats had become "the party of homosexuals," while Bush family comrade James Baker said: "He's the only man I know who could look at the swimsuit issue of *Sports Illustrated* and complain because the bathing suits weren't flame-retardant."

Far more than any policy issues, these attacks on Dukakis as unmanly and the accompanying depiction of Bush as a protective "ass-kicker" turned a huge deficit into a relatively easy Bush victory. Ducat:

> One response to a debate question would not ordinarily have such an impact. But this event was simply the climax of an electoral battle characterized by its comical but earnest performances of masculinity. While Bush, with much help, had adroitly, if temporarily, countered attributions of effeminacy, Dukakis had not been so

successful. The rhetorical assaults on his manhood had ranged from subtle innuendo to grotesque caricature, but the cumulative effect was an enduring image of the Democratic candidate as a feminized man.

The Republicans had actually begun impugning the masculinity and wholesomeness of Democratic candidates in the 1984 election, when Ronald Reagan crushed Walter Mondale. At a time when homosexuality was beginning to enter the public discourse in earnest, largely due to the emerging AIDS crisis, Jeane Kirkpatrick delivered a prime-time address to the GOP convention in which she referred five separate times to the "San Francisco Democrats."

But what was an implied and secondary theme in the 1984 election became the predominant attack in the 1988 campaign under the direction of Atwater and Ailes. And the successful depiction of George Bush as a tough guy and Dukakis as an effeminate girly-man, more than any other factor, swung the election in Bush's favor.

The cultural theme of tough, masculine, wholesome, salt-of-the-earth Republican versus the weak, emasculated, freakish, elitist Democrat reached a whole new level of viciousness in 1992, when then-president Bush was under attack from both Bill Clinton and Ross Perot. And there is no more vivid expression of the GOP slander machine than the prime-time 1992 RNC convention speech delivered by Pat Buchanan, who had shaken up the political establishment by posing a serious primary challenge to the incumbent president.

Buchanan's convention speech took what had been the implicit gender- and personality-manipulating cultural attacks on Democrats and made them explicitly clear. Wasting no time linking Democrats to transvestites, Buchanan declared,

Like many of you last month, I watched that giant masquerade ball at Madison Square Garden—where twenty thousand radicals and liberals came dressed up as moderates and centrists—in the greatest single exhibition of cross-dressing in American political history.

Following in the wake of Kirkpatrick's pioneered phrase "San Francisco Democrats," the meaning of Buchanan's attack was clear: Democrats were the party of the fags, the dykes, the gender-confused freaks. And the media, as it always does with such catty and personal smears, swooned with delight, doing more to bolster and disseminate the smear than all the paid advertising in the world could accomplish. In 2007, Chris Matthews and Pat Buchanan fondly reminisced on MSNBC about Buchanan's speech as follows:

> **MATTHEWS:** Pat, you are one of the greatest rheoreticians [*sic*] of our life. You spoke down there in Houston in '92. I mention this because it was **one of the great moments in the Republican Party.** You're down—great in a certain way. You're down there in Houston, **talking about the whole Democratic Party "cross dressing."**
> **BUCHANAN:** Well, I . . .
> **MATTHEWS: Jeane Kirkpatrick in '84 referred to the "San Francisco Democrats." Everybody got the giggle. We all get the giggle.**

"Everyone" in the press "got the giggle"—and they still do. During that 1992 speech, Buchanan (who has no children of his own) repeatedly emphasized the central importance of the traditional family as a reason to vote for Bush. And he contrasted that image by continuously invoking the specter of the frighteningly assertive wife of the would-be Democratic president, one who—despite having been married to the same man her entire life and having raised with him a daughter—did not, according to Buchanan, believe in the proper place for women or even in the institution of marriage itself:

"Elect me, and you get two for the price of one," Mr. Clinton says of his lawyer-spouse.

And what does Hillary believe? Well, Hillary believes that twelve-year-olds should have a right to sue their parents, and she has compared marriage as an institution to slavery—and life on an Indian reservation.

Well, speak for yourself, Hillary.

Friends, this is radical feminism.

Buchanan, despite having been of prime fighting age throughout the Vietnam War but avoiding all military service, sought to portray Bush as The Better Man Than Clinton when he contrasted Bush's war record to what he called Clinton's "draft dodging." That argument prompted boisterous cheers from the GOP throngs. Those are the same throngs who, a mere eight years later, would go on to elect and then venerate combat-avoiding George W. Bush. They're the same throngs who, in 2000, supported Bush over Vietnam-serving Al Gore, and in 2004 reelected him while mocking Vietnam veteran John Kerry's war medals and waving signs at that year's GOP convention depicting a Purple Heart patched with a Band-Aid. Buchanan thundered:

George Bush was seventeen when they bombed Pearl Harbor. He left his high school class, walked down to the recruiting office, and signed up to become the youngest fighter pilot in the Pacific war.

And Mr. Clinton? When Bill Clinton's turn came in Vietnam, he sat up in a dormitory in Oxford, England, and figured out how to dodge the draft.

Which of these two men has won the moral authority to call on Americans to put their lives at risk? I suggest, respectfully, it is the patriot and war hero, Navy Lieutenant J. G. George Herbert Walker Bush.

In that speech, Buchanan made as explicit an argument as had been made that elections ought to be decided not on the basis of foreign policy disagreements or even domestic policy conflicts, but rather on the basis of religious and cultural tribalism. Ominously referring again to "Clinton & Clinton"—thus elevating the emasculating "lawyer-spouse" and belittling her controlled husband—Buchanan drew the battle lines:

> There is a religious war going on in our country for the soul of America. It is a cultural war, as critical to the kind of nation we will one day be as was the Cold War itself. And in that struggle for the soul of America, Clinton & Clinton are on the other side, and George Bush is on our side.

Right-wing efforts to emasculate Bill Clinton relied at least as much on the depiction of Hillary as a threatening, excessively domineering female as it did on any attacks on Bill himself. As Ducat demonstrates through a series of countless examples, during both the 1992 campaign and for the first two years of the Clinton presidency—with Clinton's defense of "gays in the military" as the context—both the right-wing press and their allies in the establishment media repeatedly depicted Hillary as a domineering woman who shattered the proper gender role of women, in the process emasculating not only her husband but all American males.

Throughout the 1990s, twisted attacks on the femininity of Hillary Clinton dominated both right-wing demonization campaigns and mainstream political discourse. *National Review* repeatedly referred to Hillary as "that smiling barracuda." Bill Maher said of the possibility raised in the Paula Jones sexual-harassment suit that Clinton may have to have his penis physically examined to determine if it had "distinguishing characteristics": "He has to be careful around the White House because you know how

Hillary loves to shred evidence." *Newsweek* ran a cartoon show-ing Hillary lying next to Bill in bed with this thought in a bubble over her head: "Hillary Rodham Bobbitt."

Spy magazine ran a cover story titled "Hillary's Big Secret" and depicted Hillary on its cover in the mold of the famous pho-tograph of Marilyn Monroe standing on a grate with her skirt blowing up—only, Hillary's skirt blew up and revealed a penis asserting itself through her male underwear. *The American Spec-tator* featured a cover story by Fred Barnes warning of the dom-ineering Hillary's health care plan, and published a cartoon of a man held down helplessly on his back by Bill Clinton, while Hillary stood over him with a saw; the cartoon was captioned "Health Nuts." Even in 2007, this Emasculating Hillary imagery continued to roll out of the mouths and keyboards of our na-tion's frightened right-wing tough guys, as, for instance, when *National Review*'s Mark Steyn wrote a column about Hillary's newly unveiled health care plan titled "Bend Over for Nurse Hillary." On his MSNBC show, Tucker Carlson actually con-fessed about his reaction to Hillary: "There's just something about her that feels castrating, overbearing, and scary." Carlson's MSNBC colleague, Chris Matthews, referred to surrogates of the Hillary Clinton campaign and asked rhetorically: "[A]ren't you appalled at the willingness of these people to become ***cas-tratos*** in the **eunuch chorus** here or whatever thay are?" All of these creepy, revealing phrases echoed Rush Limbaugh's re-peated application of the woman-fearing phrase "testicular lock-box" when describing various Clinton policies, including her Iraq plan and health care proposals.

Despite all of that, the twice-elected and highly popular Bill Clinton was the one Democratic candidate of any significance over the last two decades whom the Republicans failed to trans-form into an effeminate, weak male. Despite the vicious efforts of the right-wing noise machine and the GOP edifice to emascu-late Clinton by portraying him as the captive of gays and a con-trolling wife, Americans perceived Clinton as a regular guy. And the reason, ironically, was that the right wing's obsessive focus on his sex life and other appetites, and their endless depictions of him as a conquering lady's man, had the opposite of the intended effect.

The Clinton sex scandals unintentionally pushed Clinton closer to the GOP image of the virile, sexually conquering, and unquestionably heterosexual male than the effeminate-loser image that had engulfed Dukakis, Mondale, and so many others. How threatening and emasculating could Hillary be, how effeminate and whipped could Bill Clinton be, if—as the right wing endlessly insisted—he was a virile sexual conquerer having his way with one woman after the next?

Right-Wing Dirt-Peddlers: From the Fringe to the Dominant Mainstream

While the right-wing political movement parades around as the morally upstanding, traditional-values-embracing, wholesome American faction, they are led by some of the most morally "untraditional" hedonists who engage in myriad decadent and filth-wallowing practices. Two of the most politically influential figures in the right-wing noise machine—Rush Limbaugh and Matt Drudge—spent virtually all of the 1990s spewing one assault after another against the Clintons based not on policy disputes but instead rooted in gender, cultural, and highly sexualized themes.

The draft-avoiding, illegal-pill-addicted, and multiple-divorced Limbaugh—burdened with one of the most decadent and degraded personal lives of any public figure anywhere—repeatedly insinuated and then outright asserted that Hillary was a lesbian, that Bill had assaulted and even raped women, and that Hillary had her lover, Vince Foster, murdered. Matt Drudge, an unmarried, reputedly homosexual recluse, supplemented Limbaugh's sexually twisted attacks with even more degrading discussions, repeatedly spewing rumors—fed to him by the tawdry, bottom-feeding likes of Laura Ingraham, George Conway, and Ann Coulter—about the marks on Clinton's penis and his alleged multiple rapes.

Remarkably—indeed, incredibly—while the decadent individuals and dirt-peddling practices that defined the Limbaugh/Drudge circle began as the unspeakable fringe, these right-wing smear merchants and their tactics have become not just mainstream but dominant. Our political culture and mainstream discourse are now shaped by the same right-wing filthmongers who spent the last two decades spewing some of the most vile and defamatory trash imaginable.

That our establishment media has been "Drudge-ified"—that is, completely taken over by right-wing dirt-peddling and twisted gender-based caricatures—is beyond dispute. The examples conclusively demonstrating that to be true are too numerous to chronicle in this one book. But the task is unnecessary, for many of our country's leading mainstream journalists, working at the top echelons of our most respected news organizations, have made the definitive case that this "Drudge-ification" reigns.

Mark Halperin was the political director of ABC News and is now senior political analyst for *Time* magazine. John Harris was the national politics editor for the *Washington Post* and is now the editor in chief of *The Politico,* a Drudge-mimicking daily Internet political newspaper. It is virtually impossible to find journalists who are more consummate Washington political media insiders than Halperin and Harris, working, as they do, for our nation's most establishment and influential news organizations.

And yet in their 2006 book, *The Way to Win,* Halperin and Harris reveal one of the most amazing and extraordinary truths about our establishment political press: that the individual who wields the single greatest influence over the process by which political news is reported—what the duo call "The Freak

Show"—is the lie-spewing, dirt-wallowing, right-wing Internet gossip Matt Drudge:

> In the fragmented, remote-control, click-on-this, did you hear? political media world in which we live, revered Uncle Walter has been replaced by odd nephew Matt. . . .
>
> Matt Drudge rules our world . . . With the exception of the Associated Press, there is no outlet other than the Drudge Report whose dispatches instantly can command the attention and energies of the most established news-papers and television newscasts.
>
> So many media elites check the Drudge Report con-sistently that a reporter is aware his bosses, his competi-tors, his sources, his friends on Wall Street, lobbyists, White House officials, congressional aides, cousins, and everyone who is anyone has seen it, too. . . .
>
> And there has been no more effective venue for promoting the Freak Show agenda in presidential pol-itics than the website run out of the Miami apartment of Matt Drudge, the impresario of **the attack-based personality-obsessed politics that is the Freak Show's signature. . . .**
>
> Members of the Gang of 500—which, according to the *New Yorker,* includes "the campaign consultants, strategists, pollsters, pundits, and journalists who make up the modern-day political establishment"—all read the Drudge Report. If the greatest challenge of any person seeking the presidency is keeping control of his or her public image, and the great obstacle to this control is the Freak Show, then Matt Drudge is the gatekeeper. In this sense, he is the Walter Cronkite of his era.

Ponder what that really means—for our country and our po-litical system. Our establishment political press, according to two of its most influential members, is *led by* a lowlife gossipmonger who, a mere ten years ago, was considered so unseemly and unreliable that he was the symbol of journalistic irresponsibility, that which was to be avoided. Yet now he is the "Walter Cronkite" of this era to our nation's press corps, setting its agenda and dictating its coverage. And our political press, in turn, is defined, first and foremost, by the "attack-based personality-obsessed politics" that Matt Drudge perfected.

More significantly still, Drudge is no mere generic dirtmonger. He is a dirtmonger with a distinctly right-wing political agenda. He was the creation of Rush Limbaugh, who, in the mid-1990s, relentlessly promoted Drudge's trashy anti-Clinton items at a time when Drudge was an obscure Internet gossip with fewer than a thousand daily readers. As a result of the attention paid to him by Limbaugh, Drudge became famous by virtue of serving as Innuendo Central for the most scurrilous sex rumors aimed at the Clintons. That he is now the leader of our political press means that he not only dragged it down to his level of "personality-based attacks," but also has dragged it distinctly *to the right.*

More incredibly still, not even the publication of outright fabrications have diminished Drudge's credibility with, and influence over, our media elite. In the midst of the 2004 presidential campaign, Drudge, looking to recapture the Glory of the Clinton Sex Scandals, ran a screaming headline announcing that John Kerry had harassed a young campaign aide, Alexandra Polier, to the point where she fled the country to Africa in order to escape his unwanted advances:

> A frantic behind-the-scenes drama is unfolding around Sen. John Kerry and his quest to lockup the Democratic nomination for President, the Drudge Report can reveal.
>
> Intrigue surrounds a woman who recently fled the country, reportedly at the prodding of Kerry, the Drudge Report has learned. . . .
>
> A close friend of the woman first approached a re-

porter late last year claiming fantastic stories—stories that now threaten to turn the race for the presidency on its head! . . .

The report in its entirety was completely false. Polier was forced to issue a statement: "I have never had a relationship with Senator Kerry, and the rumors in the press are completely false." Without ever apologizing or retracting the story, Drudge simply slinked away from it, eventually reporting that Polier was involved in a romantic relationship with a Kerry aide and then quietly whitewashing the reports from his site.

Even with the story having become completely discredited, right-wing pundits such as Rush Limbaugh continued to make use of it for months. In July—four months after the story was revealed to be a complete hoax—Limbaugh imitated the voice of Bill Clinton giving advice to Kerry:

John, whatever you do, keep that babe in Africa. Don't let her come back here. I've been there, too, and this is not a good thing. What was her name? Alex? Yeah. (Laughing) . . . Stay away from any more of these. You don't have to write a book like I had to write.

The Polier story was a lie. Limbaugh repeated it with the intent of depicting John Kerry as a lecherous menace to young women. And Drudge himself has a long record of publishing other blatantly false accusations, from falsely accusing Clinton aide Sidney Blumenthal of spousal abuse to suggesting that a bump on John McCain's head was a growing tumor. And in November 2007, Drudge prominently featured a report from a British tabloid accusing Hillary Clinton of having an ongoing lesbian affair with one of her young Muslim female aides. As part of that item, Drudge excitedly vowed: "The current campaign promises to become one of the dirtiest in modern history." Yet two full years after the Kerry intern story and multiple fabrications, Mark

Halperin and John Harris hailed Drudge as the "Walter Cronkite of their era," the individual who—more than any other—sets the agenda for what our political press covers.

This is why our political process has become so broken and corrupt. The worst elements of the far-right wing have been shaping and driving how national journalists view events, the stories they cover, and the narratives they disseminate. For Halperin and Harris to acknowledge that our political press—long deemed by the right-wing noise machine and therefore the press itself to be the "liberal media"—is in fact guided and shaped by a right-wing filthmonger and lowly gossip is extraordinary.

Indeed, Harris and Halperin explicitly acknowledge the incomparable influence that the right-wing smear machine now exerts over how the establishment press covers political issues:

> The simultaneous stumble of the Old Media and the rise of the New have had a disproportionate impact on the two warring sides in American politics. While there are plenty of conservatives who have been singed (or even burned at the stake) by the Freak Show, on the whole, these **changes have been beneficial for conservatives and bad for liberals, since the New Media overwhelmingly favors conservatives.** There is no liberal equivalent of the Fox News Channel, or Rush Limbaugh, or the Drudge Report, all of which have significant audiences and **a demonstrated ability to promote controversies and story lines that affect the Old Media.**

Imagine the uproar if Halperin and Harris instead had identified a figure associated with the Left—Michael Moore or an Air America personality—as the single most influential figure shaping coverage by the press, or if they had described a process whereby the most vicious ideologues on the Left, rather than the Right, can "promote controversies and story lines" virtually at will. Shrill protests over the "liberal media" would be even louder than they already are.

Yet the duo's confession that they and their colleagues march to the lowly, right-wing tune of Matt Drudge and the rest of the right-wing "personality-based attack" engines received little attention, and understandably so. After all, anyone who pays even minimal attention to how our media covers political figures is already well aware that they operate just as their Leader, Matt Drudge, does—namely, by reciting right-wing personality attacks designed to make liberals and Democrats appear to be weak and Republicans strong. The sleazy personality-based attacks churned out by the right wing are able to dominate our political discourse and our elections only because the establishment press so hungrily gorges on them and then spews them back, thereby establishing the dominant narratives that dictate how our political leaders are perceived.

John Harris has gone far beyond mere words in recognizing that the political press is dominated by the sort of right-wing attacks in which Drudge specializes. In 2006, Harris announced that he was leaving his prestigious position at the *Washington Post* to found and serve as editor in chief for a new political daily newspaper, to be called *The Politico*.

Harris quickly recruited some of the most establishment political journalists in the country to leave their positions and join *The Politico*, including *Washington Post* reporter Jim VandeHei and *Time* magazine White House correspondent Mike Allen. When *The Politico* was launched, VandeHei vowed to assemble "the best political reporting team in the country today and deliver the news the way people want it: fast, fair, and first." But it quickly became apparent that *The Politico* would follow completely in Drudge's footsteps, specializing in the types of right-wing personality-based attacks that, as Harris himself acknowledged, dominate our political discourse.

The Politico is funded almost entirely by the Albritton

Corporation, whose founder and CEO, Joseph Albritton, was a longtime right-wing fixture in Washington. And the publication hardly sought to conceal its leanings, as the Albritton Corporation named as *The Politico*'s CEO Frederick Ryan, an official in the Reagan White House, longtime confidant of the Reagan family and the current chairman of the board of trustees of the Ronald Reagan Presidential Library Foundation.

Virtually from the first day it began publishing, it was inescapably clear that *The Politico* would devote itself to the same types of vapid, base personality attacks on liberals and Democrats that drive our political and media culture generally. As John Harris, *The Politico*'s editor in chief, recognizes, political media outlets receive attention (and therefore readers and page hits) only by adhering to the standard script, whereby "journalists" take their cues from the Drudge/Limbaugh right-wing noise machine, ignoring substantive policy disputes and focusing obsessively on shallow personality issues and smears.

Almost immediately, *The Politico* became the prime beneficiary of the gossipmonger whom its editor in chief flattered as "the Walter Cronkite of our era." A link from The Drudge Report is like no other on the Internet; a single Drudge link generates traffic at the linked site magnitudes above any other political website's ability. Drudge is notoriously reluctant to link to new online ventures, reserving links almost exclusively for established newspapers. Yet virtually from its inception *The Politico* became one of the most linked-to—if not the single most linked-to—sites on Drudge. Sometimes on a daily basis, whatever story *The Politico* happened to churn out, The Drudge Report prominently promoted. From the most banal stories carried by every other news outlet and wire service, to the pettiest personality attacks published only by *The Politico,* the millions of daily Drudge readers were continuously sent to *Politico* stories.

On March 28, 2007, Media Matters published an analysis documenting that it had "reviewed the Drudge Report Archives and found that since *The Politico* launched on January 23 [a mere sixty-four days earlier], Drudge has linked to *Politico* items on at least 45 separate occasions."

On some occasions, Drudge promoted and linked to *Politico* stories even before *The Politico* published the story on its own site. The two websites worked in perfect tandem with each other, and no publication promoted the gossip-obsessed, right-wing Drudge agenda as extensively as did *The Politico*. Drudge, in turn, repaid *The Politico* with links so numerous and continuous that one Web analyst estimated in March 2007 that Drudge accounted for 65 percent of *The Politico*'s traffic (the next-highest source of traffic for *The Politico* was Google, at a mere 3 percent).

And it was not hard to understand this coordinated linking strategy between Drudge and *The Politico*. The latter churned out one petty, personality-based attack story after another, aimed primarily at Democrats and liberals, exactly the type of shallow and vapid smears that already pervade our political landscape and that Matt Drudge eats up.

That *The Politico,* as well as numerous other publications, crafts its stories with the hope of attracting Drudge's attention is conceded by Harris himself in *The Way to Win,* describing the perception of Drudge's importance:

> Meanwhile, although there is no system for authorized leaks to the Drudge Report at the *Washington Post,* editors at the website and main newspaper are delighted when Drudge does link to stories at washingtonpost.com. Invariably, traffic to the site soars. And there is evident frustration when the Drudge Report does not acknowledge significant *Washington Post* pieces.

Harris goes on to recount how a mere mention from Drudge single-handedly enabled Harris to get invited on major news shows to promote his new book.

The Politico has followed this Drudge-based strategy

tenaciously. The most attention-generating, petty *Politico* attack began on April 16, 2007, when former *New York Daily News* reporter Ben Smith, assigned to cover Democratic presidential candidates for *The Politico,* published an item regarding John Edwards's haircuts. The item was titled "The Hair's Still Perfect," and at the top displayed a large, informal photograph of Edwards, grinning widely. Underneath the photograph, Smith wrote: "How much you ask [*sic*] does it cost to look like that?" Smith continued:

> Well, John Edwards' campaign for president spent $400 on February 20, and another $400 on March 7, at a top Beverly Hills men's stylist, Torrenueva Hair Designs.
>
> The expensive haircut is, of course, a perennial. Bill Clinton got zinged for getting a cut from Cristophe, and Hillary was found at one point to have buried a stylist on her campaign payroll.
>
> Obama, on the other hand, gets his cut cheap and frequent—but he does take the process seriously enough to hold his calls.
>
> Only Edwards, however, has had the care he takes with his hair memorialized on YouTube.
>
> Edwards' campaign also spent money at two spas: Designworks Salon in Dubuque, and Pink Sapphire in Manchester.

Over the phrase "memorialized on YouTube," Smith provided a link to a widely disseminated video of Edwards from the 2004 presidential campaign where, prior to a television appearance, he brushes his hair in front of a mirror for thirty to forty seconds. That video was endlessly deployed by right-wing pundits and bloggers to mock Edwards during the campaign as an effeminate, vain girly-man obsessed with his hair. Not only did Smith link to the video as part of his haircut item, but the specific video he chose shows Edwards brushing his hair while blaring in the background is the song "I Feel Pretty."

That "I Feel Pretty" video alone has been viewed in excess of one million times on YouTube.

GOP operatives repeatedly referred to Edwards during the 2004 campaign as "the Breck Girl," a slur disseminated most helpfully by the *New York Times* political reporter Adam Nagourney. Nagourney, in a front-page *Times* article at the height of the 2004 campaign, actually granted anonymity to his "sources," whom he described as "Bush officials," to sling that emasculating insult at Edwards. (In this same ignominious article, Nagourney mindlessly parroted the same anonymous cowards as saying that Kerry "looks French," leading to that "observation" becoming a favorite anti-Kerry insult of the national media throughout the campaign.)

Three years later, in April 2007—in the midst of the Edwards hair "controversy"—Nagourney wrote in the *New York Times* about his 2004 hit piece, sheepishly acknowledging the significant role the "looks French" and "Breck Girl" attacks he published played in demeaning the personalities of Kerry and Edwards during the election:

> Our story may have had the result of not only previewing what the Bush campaign intended to do, but, by introducing such memorably biting characterizations into the political dialogue, helping it.

It apparently took Nagourney three years of deep contemplation to realize that turning over the front pages of the *New York Times* to anonymous partisan smear artists might actually end up bolstering their smears and cementing them in our national political dialogue.

But Nagourney's efforts were merely one component of the right-wing-machine/media onslaught that promoted—and continues to promote—the "Edwards Is a Faggot Girl" slur. Throughout 2007, with Smith's *Politico* story as the fuel, Rush Limbaugh regularly posted Photoshopped pictures on his website of Edwards as an androgynous womanly freak, with long flowing hair, eye shadow, and lipstick. The *New York Sun* published an article headlined: "Could John Edwards Become the First Woman President?" a question then repeated by the likes of Limbaugh and the *Wall Street Journal*'s James Taranto. And Ann Coulter capped the smear in April 2007 by famously appearing at one of the most prestigious conservative events and outright calling Edwards a "faggot."

From the time Smith first "broke" the Edwards haircut story on April 16 until May 2, *The Politico* itself ran no fewer than eight separate stories on Edwards's hair, at one point even publishing an "investigative piece" in which it interviewed the hairstylist and analyzed the stylist's pricing structures. Drudge prominently featured multiple Edwards hair stories.

One can see the validity of Halperin and Harris's coronation of Drudge as the leader of our nation's political press by simply reviewing the tidal wave of establishment media outlets that dutifully reported the Edwards hair story after Drudge pushed it. In fact, it is not hyperbole to say that, for the two weeks following Smith's "scoop," the Edwards haircut issue was one of the most reported political stories in the nation. And the establishment press not only reported the facts of Edwards's haircut but eagerly promoted the central derisive narrative—that his haircuts demonstrate, yet again, Edwards's girlish obsession with his hair.

The day after Drudge touted Smith's story, the Associated Press churned out an article, published by CNN (among others), that began: "**Looking pretty** is costing John Edwards' presidential campaign a lot of pennies." The Associated Press then interviewed Edwards's hairstylist and reported that the stylist confessed: " 'I do cut his hair and I have cut it for quite a while,' Torrenueva said. 'We've been friends a long time.' "

All of that led *The New Republic,* a day late but still right on script, to lament the effeminate and vain Edwards. *TNR*'s Eve Fairbanks posted an item on the magazine's website that she headlined "He Feels Pretty and Witty, and . . ." in which she let us know that she (of course) is far too sophisticated and serious to "give a damn that Edwards went to the Pink Sapphire." After dutifully reporting the item (that she is much too serious to care about), she then linked to the same three-year-old YouTube clip of Edwards brushing his hair to the "I Feel Pretty" song.

Fairbanks justified her post by claiming that "the fact that the haircut and the Pink Sapphire is a CNN top headline on a huge news day suggests that, sadly, plenty of people still think of Edwards like this," the "this" referencing the YouTube clip. In her world, the media's chatter—in which (as she herself was doing) they repeat Drudge gossip—is proof of how "plenty of people" think. As always, Drudge rules their world and they become his echo chamber. If he selects a petty, personality-smearing story to trumpet, and the media (as they always do) dutifully follows, then that alone constitutes "proof" of the story's importance, evidence that "plenty of people" care about it, which in turn justifies the media's continuous chatter about it.

Most certainly, the press will pretend to be above it all ("this is not something that we, the sophisticated political journalists, care about, of course"). But they yammer about Drudge-promoted gossip endlessly, and then insist that their own chattering is proof that it is an important story that people care about. And because they conclude that "people" (i.e., them) are concerned with the story, they keep chirping about it, which in turn fuels their belief that the story is important. It is an endless loop of self-referential narcissism—whatever they endlessly sputter is what "the people" care about, and therefore they must keep harping on it, because their chatter is proof of its importance.

Illustrating this cycle perfectly, Howard Kurtz—the media critic for the *Washington Post* and CNN—defended the intense coverage of Smith's story about Edwards's haircut, writing: "You might think that this would be too trivial to spark a major online debate, but hair matters, apparently. It's a meta-phor for . . . well, for something very important." The hair-cut item was not only highlighted, but repeatedly harped on, by virtually every significant news outlet. As Media Matters documented:

- The *New York Times* reported on the story twice, and the haircuts were the subject of *Times* columnist Maureen Dowd's April 21 column. The *Washington Post* mentioned the haircuts in five articles, while the *Los Angeles Times* mentioned them twice. *USA Today* mentioned them once.
- The AP referred to the haircuts in five articles, including the April 17 article that labeled Edwards as "pretty."
- NBC and CBS reported on Edwards's haircuts twice, and ABC reported on them once.
- CNN referred to the haircuts at least six times, MSNBC at least three times, and Fox News at least five times.

Eric Boehlert of Media Matters added:

In its Conventional Wisdom Watch column, *Newsweek* placed The Haircut directly behind the Virginia Tech massacre and Attorney General Alberto Gonzales' Sen-ate testimony as that week's most important news events.

And a *New York Times* Week in Review piece included a roundup of key news developments and highlighted the surging stock market, the rise of the British pound, the record-setting amount of mutual funds distributed to investors last year, and yes, Edwards' costly trim.

This idiocy reached its zenith when NBC News anchor Brian Williams asked Edwards about his haircuts during the April 26, 2007, Democratic presidential debate. A mere two days earlier,

Williams had appeared on *The Late Show with David Letterman* and discussed the Edwards Hair Story at length.

Williams—whose annual salary is $10 million and who, according to Boehlert, "lives in a restored farmhouse in Connecticut where he parks his 477-horsepower black Porsche GT2 (that is, when he's not decamping on the Upper East Side)"—snidely and quite improbably claimed on Letterman's show that the most expensive haircut he ever received was priced at $12. Though he agreed that the Edwards haircut story was "silly" and there was "no reason for us to continue talking about it"—even as he talked about it—Williams then proceeded two days later, during a nationally televised presidential debate, to ask Edwards about his haircuts as the second question he posed to the candidate.

Days later, Mike Huckabee raised the issue during a Republican presidential debate by remarking: "We've had a Congress that's spent money like John Edwards at a beauty shop." And amazingly, NBC's Tim Russert, while moderating a Democratic presidential debate on September 26, 2007—a full five months after Smith first "broke" the story—became the second NBC journalist to use his time in a presidential debate to inquire of Edwards about his hair:

> Your campaign has hit some obstacles with revelations about $400 haircuts, half-million dollars working for a hedge fund, $800,000 from Rupert Murdoch. Do you wish you hadn't taken money in all those cases or hadn't made that kind of expenditure for a haircut?

In December 2007, the *Wall St. Journal*'s Peggy Noonan offered up a Santa-like checklist of which presidential candidates were "reasonable" and which ones were not. In describing the attributes that Americans want in a president, she wrote, "I claim here to speak for thousands, millions." On behalf of the throngs for whom she fantasizes she speaks, Noonan proclaimed, "We are grown-ups . . . We'd like knowledge, judgment, a prudent understanding of the world and of the ways and histories of the men and women in it."

This "grown-up" then proceeded to pronounce that all GOP candidates except Mike Huckabee were "reasonable"—as were Biden, Dodd, Richardson, and Obama (though too young and inexperienced to be president)—but this is what she wrote about John Edwards:

> John Edwards is not reasonable . . . [W]e can't have a president who spent two minutes on YouTube staring in a mirror and poofing his hair. Really, we just can't.

What is notable here is not so much the specific petty attacks, but rather the method by which they are disseminated and then entrenched as conventional wisdom among our Really Smart Political Insiders and Serious Journalists. This is the endlessly repeated process that drives political coverage of our candidates:

STEP 1 A new Drudge-dependent gossip (Ben Smith) at a new substance-free political rag (*The Politico*)—or some right-wing talk-radio host (Rush Limbaugh) or some credibility-bereft right-wing blogger (a Michelle Malkin)—seizes on some petty, manufactured incident to fuel clichéd caricatures of Democratic candidates.

STEP 2 The old right-wing gossip (Drudge) employs his old, substance-free political rag (The Drudge Report) to amplify the inane caricatures.

STEP 3 National media outlets, such as AP and CNN, whose world is ruled by Drudge, take note of and begin "analyzing" the "political implications" of the gossip, thus transforming it into "news stories."

STEP 4 Our Serious Beltway Journalists and Political Analysts—in the Haircut Case, Tim Russert and Brian Williams and Adam Nagourney and the very serious and smart Substantive Journalists at *The New Republic*—mindlessly repeat all of it, thereby solidifying it as transpartisan conventional wisdom.

STEP 5 When called upon to justify their endless reporting over such petty and pointless Drudge-generated matters, these "journalists" cite Steps 1–4 as "proof" that "the people" care about these stories, even though the "evidence" consists of nothing other than their own flocklike chirping.

To observe this self-reinforcing behavior in action, one can look at *The Politico*'s tenacious follow-up on its Haircut Scoop. On May 2, *The Politico*'s so-called chief political columnist, Roger Simon, published a 674-word article—prominently touted on *The Politico*'s front page—exclusively about Edwards's haircuts, very cleverly headlined "Hair Today, Gone Tomorrow." That May 2 article by Simon was his second on this topic. Simon began his article by pronouncing:

> It is the haircut that will not die.
> He can spin it, he can gel it, he can mousse it. But it is not going away.

Simon marveled at how enduring the story is, as though there was some phenomenon keeping it alive independent of the fact that the gossipy, tiny-minded, substance-free "political journalists" plaguing our nation—from Roger Simon and Maureen Dowd, to Adam Nagourney, Mickey Kaus, and Matt Drudge—had not stopped harping on it. That is tantamount to someone who keeps chewing their food and spitting it across the room and then marveling at how filthy things are and writing columns bewilderingly examining how and why the floor is covered with food and what that all signifies.

Even *The Politico*—for which no story is too petty or Drudge-like—seemed embarrassed by its obsession. Thus, Simon claimed in his article that he "was willing never to write about the haircuts again," and *The Politico*'s front-page headline claimed: "Roger *reluctantly* takes another look at the haircut that will not die." In the article itself, Simon offered up this excuse for why he was writing his "newspaper's" eighth story in less than two weeks about John Edwards's hair:

> This is bad: When you go to Google and enter "Edwards haircut," the first item that comes up is a story by Bill Wundram in *The Quad-City Times* of Davenport, Iowa. . . .
>
> The article got 324 comments from readers. When people inside the Beltway are talking about your haircut, it doesn't matter much. When people in Iowa are talking about your haircut, you may have a problem.

So Simon used the excuse that the item in the Iowa paper received 324 comments as proof that this was a huge story outside the Beltway, that there was this spontaneous groundswell of interest in John Edwards's hair among salt-of-the-earth ordinary Iowans. Therefore, as much as he wished he could spend his time on more elevated matters, he simply had to write about it.

But what Simon omitted is that the reason the item in the Iowa paper received so many comments is that Drudge had linked to it, just as he linked to *The Politico*'s stories on this "issue." That sent hundreds of thousands of right-wing Drudge fanatics to the Iowa article, producing hundreds of comments. The slightest critical thought would have revealed that the article generated so many comments not because Americans care about the story but *because Drudge linked to it*. But critical thought was nowhere to be found in what Simon wrote. In his mind, media chatter about a "story" is proof of its importance.

During the two-week period when the political press, following Drudge's lead, was fixated on John Edwards's haircuts, the following are but a few of the stories that were never once mentioned, let alone covered, by *The Politico,* and that barely received any attention in the wider establishment political press:

- Retired Marine Corps general John Sheehan requested that his name be removed for consideration as "war czar" because our Iraq policy was being destroyed by what he called "the constant refrain by a small but powerful group that we are going to 'win,' even as 'victory' is not defined or is frequently redefined."

- The Bush administration sought vastly increased powers to spy on the telephone conversations of Americans, then threatened to begin spying again illegally and without warrants.

- It was revealed that Condoleezza Rice would meet with Syrian officials, a significant shift in Middle East policy.

- It was disclosed that Iraq's government was actually purging itself of anyone who sought to impede lawless Shiite militias.

- One of the right wing's most influential academicians, Harvard's Harvey Mansfield, published an Op-Ed in the *Wall Street Journal* explicitly advocating "one-man rule" in America, whereby the President can ignore the "rule of law" in order to fight the Terrorists.

Given the political press's eagerness to repeat and disseminate the twisted personality-based attacks on Democratic candidates cooked up by the right-wing noise machine, it was hardly a surprise when a Fox News poll in June 2007 found that an astonishing 44 percent of the electorate was able to answer "Edwards" when asked: "Do you happen to know which presidential candidate has been in the news recently for paying four hundred dollars for a haircut?"

As Greg Sargent of Talking Points Memo pointed out, a

Harris Interactive Poll from July 2006 found that only 45 percent of Americans answered "Not True" when asked whether Iraq had weapons of mass destruction when the United States invaded. As Sargent pointed out:

> Only one point more knew Saddam didn't have WMDs—a statistically identical amount. That's right—**the same number know about Edwards' haircut that knew the truth last year about Saddam and his phantom weapons.**

Far worse still, a *Washington Post* poll taken in September 2003—a full two years after the 9/11 attack and a full *six months after the United States invaded Iraq*—revealed that a truly depressing 69 percent of Americans believed it "likely" or "very likely" that "Saddam Hussein was personally involved in the September 11 attacks." As Sargent concluded:

> **So nearly 20 percent more know about Edwards' haircut than believed Saddam wasn't behind 9/11—**
> two years after the attacks and six whole months after the invasion.
>
> Something's wrong here.

What is "wrong here" is that our political press has been consumed by the filthiest, most slothful, and pettiest personality attacks—engineered by the likes of their leaders, Matt Drudge and Rush Limbaugh—while the vast bulk of its "journalists" ignore substantive stories except to repeat government claims about them uncritically and mindlessly. The political discourse engendered by our nation's media is thus suffused with an unceasing parade of juvenile "discussion" about patent nonstories, and even our presidential elections are decided more by contrived personal imagery than by any real consideration of policy and substantive issues.

Indeed, comprehensive surveys of media coverage demon-

strate that discussions of actual issues are excluded almost completely from press discussion even of our elections. An October
2007 report from the Pew Research Center examined press coverage of the 2008 presidential campaign and found that a minus-
cule 12 percent had anything to do with "how citizens might be
affected by the election." The overwhelming bulk of the coverage was instead devoted to campaign tactics, polling chatter,
and gossip about the candidates. Worse still, *virtually none* of
the discussions of the candidates involved their record or past
performance:

> In all, 63% of the campaign stories focused on political
> and tactical aspects of the campaign. That is nearly four
> times the number of stories about the personal back-
> grounds of the candidates (17%) or the candidates' ideas
> and policy proposals (15%). And **just 1% of stories ex-
> amined the candidates' records or past public per-
> formance,** the study found.

Thus, a very well-funded new political magazine, staffed by
some of the nation's most establishment political journalists,
jumped immediately into the Drudgian attack muck because, in
our political culture, that is where the real action is. Ground zero
for our political discourse among our establishment media are
scurrilous, personal smears and attack gossip dredged from the
Beltway gutters.

The fact that such adolescent smears are directed primarily—
or at least most potently—at liberals and Democrats was demonstrated by the virtually complete silence in the wake of a *Politico*
item concerning Mitt Romney. In July 2006, *The Politico*'s Ken-
neth Vogel published a 360-word article reporting that " 'communications consulting' is how presidential candidate Mitt
Romney recorded $300 in payments to a California company
that describes itself as 'a mobile beauty team for hair, makeup
and men's grooming and spa services.' " The Romney campaign

"confirmed that the payments—actually two separate $150 charges—were for makeup." Vogel's article included an interview with one of the makeup artists who worked on Romney:

> Stacy Andrews, who made up Romney for Hidden Beauty, said he barely needs makeup.
>
> "He's already tan," she said. "We basically put a drop of foundation on him . . . and we powdered him a little bit."

Despite its obvious similarities to the Edwards haircut story, this item went nowhere, as it was ignored almost completely by the establishment press. While Drudge heavily promoted the Edwards story, he completely ignored the Romney item. A 2007 article by *Salon*'s Michael Scherer sheds light on the likely cause of Drudge's lack of interest in the Romney "makeup" story:

> Matt Rhoades, Romney's communications director, has a long history as the source for Drudge headlines, having previously served as the research director for the Republican National Committee during the 2006 campaign. In their book *The Way to Win, Time*'s Mark Halperin and *The Politico*'s John Harris recount that Rhoades traveled to Florida for a friendly steakhouse dinner with Drudge when he took the research director job in 2005.

Drudge aggressively promoted the Edwards haircut story; therefore, it became one of the most covered items from the political press he leads. Drudge ignored the Romney story; therefore, it was ignored almost entirely by his journalistic followers. A LEXIS search reveals that the Edwards haircut story was mentioned 2,372 times in the media from the time it was first reported by *The Politico* through October 2007. A similar LEXIS search reveals that Romney's $300 makeup expenditure, during the same period, was mentioned a grand total of 21 times. Drudge rules their world.

The Politico's immediate effort to court and copy Drudge is by far not the only evidence demonstrating the supremacy of this strain of "journalism." In October 2007, Jim Rutenberg of the *New York Times* explored Drudge coverage of Hillary Clinton's campaign in an article headlined "Clinton Finds Way to Play Along with Drudge." That article, echoing the Halperin/Harris confession, made clear that Drudge single-handedly continues to rule the political press. Rutenberg documented coordinated efforts by the Clinton campaign to court the ruler of the media world:

> Mrs. Clinton is learning to play nice with the Drudge Report and the powerful, elusive and conservative-leaning man behind it. . . .
>
> [I]t also speaks to the enduring power of the Drudge Report, which mixes original reporting with links to newspaper, Internet or television reports far and wide. . . .
>
> Aides in both parties acknowledge working harder than ever to get favorable coverage for their candidates—or unfavorable coverage of competitors—onto the Drudge Report's home page, knowing that television producers, radio talk show hosts and newspaper reporters view it as a bulletin board for the latest news and gossip.
>
> Because of the sheer number of people who look at it and because of the attention it gets from the media, **what appears on Drudge can, for a few minutes or an entire day, drive what appears elsewhere, making it, "a force in the political news cycle for both the press and the campaigns," said David Chalian, the political director at ABC News. . . .**
>
> On the Republican side, a generation of campaign consultants has grown up learning to play in Mr. Drudge's influential but rarefied world. They have spent years studying his tastes and moods while carefully

building close relationships with him that are now bene-
fiting some Republican presidential campaigns—and that
others are scrambling to match.

That these establishment political journalists, following in
the Harris/Halperin footsteps, admit—without the slightest
trace of shame—that Matt Drudge determines the coverage
choices for America's political media outlets is utterly astound-
ing. After all, much of Drudge's reporting is, as the *New York
Times* article put it, "delivered with no apparent effort to determine its truth."

And yet America's most respected journalists casually praise
this fabricating smear artist as their leader. As Philip Weiss reported in *New York* magazine:

> "This is America's bulletin board, and much more than
> that," NBC's Brian Williams said recently. "Matt Drudge is
> just about the most powerful journalist in America," said
> Pat Buchanan.

The caption underneath the photograph accompanying the
New York Times story read: "*News reporter* Matt Drudge, publisher of the Drudge Report Web site, attends the White House
Correspondents' Dinner at the Washington Hilton Hotel on
April 30, 2005." Notwithstanding the avalanche of smears and
outright fabricated stories, political journalists consider Matt
Drudge not merely one of their own—a "news reporter"—but
their leader. The *Times* article quoted Jim Dyke, a Giuliani strategist and the communications director for the RNC in 2004, as
proclaiming: "No single person is more relevant to shaping the
media environment in a political campaign."

As Rutenberg documented, the highest levels of the Bush
2004 reelection campaign were devoted to placing "embarrassing tidbits" about Kerry with Drudge that establishment reporters were reluctant to cover. Like clockwork:

An item's appearance on Drudge would drive it into mainstream news coverage: A video clip of Mr. Kerry contradicting himself, or a photograph of him wearing a protective germ outfit.

"It's the stuff that speaks to the absurdity of politics, and it's done with devastating effect," a former Bush campaign aide said.

Despite the efforts of Hillary Clinton's aides to develop a rapport with Drudge—and notwithstanding the right's constant yammering about the "liberal media"—the most influential force in American political press coverage is decisively right wing and pro-Republican. As Weiss observed in *New York:*

> In 2000, he helped defeat Al Gore by turning up the volume on such stories as Al Gore's fund-raising appearance at a Buddhist temple. In 2004, he did more than anyone to upend Kerry by playing up a small ad buy by the Swift Boat Veterans. In this campaign season, he has made a virus of the John Edwards $400 haircut. . . .
>
> His audience is decidedly right-wing. According to the online advertising company linked to his site, the audience is 78 percent male, 60 percent Republican, only 8 percent Democratic.

For all the ink spilled on media criticism, the fact that the most potent influence on our political press is a right-wing dirtmonger specializing in often false personality smears is all one needs to know about the state of American political discourse.

Willing Puppets

When confronted with this shameful reality, the reaction of our leading journalists is quite telling. In October 2007, there was an intense debate over whether to expand a government health care program for children, known as S-CHIP. In defense of their efforts to expand the program, the Democrats put forward a message from Graeme Frost, a twelve-year-old whose life was likely saved by virtue of having S-CHIP health care coverage after he was in a near-fatal car accident. Almost immediately thereafter, a slew of right-wing bloggers and pundits unleashed a vicious attack on the Frost family, depicting them as wealthy defrauders who deserved no government-supplied insurance, culminating with Fox News's Michelle Malkin driving to the Frosts' home, writing about their house, and speaking to their neighbors.

The right-wing bloggers' attacks on the Frost family proved to be based on multiple falsehoods about the family's economic status, and those hit pieces generated widespread revulsion. Soon thereafter it was revealed that—contrary to the false denials of Senate Minority Leader Mitch McConnell—McConnell's office had sent to various journalists a memorandum about the Frosts disseminating the false attacks in order to encourage reporters to highlight the smears.

CNN's John Roberts dutifully went on the air and mindlessly repeated what he read in the McConnell smear memo, provided to him—"off the record," of course—by McConnell's top aide. This is how our journalists report on the political issues they cover. From the McConnell memo sent to Roberts:

> Apparently, there's more to the story on the kid (Graeme Frost) that did the Dems' radio response on S-CHIP. . . .
> **Could the Dems really have done that bad of a job vetting this family?**

This claim traveled from the off-the-record Republican dirtmongering machine out of the mouth of CNN's Roberts, with no stopping for investigation. Hence, Roberts, after quoting from Malkin's blog, reported:

Some of the accusations [against the Frosts] may be exaggerated or false. But did the Democrats make a tactical error in holding up Graeme as their poster child?

In language taken almost verbatim from the McConnell memo, Roberts's story then flashed to a "CNN political analyst," who placed the blame squarely on the Democrats' shoulders: "I think in this instance what happened was **the Democrats didn't do as much of a vetting** as they could have done on this young man, his situation, his family."

This was but one instance—a highly illustrative one—demonstrating how so much of our press coverage is shaped by petty, personality-based dirt and smears fed by anonymous Republican operatives to gossip-hungry, slothful journalists, who then uncritically repeat it all. About this right wing/press synergy, the widely quoted liberal political blogger Digby wrote:

> Journalists will say that using political "oppo research" is a legitimate way to get tips, as long as they always check them out before they run with them. Fair enough. But what they fail to acknowledge is that this allows the best story-planters to set the agenda for coverage, and the best story-planters are those who know how to get the media interested.
>
> And after watching them for the past two decades very closely, I think it's obvious that what interests the media more than anything is access and gossip and vicious little smears piled one atop the other. And why not? They are easy to report, require no mind-numbing shuffling of financial reports or struggling through arcane policy papers.
>
> In fact, the press has made a virtue of the simple-mindedness by calling what used to be known as gossip, "character issues," which are used to stand in for judgment about policy.

The press, therefore, will go to great lengths to protect the people who give them what they crave, most of whom happen to be Republicans since character smears are their very special talent. There was a reason why Rove and Libby [in response to Ambassador Joe Wilson's Iraq Op-Ed] used "the wife sent him on a boondoggle" line. Stories about Edwards and his hair and Hillary and her cold, calculating cleavage are the coin of the realm.

In the *Washington Post,* media critic Howard Kurtz responded to Digby's essay. His reply provided great (albeit unintentional) insight into the mind-set of our political press.

Initially, Kurtz—who is married to GOP media consultant Sherri Annis—simply could not tolerate the notion that the press corps' dirtmongering favors Republicans. One of the Central Principles of Beltway journalists is "equivalence"—always to insist that everything is the same between the two sides, regardless of whether it actually is. To demonstrate this claim of media balance, Kurtz refuted Digby's description of how our political press functions:

I agree that leakers often get to set the story line, but I also know that Democrats are not unfamiliar with the practice. (Remember the Bush DUI leak just before the 2000 election?) And those who leaked information about domestic surveillance, Abu Ghraib and secret CIA prisons also had an impact.

Leave aside the fact that Kurtz is so desperate to defend Republican operatives that he just recklessly asserts things as fact here even though he has no idea whether they are true. Kurtz has absolutely no knowledge of who leaked the NSA surveillance story to the *New York Times*'s Jim Risen and Eric Lichtblau, and cannot know whether the leakers are Democrats. The same is almost certainly true of the *Washington Post*'s Dana Priest's sources for her CIA "black site" story, whom Priest described as "U.S. and foreign officials" and "current and former intelligence officials and diplomats from three continents"—she did not identify them as "Democrats."

Worse, the Abu Ghraib whistle-blower was U.S. Army Sgt. Joseph Darby, not a Democratic Party operative. And the Bush DUI story was uncovered by a local reporter in Maine through actual, old-fashioned investigative journalism—pursuing a copy of the arrest record and interviewing the arresting officer. But Kurtz, like most Beltway journalists, has such a compulsion to assert equivalencies that he literally just invented facts—Democrats leaked these stories—in order to support his balance mantra.

But far more significant than Kurtz's willingness to invent facts is that he sees no distinction between (a) revelations that the Bush administration is torturing detainees, holding them in secret prisons, and spying on Americans in violation of the law and (b) what Digby described as "stories about Edwards and his hair and Hillary and her cold, calculating cleavage."

The whole point here is that Republicans dominate political press coverage because they feed vapid, slothful, tiny-minded "journalists" with vapid, tiny-minded, malicious gossip that reporters eat up and spew out in lieu of reporting on actual matters of substance. To rebut this claim, Kurtz argued that Democrats do it, too—and then cited the leaks about *torture, secret prisons, and warrantless surveillance* as his proof.

The most extraordinary political fact over the last seven years is that the Bush administration has been free to pursue such blatantly radical and extremist policies as indefinite detention, torture, and illegal surveillance with barely a peep of protest. The nation remains in a war in Iraq that the vast majority of the country opposes and the Bush administration long threatened new wars against the wishes of the overwhelming majority of the American citizenry. The alarming issue is not merely that the Republicans have succeeded in foisting upon this country such grossly destructive policies, ones that contravene every core political principle that has defined the United States for decades. It is that they have foisted them with so little critical analysis from our political and media elite.

But it is easy to see why this is so. These policies have become normalized, entirely mainstream, because our elite media does not see anything noteworthy or significant about them, let alone alarming or radical, and—with rare exceptions—they have no desire, and no ability, to take any of these stories on. They are interested in doing nothing other than repeating what they are told by their government sources, and hence that is what they do.

Rendition, warrantless eavesdropping, and expansive executive lawbreaking are just dreary, boring stories to pick at for political fodder when our media stars are forced—between gossipy sessions over Hillary's coldness and Edwards's gayness and the size of his house and the content of newspaper advertisements from MoveOn.org—to pay them any attention at all. The last thing they are interested in doing is alienating their secret, inside sources who feed them the prepackaged dirt by trying to expose any actual corruption or wrongdoing in our government. There is a cost to undertaking the latter; it takes work and energy. And our coddled media stars have no interest in endeavors entailing any of that.

That is why Kurtz and his colleagues view torture and NSA lawbreaking stories as the equivalent of what Digby calls "those delightfully bitchy tidbits" fed to them by right-wing dirtmongers. It is because most journalists treat them the same, except that they're far more interested in the latter than the former. Matt Drudge rules their world.

One of Kurtz's *Washington Post* colleagues, political reporter Shailagh Murray, is a blazing example of the media's preference for spoon-fed filth over substantive issues. Murray embodies every decadent, petty, and rotted attribute of the Beltway journalist, enabling one to understand vividly how corrosive our political discourse is simply by observing her behavior.

When Lewis Libby, the top aide to Dick Cheney and one of President Bush's top advisors, was convicted of multiple felonies in a federal court and sentenced (by a Bush-appointed federal judge) to almost three years in prison, George Bush intervened in the case and announced that he would commute Libby's sentence to ensure that he never spent a day in jail. When asked during a *Washington Post* online chat about this extraordinary event, Murray—the national political reporter of the *Washington Post*—could barely contain her boredom. She strutted around in a posture of faux sophistication, declaring that she regarded the whole affair as merely "the Libby flap," and that her reaction could be summed up in one word: "YAAWWN" [*sic*].

That is the hallmark of most of the media elite's reaction to any issues that actually matter—"YAAWWN." And our political dialogue is thus awash in petty, adolescent gossip and smears that require little work—and even less thought—to churn out. Indeed, in November 2007, the media was obsessed for almost a full week with the story that one of the questioners at a Hillary Clinton campaign event had been "planted"—that is, told what to ask the candidate by a Clinton staffer. Murray unsurprisingly found this irrelevancy full of meaning:

> But some stories stay alive longer than others because they reveal a more serious vulnerability. In Iowa, planting questions calls into question your authenticity— something Clinton struggles to demonstrate on the best of days, because she's just not a gal who wings it. **This episode sort of reminds me of the John Kerry windsurfing photo. It's the sort of thing that can linger in the mind.**

As always, petty personality stories fascinate our political reporters. John Kerry windsurfs! Hillary Clinton is controlling!

Substantive matters—such as the President's decision to protect one of his highest aides from prison—bores them to tears.

In October 2007, one of the first significant events in the presidential race that was a dispute over an actual substantive issue occurred. Throughout 2007, the Bush administration had been demanding that Congress grant retroactive immunity—or amnesty—to telecommunications companies such as AT&T and Verizon that had repeatedly broken the law since 2001 by allowing the administration to spy on Americans without the warrants required by numerous federal laws. Amnesty would mean that the telecoms—which had been losing a series of battles in federal court—could never be held accountable by any court of law.

The telecom industry has given well over $100 million in campaign contributions to members of Congress from both parties. Many, many magnitudes greater are their expenditures on lobbyists, former government officials who sell their influence to corporations to secure favorable legislation. And in 2007, the telecoms and their executives suddenly began making huge contributions to Democratic senator Jay Rockefeller of West Virginia, who—as the chairman of the Senate Intelligence Committee—was the key legislator for passing their eagerly sought amnesty bill.

In October, Senator Rockefeller announced that, pursuant to a deal he had reached with Vice President Cheney, he would support legislation granting full retroactive immunity to the telecoms, relieving them of all liability for their blatant lawbreaking. His committee quickly voted on a bipartisan basis, 13–2, to bestow on the telecom industry this extraordinary special protection—protection that literally exempts these companies from the rule of law.

The travesty of telecom amnesty united a broad array of civil liberties and privacy groups, grassroots activist organizations, and bloggers, enclaves that in the aggregate represent millions of politically engaged American citizens. These groups and their members and readers began calling for someone in Congress—anyone—to take a principled stand against this outrage, to take meaningful action to prevent singling out an influential industry and bestowing on it license to break the law.

On October 18, 2007, Senator Chris Dodd of Connecticut—who for months had been emphasizing the need to restore the rule of law and our constitutional framework as the centerpiece of his presidential campaign—responded by announcing that he would place a senatorial "hold" on any telecom amnesty legislation and would actively filibuster it if necessary. Dodd tied the attempt to grant telecom amnesty to the litany of abuses over the last six years and proclaimed:

> The Military Commissions Act. Warrantless wiretapping. Shredding of Habeas Corpus. Torture. Extraordinary Rendition. Secret Prisons.
>
> No more.
>
> I have decided to place a "hold" on the latest FISA bill that would have included amnesty for telecommunications companies that enabled the President's assault on the Constitution by illegally providing personal information on their customers without judicial authorization.
>
> I said that I would do everything I could to stop this bill from passing, and I have.
>
> It's about delivering results—and as I've said before, the FIRST thing I will do after being sworn into office is restore the Constitution. But we shouldn't have to wait until then to prevent the further erosion of our country's most treasured document. That's why I am stopping this bill today.

Dodd's pledge triggered intense enthusiasm and passion among tens of thousands of Americans hungry for anything resembling actual leadership on these issues. As *Time*'s Karen Tumulty reported,

> Senator Dodd's campaign communications director Hari Sevugan tells me that $150,000 in small contributions have poured into Dodd's campaign in the past 24 hours. . . . Dodd has raised **more small-dollar contributions in the last 24 hours than he did in the previous month.** Sevugan also says the number of visits to his website is up tenfold, as is the number of people registering their e-mail addresses there.

It is difficult to recall any single act by an American political leader over the last several years that generated such impassioned support at the grassroots level. Indeed, it was an exercise of democracy that is as noble as it is now rare—American citizens calling for their elected representatives to take a stand on a vital issue in defense of basic constitutional protections, and having an elected official actually respond.

Shailagh Murray wrote about this story on the *Washington Post*'s political blog the day following Dodd's announcement. As had been true from the moment the controversy over telecom amnesty erupted, Murray had absolutely nothing to say about the substance of the issue—zero. Is amnesty a total evisceration of the rule of law? Do the hundreds of millions of dollars telecoms pour into the Beltway enhance their ability to obtain such extraordinary legislative license to break the law? Why are lawmakers from both parties so willing to grant such extreme protections to these companies, even though the Bush White House continues to keep them completely in the dark about what these telecoms actually did in enabling illegal spying on their customers? After six years of radical lawbreaking theories emanating from the Bush White House, what signal would amnesty send about the rule of law in America?

None of those issues was addressed in most of our establishment press's examination of this matter, when they bothered to examine it at all. And those issues were certainly nowhere to be found in anything Murray wrote about it. Instead, Murray—as is virtually always true of her and most of her colleagues—spewed only the pettiest, most substance-free commentary.

Lip-curling mockery was her opening sentence: "Here's a first for a Senate presidential candidate: blocking a bill that doesn't exist yet." In her next sentence, she derided Dodd's tone, referring to his "announce[ment] in a breathless press release this afternoon"—as though only someone shrill and overwrought would possibly get worked up over the rule of law, warrants for spying on Americans, and retroactive immunity for an entire lawbreaking industry. Murray's snide derision of Dodd's purportedly "hot rhetoric" was not accompanied by a single substantive comment.

She concluded her column with a most revealing insinuation—that there was nothing remotely authentic about Dodd's stance, but that instead it was merely a desperate attempt to salvage his failing campaign:

> Assuming all goes smoothly, the legislation could hit the floor in mid-November, although senior Senate aides said late November or early December is a more likely time frame.
>
> Whenever that big day comes, Dodd—as the keeper of the "hold"—must return from the campaign trail to officially block debate on the bill. That entails standing around on the Senate floor, forcing procedural votes, avoiding the furious glares of colleagues who don't share the same concerns. The standard duration of such showdowns is about a week—time that Dodd, who is trailing badly in early primary polls, can scarcely afford.

That Murray wrote a jaded and outright snotty dismissal of Chris Dodd's stance against warrantless spying on Americans and amnesty for *lawbreaking telecoms* reveals all one needs to know about our sorry Beltway media culture. So, too, does the fact that she views as "breathless" and "hot rhetoric" Dodd's calmly stated objections to things such as "The Military Commissions Act. Warrantless wiretapping. Shredding of Habeas Corpus. Torture. Extraordinary Rendition. Secret Prisons."

Our Beltway media elite believe that their petty, above-it-all, junior-high coolness is a sign of their sophistication and insight. Conversely, they think that political passion and conviction is the province of the lowly, ignorant masses, the overly serious nerds. Moreover, mere citizens have no role to play in our political system other than to keep quiet and allow the Serious Beltway Officials and Experts—the ones who whisper gossip into Murray's hungry ear and flatter her with access and attention—to make the right, Serious decisions. As Murray explained once before, during a January 2007 *Post* chat, when the President announced he would escalate the war in Iraq despite pervasive opposition to the war among Americans:

> **Washington, D.C.:** I am somewhat surprised at the debate about the surge. In October, the *Post*'s own polling showed that 19% of voters favored an immediate withdrawal. Yesterday, CNN reported that more than 50% want an immediate or by year's end withdrawal. Still, the politicians debate more or less, not sooner or later. Why won't the politicians follow the polls when it comes to leaving Iraq?
>
> **Shailagh Murray:** Would you want a department store manager or orthodontist running the Pentagon? I don't think so.

The snickering over Dodd's stand and the enthusiasm it triggered are quite similar to how the Beltway media spent all of 2006 reporting on Senator Russ Feingold's lonely attempt to impose some accountability on the Bush administration for its blatant lawbreaking in eavesdropping on our conversations without warrants. When Feingold endlessly protested the NSA law-breaking, then announced his intention to introduce a resolution censuring Bush for *breaking the law,* in unison the establishment political press chuckled oh-so-knowingly and dismissively.

Nothing could interest them less than matters of constitutional safeguards on government spying, or Republican lawbreaking at the highest levels of government. With regard to the weightiest issues, those who dwell in Matt Drudge's kingdom are capable only of jaded, adolescent mockery of those who do care about the erosion of the Constitution and expansive executive-branch lawlessness.

Our very sophisticated Beltway media stars explained to the masses that this was nothing more than Feingold's cheap political ploy to pander to the "Far Left" in order to gain their support for his presidential campaign. The very first line of an Associated Press article on Feingold's censure resolution asserted: "The idea is increasing his standing among many Democratic voters as he ponders a bid for the party's presidential nomination in 2008."

The *Washington Post* reported that Republicans "denounced the censure resolution as a political stunt by an ambitious lawmaker positioning himself to run for president in 2008." And even some Senate Democrats got into the act, with Minnesota's Democratic senator Mark Dayton claiming that Feingold's move is "an overreaching step by someone who is grandstanding and running for president at the expense of his own party and his own country."

As is so often the case, the Beltway establishment's contempt for political passion and opposition to GOP lawbreaking was expressed most vigorously by those assigned to play the role of "liberal pundits." As they so reliably do in almost every case, they led the way in cynical mockery of Feingold's motives, as well as any other efforts to hold the Bush administration accountable for its radical actions. In *Newsweek,* Eleanor Clift insisted that Feingold was pursuing a frivolous agenda solely in order to advance his own political interests:

Republicans finally had something to celebrate this week when Democratic Sen. Russ Feingold called for censuring George W. Bush. Democrats must have a death wish. Just when the momentum was going against the president, Feingold pops up to toss the GOP a life raft.

It's brilliant strategy for him, a dark horse presidential candidate carving out a niche to the left of Hillary Clinton. . . . There is a vacuum in the heart of the party's base that Feingold fills, but at what cost? . . .

The broader public sees it as political extremism. Just when the Republicans looked like they were coming unhinged, the Democrats serve up a refresher course on why they can't be trusted with the keys to the country.

Time's Joe Klein echoed these sentiments in a January 2006 article titled "How to Stay Out of Power," warning that opposing Bush's illegal eavesdropping would be politically fatal for Democrats: "Until the Democrats make clear that they will err on the side of aggressiveness in the war against al-Qaeda, they will probably not regain the majority in Congress or the country." And *The New Republic,* courtesy of Ryan Lizza, chortled at the political stupidity of Feingold's censure resolution, but Lizza of course understood the base and cynical motives driving Feingold:

Feingold is mystified by the reaction. Democrats, he said this week, are "cowering with this president's numbers so low." The liberal blogosphere, aghast at how wimpy Democrats are being, has risen up in a chorus of outrage: . . .

The nature of the split is obvious. **Feingold is thinking about 2008. Harry Reid, Charles Schumer, and other Democrats are thinking about 2006. Feingold cares about wooing the anti-Bush donor base on the web and putting some of his '08 rivals—Hillary**

Clinton, Joe Biden, and Evan Bayh—in uncomfortable positions. Reid and Schumer care about winning the six seats it will take for Democrats to win control of the Senate.

Our most influential political journalists do not express a single thought of substance. Over the last seven years, the most they have been able to say about any legislator's efforts to stem the tide of Bush radicalism and warmongering is to spout platitudes about the political implications and insist that such efforts are motivated by cynical and base self-interest. The substance of those issues bores them.

That Feingold represents a decidedly unliberal state (Kerry barely won Wisconsin in 2004: 50–49), and thus takes real political risks by pursuing these positions in defense of the rule of law and constitutional liberties, never causes the Beltway parrots a moment's thought about whether he actually believes in what he is saying. Additionally, when Feingold, a few months after announcing his censure resolution, revealed that he actually *did not intend to run for president,* yet continued to pursue these positions with equal vigor, the idea that perhaps he believed in what he advocated still never occurred to the media elites.

That realization *cannot* occur to them. The idea that Feingold—or Dodd or any other political figure of significance—actually believes in what they are saying and doing is beyond the comprehension of Beltway journalists. For they are empty and self-absorbed, abiding in the world Drudge rules, and thus are consumed with pettiness; they believe in nothing, and thus assume that everyone else is as barren and vapid as they are. Hence they see no distinction between catty chatter about Edwards's haircuts, on the one hand, and alerting Americans to how radical this government has become on the other. Indeed, those who harp on the latter are dreary killjoys who ruin the fun and ease of wallowing in the former.

This is why we have become a country that has stood by

passively while the President has seized the power to *imprison American citizens with no charges,* has tortured and broken the law at will, and has endlessly pursued a war agenda that most of the country opposes. Most of our political journalists are largely uninterested in such matters. As Murray put it: YAAWWN.

Media Hypocrites Love a Beauty Contest

The core attitude of the political press—and the dominant theme of our political dialogue for the last two decades—was summarized perfectly by the media's unrestrained id, Chris Matthews. While speaking with Democratic National Committee chair Howard Dean in September 2007, Matthews lamented that Democrats continuously nominate "weird" geeks and losers while the Republicans put forth strong, "charming" tough guys:

> **MATTHEWS:** Why do Democrats keep running these weird presidential candidates, who always seem—ever since Jack Kennedy and maybe, well, Bill Clinton, they always lose the personality question. They always seem geekier, nerdier than the Republican guy. Why is that the case?
>
> **DEAN:** How do you really feel about that, Chris?
>
> **MATTHEWS:** Well, it's true. It's an objective assessment. Look at Dukakis in the tank. That's an objective reality. I mean, Mondale.
>
> **DEAN:** Let me tell you—let me tell you what we have to do.
>
> **MATTHEWS:** Jesus, a good guy, but unacceptable on television.
>
> The Republicans, they get the charm school. They got Reagan. They have got this guy George W. Bush. You know, they seem to run charming people.
>
> **DEAN:** What Democrats have to do is talk about their val-

ues. People vote on values. They don't vote on position
papers.

MATTHEWS: No, they vote on personalities.

Earlier in the year, in August, Matthews announced that the
Democratic presidential field suffered from a major deficiency:

> I don't see a big, beefy alternative to Hillary Clinton—a
> big guy. You know what I mean? An . . . everyday big
> guy. I don't see one out there. I see a lot of slight, skinny,
> second- and third-rate candidates.

The vast bulk of our political press has a single-minded, adolescent obsession with the petty personality traits of political
candidates in lieu of any interest in their positions or abilities.
Here was the *Washington Post*'s Joel Achenbach's analysis of the
1988 presidential election:

> That's one reason people like Bill Richardson: He looks
> like a good eater. They liked that about Bill Clinton,
> too. . . .
>
> Years ago I heard an anecdote about Mike Dukakis,
> and I'm sure I'll mangle it, but here's the gist as I dimly
> recall it: Coupla big union guys, beefy fellows, came to
> see Dukakis at his home in Brookline, thinking about en-
> dorsing him. Dukakis asked them if they wanted a beer.
> Sure, they said. So he gets out a beer and two glasses,
> and pours half the beer in one glass and half the beer in
> the other.
>
> Lost the election right there.

Achenbach went on to explain that Mitt Romney picks the
cheese off his pizza, which was a significant liability, since "I just
can't imagine the American people electing as president someone

who does that to pizza." As always, they justify their vapid gossip by patronizingly claiming that it's what the little people are interested in—all grounded in their condescending fantasies about the political assessments of the salt-of-the-earth simpletons who comprise the voting masses—but this sort of childish, barren yapping is, in reality, representative of nothing other than how our empty Beltway media thinks.

That has been the dominant media theme for the last two decades in our political discourse, and particularly in our national elections. Leave policy and ideology to the side. Just ignore it. What matters is that Democrats and liberals are weak, effete, elitist, nerdy, military-hating, gender-confused losers, whose men are effeminate, whose women are emasculating dykes, and who merit sneering mockery and derision. Republican right-wing male leaders are salt-of-the-earth, wholesome, likable tough guys—courageous warriors and normal family men who merit personal admiration and affection.

The Republican Party pioneered by Lee Atwater, Roger Ailes, and Karl Rove will redeploy these same personality-based themes in the 2008 election because it is all they know and, more important, because nothing has yet ended the efficacy of such deceitful strategies. A shallow and gossipy press continues to eat it up.

Indeed, the GOP has been able to pervert our political process this way only because of the indispensable aid of the establishment media, which reflexively views the political landscape through the lens of this GOP-generated mythology. The strain of petty personality-based gossip in which the GOP has come to specialize appeals to our media stars for a whole range of reasons. Catty attacks are cheap and easy to cover, and require few resources and even less critical thought to convey. Even the shallowest and most slothful reporters are able to dish about the Clintons' marital problems or how Barack Obama looks in a bathing suit.

Herd behavior, peer pressure, and desperation for attention fuel this lowly process further. Reporters are invited on television by Tim Russert and Chris Matthews—and are promoted by Matt Drudge—if they are skilled in gossiping gleefully about the candidates, but not if they drone on about boring substantive policy matters or political corruption or lawbreaking scandals. Cheap gossip and vapid chatter thus become the primary currency of our coddled Beltway media stars.

And, perhaps most significantly of all, the pressures created by the GOP smear machine perfectly re-create the social dynamic of high school and college, where one can reap the rewards of being favored as the popular jock and cheerleader or relegated to the realm of the losers and nerds. It's so much more fun and personally fulfilling to be liked and flattered by the triumphant War President—the "Commander-in-Chief" prancing around in "victory" on an aircraft carrier—while cackling at the weak, boring loser in the windsurfing tights, or the earnest nerd hilariously droning on about telecom amnesty and surveillance lawbreaking.

Perhaps more than anyone, Karl Rove exploited this sad social dynamic among reporters to keep them enthralled by his message machine. In a September 2007 column touting the genius of Rove, Gloria Borger of *U.S. News & World Report* unintentionally illustrated the GOP's complete domination of the establishment media:

> Karl Rove knew exactly what he was doing. In a round of interviews as he exited the White House, the man President Bush called the "architect" of his re-election was designing something else: a push for Hillary Clinton's nomination. "I think she's likely to be the nominee," he told Rush Limbaugh. "And I think she's fatally flawed."
>
> All observations that, coming from anyone else, might be considered routine punditry. **But when Rove speaks, the political class pays attention—usually with good reason.**

The rest of Borger's column is devoted to hailing the brilliance of Rove's plot to induce Democrats to nominate Clinton because of how vulnerable a candidate she is. Beltway media mavens like Borger have spent the last seven years awash in true reverence for Karl Rove. Rove's function, like all political operatives, is to manipulate the media, conceal information from them, and induce them to say what is politically beneficial to his boss, the President. In a world where political journalism performs its most basic functions, media manipulators like Rove are the natural enemy of journalists.

But for our journalist class, Karl Rove is the North Star of what they do—he provides their instructions, their leaks, their scoops, their access. As the purveyor of Beltway political power, he is their most admired leader. "When Rove speaks, the political class pays attention—usually with good reason," Borger proclaims. That's because by taking their cues from Rove, sitting as he did for so long at the center of power (near the high school quarterback at the jocks' table in the cafeteria), they are rewarded, patted on the head, given the treats they crave.

From the dean of the Washington press corps David Broder's bold confession of Rove admiration ("Let me disclose my own bias in this matter. I like Karl Rove . . . The other reason for inviting Rove was his wealth of information on the forces shaping the biggest single change in American politics— the emergence of the Republican South. . . . He generally tries to return calls in the same week—if not day—they are placed") to Broder's decree that various media outlets "owe Karl Rove an apology" for criticizing his role in the Valerie Plame case, it has long been apparent that most of our nation's leading journalists believe that Rove is filled with wisdom and merits the greatest respect.

After the 2006 midterm elections, Eric Boehlert—in an article titled "The Karl Rove Crush"—examined how reporters throughout 2006 were overwhelmingly warning of disaster for the weak and hapless Democrats because that is what Rove was saying, and they thus repeated it, even though all evidence pointed to the opposite outcome. As but one example, the odious Mark Halperin—then of ABC News, now of *Time*—said: "If I were them [Democrats], I'd be scared to death about November's elections." It was the same Mark Halperin who told right-wing radio talk-show host Hugh Hewitt the following:

> Let me say one thing we say in the book about Karl Rove, **who I respect and enjoy . . . I enjoy his company.** If you look at the allegations of Karl Rove that have been propagated in Texas and in Washington by the media, the liberal media, and by Democrats, and you look at the allegations, there's—except for the useful indiscretions to which Karl has admitted, there is no evidence for the allegations against him.
>
> And the ability of the press to paint him as this evil guy, and say that accounts for his success, is fundamental and **outrageous.**

This is the dynamic that has shaped the media's political coverage for years. Right-wing operatives feed the media shallow story lines, and they dutifully repeat it. Critically, the more this process works to manipulate media coverage, *the more our media stars come to admire, and want to please and follow, these right-wing operatives.* As NYU journalism professor Jay Rosen put it in his excellent 2007 essay on the relationship of Washington journalists to Rove's GOP political machine:

> Savviness is what journalists admire in others. Savvy is what they themselves dearly wish to be. (And to be unsavvy is far worse than being wrong.) Savviness—that quality of being shrewd, practical, well-informed, perceptive, ironic, "with it," and unsentimental in all things political—is, in a sense, their professional religion. They make a cult of it. And it was this cult that Karl Rove

understood and exploited for political gain. What is the truest mark of savviness? Winning, of course! Everyone knows that the press admires an unprincipled winner. (Of a piece with its fixation on the horse race.) Josh Green, a reporter for the *Atlantic Monthly* who actually took the time to understand Rove's career, totaled up his winnings in a 2004 article ("Karl Rove in a Corner") that I highly recommend.

"As far as I can determine, in races he has run for statewide or national office or Congress, starting in 1986, Rove's career record is a truly impressive 34–7." This record, he notes, "would be impressive even if he used no extreme tactics. But he does use them." Again and again, Green observes. Rove tries to destroy people with whispering campaigns. He makes stuff up. He transgresses and figures no one will stop him. He goes further than others in the game. These are things you would think journalists would recoil at, or at least observe with regularity.

Karl Rove is "savvy" in exactly the way Lee Atwater and Roger Ailes were savvy. He keeps the press in line—half intimidated and half reverent. The dangers of the media's reverence for the President's top political operatives are as numerous as they are obvious. The media virtually never takes seriously any administration lawbreaking and corruption scandals because the people at the center of those scandals are those whom they deeply admire. They do not want political operatives they admire to be investigated, let alone prosecuted. They do not subject White House claims to scrutiny because they hear those claims from operatives with whom they identify and for whom they have deep affection. And they adopt GOP-fed narratives and blindly recite them because they are convinced that those who feed them those claims are individuals who possess the greatest insight.

Borger's high praise for Rove's wisdom—and her admission

that when he speaks, the "political class" (i.e., her and her media colleagues) listens—illustrates one of the principal reasons the White House has been so adept in keeping our political press meek and deferential. In their insular world, Rove has been the winner, Democrats have been the losers, and our Beltway journalists—followers and power-worshipers first and foremost—want to please those who possess power. That desire, of course, is the opposite instinct of what drives good political journalism. But the fact that this obsequious desire—whereby journalists seek the approval of our most powerful political operatives—defines much of our political press is a principal reason why we have so little real political journalism.

In American culture, there are few personality traits more popular and appealing than the swaggering tough guy and über-masculine warrior. That is the theme promoted time and again by Hollywood and Madison Avenue. As documented in the next chapter, this is the template for how the Republican Party endlessly depicts its leaders, even though virtually none of them has those attributes in reality. But with our broken and vapid press corps, fantasy easily trumps reality. And our media stars thus swoon when presented with the faux tough guys of the Republican Party, and cackle in derision at the Democratic weaklings and losers. That is the twisted story line and the corrupt methods that have dominated our political discourse and determined our elections for decades.

CHAPTER THREE

Tough Guise

Central to the right-wing mythmaking machine is the depiction of their male leaders as swaggering tough guys in the iconic mold of an American cowboy and brave, steadfast warrior. Above all else, Republican leaders are invariably held up as exuding the virtues of traditional American masculinity—courage, physical strength, "regular guy"ness, and most of all, a willingness and ability to stare down America's various and numerous enemies—in war, if necessary—and defeat them through superior strength.

Vital to this masculinity marketing campaign is the demonization of Democrats and liberal males as weak, sniveling, effeminate, effete cowards—spineless little creatures whose cowardice and lack of manliness make them laughingstocks. While right-wing leaders are the football players and swaggering tough guys, liberal males are the glasses-wearing nerds, the woman-controlled, gender-confused, always-vaguely-gay losers who are as feminine and weak as their women are masculine and threatening.

The reality, in virtually every case, is the opposite. Those who end up as leaders of the right-wing movement in America have nothing in their lives to demonstrate any actual courage, physical strength, or any of the warrior virtues they desperately strive to exude. They are, with extremely rare exceptions, draft dodgers, combat avoiders, pencil pushers, career government lawyers, coddled corporate lobbyists, bloated pill addicts. Their only "toughness" or masculine "tough guy" credentials are from cheerleading as they send others off to fight wars, never to fight in any themselves. Just like John Wayne, their masculine toughness comes from the costumes they wear, the scripts they read, the roles they play—never from the reality of their own lives.

Few events illustrate the central importance to the right-wing movement of these twisted themes more than the March 2007 speech by Ann Coulter to the Conservative Political Action Conference, when she famously called John Edwards a "faggot." What matters is not Ann Coulter but the role she plays in the right-wing movement and its full-scale embrace of her as its bestselling author and, by far, most popular speaker.

The CPAC is one of the most prestigious events held by the conservative movement, attracting the highest-level Republican political officials and most influential pundits. Coulter's 2007 appearance was not the first time she created controversy at the CPAC event. In 2006, the event was attended by virtually the entire leadership of the Republican Party: Vice President Dick Cheney, Republican National Committee chairman Ken Mehlman, then–2008 presidential hopeful Senator George Allen, then–Senate Majority Leader Bill Frist, and Newt Gingrich.

In addition to those luminaries, Ann Coulter was invited to be a featured speaker despite (or because of) her history of repeatedly urging the murder of her domestic political opponents and government officials by methods ranging from terrorist attacks ("My only regret with Timothy McVeigh is he did not go to the New York Times Building") to assassinating Supreme Court

Justices ("We need somebody to put rat poison in Justice Stevens's crème brûlée") to skull-bashing ("I think a baseball bat is the most effective way these days to talk to liberals"). None of those violence-advocating comments ever prevent the most prominent Republican groups from inviting her to speak, nor do they prevent the most prominent Republican politicians from appearing next to her without ever condemning her remarks.

To the contrary, with that repugnant history well known, Coulter—in 2006—was invited to share top billing at the most prestigious right-wing event of the year, and she did not disappoint. Her 2006 speech included unsurprising gems such as: "I think our motto should be, post-9/11, 'Raghead talks tough, raghead faces consequences' " and "If we find out someone [referring to a terrorist] is going to attack the Supreme Court next week, can't we tell Roberts, Alito, Thomas, and Scalia?"

According to one of her blogging fans in attendance, five thousand conservatives reverently sat there and listened to her and did nothing to indicate disapproval. To the contrary—as reported by The Huffington Post's Max Blumenthal—her urging of violence against "ragheads" specifically "prompted a boisterous ovation." The blogger Rick Moran, brother of ABC News reporter Terry Moran, observed that Coulter's speech was "well received by the audience."

So it was owing to that 2006 CPAC appearance, along with her history of similar remarks, that Coulter was again invited in 2007. Prior to her speech, Mitt Romney addressed the conference and excitedly announced: "I am happy to hear that after you hear from me, you will hear from Ann Coulter. That is a good thing. Oh yeah!" The CPAC attendees screamed and cheered with approval.

And it was then that she referred to John Edwards as a "faggot." As the Center for American Progress described, with an accompanying video confirming its description, "Audience members said 'ohhh' and then cheered." Andrew Sullivan, who was in attendance for the Coulter speech, reported:

> When you see her in such a context, you realize that she truly represents the heart and soul of contemporary conservative activism, especially among the young. The standing ovation for Romney was nothing like the eruption of enthusiasm that greeted her. . . .
>
> Her endorsement of Romney today—"probably the best candidate"—is a big deal, it seems to me. McCain is a nonstarter. He is as loathed as Clinton in these parts. Giuliani is, in her words, "very, very liberal." One of his sins? He opposed the impeachment of Bill Clinton. That's the new standard. She is the new Republicanism. The sooner people recognize this, the better.

Coulter's "faggot" comment was far from the first time Coulter had explicitly suggested that leading Democrats were gay. Previously, Coulter has placed what she called "even money" on Hillary Clinton's "[c]oming out of the closet." She said that Bill Clinton shows "some level of latent homosexuality," and—on MSNBC's *Hardball* with Chris Matthews—she labeled Al Gore a "total fag." During her speeches on college campuses and elsewhere, Coulter routinely accuses male liberals of being gay or effeminate.

And her remarks fit in comfortably at the CPAC event, which year after year embraces and promotes her. In addition to Coulter's tawdry hatemongering, the conference was graced with such dignified and honorable sentiments as these: T-shirts proclaiming "Straight Pride"; appearances by members of "Exodus International," encouraging gay people to become "ex-gays"; and bumper stickers declaring "Happiness is Hillary's face on a milk carton."

Ann Coulter *is* the face of what the hard-core Republican

Party has become, particularly during the Bush presidency. That is why she holds such a central position in that movement. It is why Mitt Romney was giddy with glee when her name passed his lips. He knows that her endorsement is valuable precisely because she holds great sway within the party, and she holds great sway because the hard-core party faithful consider her a heroine for expressing the thoughts that they themselves believe but that other, less courageous Republican figures are afraid to express.

This is not about a single comment or isolated remark. The more Ann Coulter says these things, the *more popular* she becomes in this movement. She reflects exactly what sort of political movement this is, its true impulses and core beliefs. If that were not the case, why would she continue to receive top billing at their most prestigious events, and why would she continue to be lavished with rock-star adoration by the party faithful?

In a very vivid way, the Ann Coulter "faggot" episode shone a light on the right-wing movement that is so bright, even our establishment press would have been able to recognize some important truths if they just looked even casually. Although some conservatives politely distanced themselves from Coulter's specific "faggot" remark, most refused to do so, and—as always—she suffered no loss of standing of any kind, either in the movement or in the attention and admiration lavished on her by our national journalists (as but one example, Chris Matthews, months later, had her on his show for an entire hour to commemorate the publication of her new book).

Coulter cannot be repudiated precisely because she embodies the soul of the current incarnation of the Republican Party. To repudiate her is to repudiate all of the hypocrisies.

The day following Coulter's "Edwards is a faggot" speech, Bill O'Reilly devoted a segment of his show to discussing the controversy. Kirsten Powers, a so-called Democratic strategist, was on the show along with right-wing blogger Michelle Malkin. Powers managed to ask the key question—the only one that was actually significant with regard to the entire affair—thereby forcing Malkin to make the critical concession, the one that right-wing pundits were desperate to avoid:

KIRSTEN POWERS: [Coulter] has said a lot of horrible things . . . she's done all these things. And I don't understand why if this is the preeminent conservative movement place to be speaking, why she is chosen as a person to speak . . .
BILL O'REILLY: Why do you think they invited her, Michelle?
MICHELLE MALKIN: She's very popular among conservatives. And let me say this. I have been a longtime admirer of much of Ann's work. She has done yeomen's work for conservatism.

This is why—the only reason—Coulter's remarks and Coulter herself are so significant. And the significance lies not just in this specific outburst at the 2007 CPAC event but in the whole array of hatemongering, violence-inciting remarks over all these years. Their significance lies in the critical fact that Malkin expressly acknowledged: "She's very popular among conservatives."

And Coulter herself knows quite well how indispensable she is, how impossible it is for Republicans to repudiate her. The day following her Edwards "faggot" speech, she appeared on Fox News alongside her good friend Sean Hannity, and she repeatedly made clear—when Hannity asked her about the "consequences" of the controversy—that nothing will change as a result of these comments. As she correctly observed: "This is my seventeenth allegedly career-ending moment."

Coulter plays a vital and irreplaceable role in the right-wing movement that dominates the Republican Party, but she is hardly unique. She is but the most overt provider of the rhetorical tools they use not only to keep themselves in power but, more important, to keep their needy, confused, and scared base feeling strong and protected. As the blogger Digby put it the day following Coulter's CPAC speech:

The underlying premise of the modern conservative movement is that the entire Democratic party consists of a bunch of fags and dykes who are both too effeminate and too masculine to properly lead the nation. Coulter says it out loud. [The *New York Times*'s Maureen] Dowd hints at it broadly. And the entire press corps giggles and swoons at this shallow, sophomoric concept like a bunch of junior high pom pom girls.

The online journalist Bob Somerby of *The Daily Howler* has spent years vigilantly documenting the constant use by our most prestigious establishment journalists of exactly the same attack themes that are Coulter's signature. As he wrote in the aftermath of the Coulter "faggot" speech—in a post titled "When you read Dowd, you're riding with Coulter":

But then, why should pundits criticize *Coulter* when she describes Dem males as big "f*ggots"? It's very similar to the gender-based "analysis" their dauphine, the Comptesse Maureen Dowd, has long offered. In Dowd's work, John Edwards is routinely "the Breck Girl" (five times so far—and counting), and Gore is "so feminized that he's practically lactating."

Indeed, two days before we voted in November 2000, Dowd devoted her entire column, **for the sixth time,** to an imaginary conversation between Gore and his bald spot. "I feel pretty," her headline said (pretending to quote Gore's inner thoughts). That was the image this idiot wanted you carrying off to the voting booth with you! Such is the state of Maureen Dowd's broken soul. And such is the state of her cohort.

And as Somerby documents, the junior-high press corps, led by Dowd, its "Queen Bee," made great strides in 2007 in applying Coulter's themes to the emerging field of Democratic candidates:

[I]n the spirit of fair play and brotherhood, [Dowd] is extending this type of "analysis" to Barack Obama. In the past few weeks, she has described Obama as "legally blonde" (in her headline); as "Scarlett O'Hara" (in her next column); as a "Dreamboy," as "Obambi," and now, in her latest absurd piece, as a "schoolboy." . . .

But as we've noted, Dowd *persistently* mocks Dem males as a race of big girlie-men. They feel pretty—and they're the Breck Girl. Now, Obama is constantly some sort of "boy"—or an iconic white woman.

Big Dem men are constantly girls. And big Dem women? Keep reading:

DOWD: "I'm just not certain, having watched the fresh-faced senator shy away from fighting with **the feral Hillary** over her Hollywood turf, that he understands that a campaign is inherently a conflict."

Big Dem women are "feral"! Indeed, when we get to paragraphs 4 through 6, Dowd spells it out just as clear as a belle at a ball. Added warning! When Dowd refers to Obama as "Barry," it's one more snide diminution.

After David Geffen made critical comments about Hillary, she seized the chance to play **Godzilla stomping on Obambi.**

DOWD: "As a woman, [Hillary] clearly feels she must be aggressive in showing she can 'deck' opponents, as she put it—whether it's Saddam with her war resolution vote or Senator Obama when he encroaches on areas that she and Bill had presumed were wrapped up, like Hollywood and now the black vote.

If Hillary is in touch with her masculine side, Barry is in touch with his feminine side."

Leave aside the persistent infantilism involved in images like "Godzilla" and "Bambi." Here, Dowd states her endless—and vacuous—theme: Big Dem males (like "Barry") are girls. And big Dem women are men.

In November 2007, following a Democratic presidential debate, Dowd devoted an entire truly twisted column to depicting Hillary Clinton as an "icy," vicious "dominatrix" and Barack Obama—"Obambi"—as her emasculated, intimidated, submissive slave. And she contrasted "Obambi" with Rudy Giuliani, who is far too masculine to be "kept in line" by Hillary's whip:

> The debate dominatrix knows how to rattle Obambi. . . .
> Mistress Hillary started disciplining her fellow senator last winter, after he began exploring a presidential bid. . . . She has continued to flick the whip in debates. . . .
>
> With so much at stake, she had to do it again in Vegas, this time using her voice, gaze and body language to such punishing effect that Obama looked as if he had been brought to heel. . . .
>
> Other guys, like Rudy, wouldn't even be looking for a chance to greet Hillary, as Obama always does. Other guys, like Rudy, wouldn't care if she iced them. . . . Obama may be responsive to Hillary's moods because he lives with another strong woman who knows how to keep him in line. She is a control freak—that's why her campaign tried to coach wonky Iowa voters to ask wonky questions—and her male rivals are letting her take control. . . .
>
> If Rudy's the nominee, he will go with relish to all the vulnerable places in Hillary's past. . . . Hillary has her work cut out for her. Rudy will not be so easy to spank.

This is the columnist occupying the most influential punditry space in the country—the Op-Ed page of the "liberal" *New York*

Times. And like so many of her journalistic colleagues, she has for years written about our political culture with these same themes asserted over and over: Democratic males are weak, effeminate, girly. Democratic women are emasculating, freakish, "feral." GOP males are true men. Ann Coulter can barely say it better herself.

Following her Edwards "faggot" speech, Coulter insisted that she did not intend the remark as an anti-gay slur—that she did not intend to suggest that John Edwards, husband and father, was gay—but instead used the word only as a "schoolyard taunt," to call him a sissy. And that is true. Her aim was *not* to suggest that Edwards is actually gay, but simply to feminize him, as the Republican Party attempts to do with all male Democratic or liberal political leaders.

But for multiple reasons, nobody does that more effectively or audaciously than Coulter, which is why they need her so desperately and will never jettison her. There are few things that can match the efficacy of a thin white woman with long blond hair running around mocking the lack of masculinity of liberal males. She is the id of the right-wing faction that controls the Republican Party, the banshee that screams its most valuable rhetorical device. How could they possibly shun her for engaging in tactics on which their entire movement depends? They cannot, which is why they do not and will not.

Grand Masquerade Party

The converse to this whole process is equally vital. As critical as it is to right-wingers to feminize Democratic and liberal males (and to masculinize the women), it is equally important to create false images of masculine power and strength around their own authority figures. The reality of this masculine power is almost always nonexistent. The imagery is all that counts.

This functions exactly the same as the images of moral purity that they work so hard to manufacture, whereby the leaders they embrace—such as Gingrich, Limbaugh, Bill Bennett, even the divorced and estranged-from-his-children Ronald Reagan and Coulter herself (with her revolving door of boyfriends and broken engagements)—are plagued by the most morally depraved and reckless personal lives, yet still parade around as the heroes of the "Values Voters." Just as what matters is that their leaders present themselves as moral (even while deviating as far as they want from those standards), what matters to them also is that their leaders *playact* as strong and masculine figures, even when there is no basis, no reality, to the playacting.

Like John Wayne, Ronald Reagan never got anywhere near war (claiming eyesight difficulties to avoid deployment in World War II), and he spent his life as a Hollywood actor, yet to this day, conservatives swoon over his masculine role-playing as though he was some sort of super-brave military hero. Meanwhile, Jimmy Carter, who served on real live nuclear submarines, as well as George McGovern (a combat veteran who volunteered to serve in World War II), are mocked as weak. As McGovern put it in a 2007 *Los Angeles Times* editorial, responding to accusations from Dick Cheney equating "McGovernism" with cowardice and surrender:

> In the war of my youth, World War II, I volunteered for military service at the age of 19 and flew 35 combat missions, winning the Distinguished Flying Cross as the pilot of a B-24 bomber. By contrast, in the war of his youth, the Vietnam War, Cheney got five deferments and has never seen a day of combat—a record matched by President Bush.

While Republicans have ensured that virtually every asset of America bears the name of Ronald Reagan—including a glorious battleship, the USS *Ronald Reagan*—right-wing tough guys who never spent a day in the military protested and mocked endlessly when it was announced, in 2005, that a submarine would be named after the Navy veteran Jimmy Carter. Carter is a graduate of the Naval Academy, having attended during World War II. In the Navy he became a submariner, serving in both the Atlantic and Pacific fleets, and he rose to the rank of lieutenant. He was personally selected by Admiral Hyman Rickover, known as "Father of the Nuclear Navy," for the top-secret nuclear submarine program, where Carter enrolled in graduate work in reactor technology and nuclear physics, and served as senior officer of the precommissioning crew of the *Seawolf,* America's second nuclear submarine.

Despite a history of military service that few right-wing warriors can come close to matching, conservatives heaped endless scorn and ridicule at the decision that a nuclear submarine would bear Carter's name. At *National Review* alone—filled to the rim with absurd, swaggering, pretend tough guys—Steve Hayward referred to the "oxymoronic Jimmy Carter attack submarine"; Jonah Goldberg published an e-mail spouting that "naming this boat for Carter resounds with irony" and another stating that "the USS *Jimmy Carter* will be *The Best* submarine in the Navy, precisely because of the jokes"; and Goldberg himself wrote:

> You do have to feel sorry for the crew of the USS *Jimmy Carter.* I'm sure they'll be very well qualified and all that. But as several readers have noted, they're just never going to hear the end of it.

Goldberg continued: "If a Russian sub attacks undefended ships, will the USS *Jimmy Carter* immediately boycott the U.S.-Russian softball game in Guam?" His colleague Kathryn Jean Lopez sneered: "I can't get over how ridiculous the sound of a Jimmy Carter attack sub is. The enemy trembles."

In the world of right-wing Republicans, actual bravery, courage, and military service are irrelevant. What matters is a willingness to *strike the pose* of a warrior.

The ultimate expression of faux, empty, masculine courage is, of course, the Commander-in-Chief himself, George W. Bush—the Glorious Leader whom John Podhoretz hailed in the title of his worshipful cult book *The First Great Leader of the 21st Century*—with the ranch hat and brush-clearing pants and flight-suit outfits that would make the Village People seethe with jealousy. Just behold this poster, which was in great demand at past CPAC events:

That laughable absurdity really reveals the heart of the Republican Party movement. They have transformed themselves into a cult of contrived hypermasculinity—whereby leaders and followers alike dress up as male archetypes such as cowboys, ranchers, tough guys, and, most of all, warriors—even though they are nothing of the kind.

Numerous commentators, such as former Nixon White House counsel John Dean and psychology professor Bob Altemeyer, have definitively and convincingly documented this dynamic. People who feel weak and vulnerable crave strong male leaders to protect them and to enable them to feel powerful. And those same people will throng to a political movement that gives them those sensations of power, strength, and triumph, and will devote absolute loyalty to any political leader who can provide them with that.

This is also the basic dynamic of garden-variety authoritarianism, and it is what the right-wing Republican Party has become at its core—far more than a set of political beliefs or geopolitical objectives or moral agendas. All of it—the obsessions with glorious "Victory" in an endless string of wars; vesting more and more power in an all-dominant centralized Leader; the forced submission of any country or leader who does not submit to the Leader's Will; the unquestioning Manichaean certainties; the endless stigmatization of the whole array of Enemies as decadent, depraved, and weak; and most of all, the canonization of their male Leaders as Strong, Powerful, Brave, and Über-Masculine—it's just base cultural tribalism geared toward making the followers feel powerful and falsely secure.

The Coulter/Hannity/Limbaugh–led right wing is basically the Abu Ghraib rituals finding full expression in an authoritarian political movement. There is a reason that individuals such as Rush Limbaugh were not bothered by that horror show, but actually took perverse delight in and were tickled by the sadism displayed there and other revelations of American torture, barbarism, and cruelty. It is because that is the full-blooded manifestation of the impulses underlying this movement—feelings of power and strength from the most depraved spectacles of force. As Limbaugh—by far the most popular and important conservative pundit in America—said of the disgusting revelations of Abu Ghraib:

I'm sorry, folks. I'm sorry. Somebody has to provide a little levity here. This is not as serious as everybody is making it out to be. My gosh, we're all wringing our hands here. . . .

I mean, it's ridiculous. It's outrageous what's happening here, and it's not—and it's not because I'm out of touch; it's because I am *in touch,* folks, that I can understand. This is a pure, media-generated story. . . .

This is no different than what happens at the Skull and Bones initiation, and we're going to ruin people's lives over it, and we're going to hamper our military effort, and then we are going to really hammer them because they had a good time. You know, these people are being fired at every day. I'm talking about people having a good time, these people, you ever heard of emotional release? You [ever] heard of need to blow some steam off?

Limbaugh is a physically weak individual, wallowing in a life of depraved hedonism, who has never displayed a single act of physical courage. He avoided combat in Vietnam by claiming that an anal boil rendered him unfit for service (and, once he became famous as an über-warrior, said nothing when a Limbaugh biographer falsely claimed it was due to a football injury). Thus, he takes pleasure in observing acts of American cruelty and barbarism. He finds "levity" in it and cheers it on. It makes him feel powerful and strong, feelings he—understandably—is unable to obtain from his own life and actions. With pulsating power from having defended the Abu Ghraib conduct, Limbaugh addressed his pretend troops, masquerading as the general he fantasizes himself to be. From his website's transcript of his monologue about Abu Ghraib (emphasis in original):

I don't understand what we're so worried about. These are the people that are trying to kill us. What do we care what is the most humiliating thing in the world for them? . . .

There's only one thing to do here, folks, and that's achieve *victory* over people who have targeted us for a loooong, long time, well over 15, 20 years. It's the only way to deal with this, and that's why obsessing about a single incident or two of so-called abuse in a prison is nothing more than a giant distraction and could end up being something that will really ties [*sic*] our hands and handcuffs us in what the *real* objective is here, which is the preservation of our way of life and our country. . . .

[B]ut the world is joining in now trying to taint us as a nation, as a people, and as a culture by virtue of these pictures on the basis that we have humiliated these people. What is hijacking our own airplanes and flying them into the World Trade Center and the Pentagon? How humiliating is it to blow up American civilians in a convoy and have their charred bodies dragged from the car and dragged through the streets? There seems to be no sensitivity, concern or outrage for any of this any-where in the world. So pardon me if my patience is a little short.

While the civilized world has recoiled in horror at the ex-cesses and war-hungriness of the United States over the last six years, the only real complaint from our right-wing war cheer-leaders about the Commander-in-Chief is that he has not given them enough torture, secret prisons, wars of aggression, bar-baric slaughter, and liberty infringement. Their hunger for those things is literally insatiable, because they need fresh pretexts for feeling strong. And nothing provides those feelings of strength better than revering a tough-guy male leader and mocking lib-eral males as weaklings and losers.

The True Meaning of Chicken Hawks

The central reason Republicans so relentlessly parade around as tough guys with warrior virtues is that their leaders are invariably the precise opposite. The playacting masks the sad reality. Just as drag queens must use wildly exaggerated female costumes, makeup, and gestures to mask their masculinity, right-wing leaders must use increasingly flamboyant warrior disguises—and an increasingly war-hungry agenda—to obscure what really lurks behind those disguises.

Indeed, the second most astonishing political scam of the last six years—behind only the permanently jaw-dropping fact that 69 percent of Americans believed as late as September 2003 that Saddam Hussein personally participated in the planning of the 9/11 attacks—is that the 2004 presidential candidate who fought in actual combat in Vietnam was the one depicted as the weak, subversive coward. By contrast, the candidate who used powerful family connections to avoid fighting was depicted as the brave, masculine fighter-warrior who had the backbone to stand down the Evil Enemies and protect us all.

That is why so many right-wing hypocrites who have never been anywhere near the military—and will never go near it even as their wars are burdened by a lack of volunteers—have a monomaniacal obsession with military glory. They revel in constant rhetorical displays of how resolute and courageous they are, with notions of forced submission and humiliation of their opponents (just take notice of how central a role those concepts play in neoconservative arguments), and with depicting those who oppose war as cowards (even when the cowards in question, such as Jack Murtha, are decorated Marines with thirty years of service).

The term "chicken hawk" (in the context of war) is much used, debated, and discussed, but its true, most revealing meaning is rarely made explicit. Although there is no formal definition for it, the chicken-hawk criticism is *not* applicable to someone who merely (a) advocates a war and also (b) will not fight in that war and/or has never fought in any war. After all, the vast majority of Americans in both political parties meet *that* definition. The war in Afghanistan was supported by roughly 90 percent of Americans, as was the first Persian Gulf War, even though only a tiny fraction of war supporters actually fought in them.

Something more than mere support for a war without fighting in it is required to earn the chicken-hawk label. Chicken-hawkism is the belief that advocating a war from afar is a sign of personal courage and strength, and that opposing a war from afar is a sign of personal cowardice and weakness. A "chicken hawk" is someone who not only advocates a war but believes that that advocacy is proof of the same courage required of those who will actually engage in combat.

One of the nation's most consummate chicken hawks is, unsurprisingly, one of the loudest advocates of sending others off to fight in endless wars: *The Weekly Standard* editor, Fox News contributor, and *New York Times* columnist Bill Kristol. Kristol's central political view is that those who advocate sending other Americans off to fight in more and more Middle Eastern wars are themselves strong, resolute, principled, and brave. But those who oppose sending others off to fight in those wars are weak, cowardly, spineless appeasers.

As but one example, Kristol, writing in the June 2006 *Weekly Standard,* urged U.S. intervention in the Israeli war against Hezbollah, claiming that those who want the United States to enter that war are "strong horses" and those who oppose it are "weak horses." Thus, said Kristol, individuals such as E. J. Dionne, Richard Cohen, and George Will are all "weak horses" because they wrote columns arguing against increased U.S. involvement in Middle Eastern wars. By contrast, Kristol is a "strong horse" because he wrote a magazine column advocating that war.

As is true of most right-wing war cheerleaders who dominate today's Republican Party, Kristol believes that his desire for other people to fight more wars in the Middle East makes him not only wise (which is arguable) but also strong and brave (which it inarguably does not). He assigns to himself the courage and strength of those who will actually fight in a war, simply because he sits in his office, protected and safe, and advocates for war.

One of the most illustrative specimens of the chicken-hawk strain is Norman Podhoretz—the leading right-wing warmonger, "Godfather of Neoconservatism," top foreign-policy guru to Rudy Giuliani, and loudest advocate of starting a new war with Iran. In a mid-2007 article in the *Wall Street Journal,* Podhoretz urged George Bush to bomb Iran, saying that he "hopes and **prays every day**" for such an attack. Thereafter, he released a book titled *World War IV: The Long Struggle Against Islamofascism,* which, as *Publishers Weekly* put it, argues that "we are in the middle of the fourth world war" and "attempts to steel us for the years of conflict to come." Its purpose, said *Booklist,* is to argue for still more "regime change, preemptive war, and propagation of democracies in the Middle East."

Podhoretz's entire career has been devoted to urging the United States to wage wars against one Muslim country after the next. And as is true of so many combat-avoiding right-wing pundits, war cheerleading (from a safe distance) is a family affair for the Podhoretzes. His son, John, zealously supports current and additional wars in *National Review, Commentary,* and the *New York Post,* and Norman's wife, Midge Decter, has long been one of neoconservatism's most admired pro-war theorists. None of the Podhoretzes ever serve in the military, of course. None ever risk their lives for the wars they cheer on. They only demand that other families' sons and daughters be sent off to the Middle East to fight and die in the new wars for which they constantly agitate, while they—the Podhoretzes—prance around as Churchillian warriors.

In understanding the right-wing chicken hawks' perverse

desire for war, one of the most revealing articles ever written is a 1963 essay in *Commentary* magazine by Podhoretz, titled "My Negro Problem—and Ours." In it, Podhoretz argues that "I am convinced that we white Americans are . . . so twisted and sick in our feelings about Negroes that I despair of the present push toward integration." But it isn't the smarmy racism that is so appalling—such open expressions of pure racism were common in 1963 and Podhoretz would undoubtedly claim that he has left such sentiments behind. Rather, what is most significant is Podhoretz's description of his psychology and view of himself that illuminates so much of the vicarious warrior culture that dominates our political system today (emphasis in original):

To me, at the age of twelve, it seemed very clear that Negroes were better off than Jews—indeed, than **all** whites. . . . [I]n my world it was the whites, the Italians and Jews, who feared the Negroes, not the other way around. The Negroes were tougher than we were, more ruthless, and on the whole were better athletes. . . . I was still afraid of Negroes. And I still hated them with all my heart. . . .

The orphanage across the street is torn down, a city housing project begins to rise in its place, and on the marvelous vacant lot next to the old orphanage they are building a playground. . . . A week later, some of us are swatting flies on the playground's inadequate little ball field. A gang of Negro kids, pretty much our own age, enter from the other side and order us out of the park. We refuse, proudly and indignantly, with superb masculine fervor. There is a fight, they win, and we retreat, half whimpering, half with bravado. My first nauseating experience of cowardice. . . .

Gradually we abandon the place and use the streets

instead. The streets are safer, though we do not admit this to ourselves. We are not, after all, sissies—the most dreaded epithet of an American boyhood. . . .

That day in school the teacher had asked a surly Negro boy named Quentin a question he was unable to answer. As usual I had waved my arm eagerly . . . and, the right answer bursting from my lips, I was held up lovingly by the teacher as an example to the class. I had seen Quentin's face—a very dark, very cruel, very Oriental-looking face—harden, and there had been enough threat in his eyes to make me run all the way home for fear that he might catch me outside. . . .

For me as a child the life lived on the other side of the playground and down the block on Ralph Avenue seemed the very embodiment of the values of the street—free, independent, reckless, brave, masculine, erotic. . . .

The hatred I still feel for Negroes is the hardest of all the old feelings to face or admit, and it is the most hidden and the most overlarded by the conscious attitudes into which I have succeeded in willing myself. It no longer has, as for me it once did, any cause or justification (except, perhaps, that I am constantly being denied my right to an honest expression of the things I earned the right as a child to feel). How, then, do I know that this hatred has never entirely disappeared? I know it from the insane rage that can stir in me at the thought of Negro anti-Semitism; I know it from the disgusting prurience that can stir in me at the sight of a mixed couple; and I know it from the violence that can stir in me whenever I encounter that special brand of paranoid touchiness to which many Negroes are prone. . . .

There were plenty of bad boys among the whites— this was, after all, a neighborhood with a long tradition

of crime as a career open to aspiring talents—but the Negroes were **really** bad, bad in a way that beckoned to
one, and made one feel inadequate.

There will never be enough bombings to erase those feelings of weakness and inadequacy. But Podhoretz and his bloodthirsty right-wing followers—including his combat-avoiding
protégées such as Rudy Giuliani and George W. Bush—will
never stop trying. Demanding an attack on Iran was but the latest—hardly the last—war they crave in order to demonstrate
their manliness. To see how true this is, one need only review
this amazing passage that appeared in *Time* magazine back in
July 2004, in an article titled "What to Do About Iran":

> But just as Tehran is divided over how to deal with
> Washington, so is Washington split over how to deal with
> Tehran. The **neo-conservative ideologues in the Bush
> administration have never made any secret of their
> desire to see the U.S. military pursue "regime
> change" in Tehran next. "Real men go to Tehran"
> was one of their playful slogans** during the buildup to
> Operation Iraqi Freedom.

The passage contains two critical insights into how our country
has functioned over the last seven years. Right-wing warriors
think they become "real men" by sending others into new wars
(with Iran as the ultimate prize), while our leading media organs
consider such twisted militarism to be "playful."

Revealingly, among the country's most influential neoconservatives, beyond just the war-cheerleading Podhoretzes, one
finds extremely pervasive nepotism. A conspicuously high percentage of war-loving tough guys have had their careers created, shaped, and fueled by their parents. They have been
dependent on the accomplishments of their parents, especially

their fathers, whose political views they regurgitate almost without deviation. Just consider the intertwined neoconservative axis that spawned the two leading Iraq "surge" advocates, Bill Kristol and Fred Kagan.

Bill Kristol's parents are Irving Kristol, the so-called Godfather of Neoconservatism (along with Podhoretz) and Gertrude Himmelfarb, whose defining political stance was paying homage to the virtues of Victorian morality at the American Enterprise Institute, the neoconservative "think tank." Bill followed in his parents' footsteps almost completely—the same career, a common political circle, and political beliefs nearly indistinguishable from those of his mother and father. And Bill's career was shaped by his parents from the outset.

Fred Kagan followed the same life map as Bill Kristol, scrupulously tracking the career and mind-set of his father. Just as with Kristol *père,* the *Washington Post* labeled Kagan's dad, Donald, "a beloved father figure of the ascendant neoconservative movement." Fred Kagan even went so far as to coauthor a 2000 book with his father titled *While America Sleeps: Self-Delusion, Military Weakness and the Threat to Peace Today,* a book that—pre-9/11—advocated many of the same militaristic policies that today they justify by the 9/11 attacks.

Fred Kagan's brother, Robert, is forged in the same mold. Along with Bill Kristol, Robert cofounded the Project for the New American Century, which, among other things, spent the years prior to the 9/11 attacks urging regime change in Iraq. Fred's wife, Kimberly Kagan, now regularly authors paeans in the *Weekly Standard* and the *Wall Street Journal* to her husband's glorious "surge" plan, and claims it is leading America to Victory in the War.

This sprawling nepotistic web weaves on and on even as one descends to the lower neoconservative ranks. The career of right-wing, pro-war Jonah Goldberg—*National Review* editor and *Los Angeles Times* columnist—was created and shaped by his mother, Lucianne, whose political beliefs he mirrors. Jonah came to national prominence by attaching himself to his mother as she milked her role in the Lewinsky scandal (during that time, Jonah, twenty-nine, was "vice president" of his mom's company). Via his mother's hard work exploiting their joint dirtmongering in that scandal, Jonah became a *National Review* editor—as recorded by this superb and darkly amusing 1998 *Salon* profile, titled "The Jester of Monicagate: How Lucianne Goldberg's Son Jonah Has Turned His 15 Minutes of Fame into a Full-Time Job":

> Jonah, agent fatale Lucianne Goldberg's 29-year-old son, entered the national stage when he listened to the Linda Tripp tapes with his mom. . . .
>
> From an early age, his mother, who has acknowledged being an undercover Republican political operative during the McGovern campaign, exposed her son to feisty right-wing hi-jinks—and instilled in him a strong sense of family loyalty and affection. Indeed, Goldberg says he first entered the media fray "to defend my mom" from those who deemed her the money-grubbing Wicked Witch of the Upper West Side.

Of course, like all right-wing *National Review* tough guys, Jonah hates handouts; believes strongly in the glorious virtues of self-sufficiency and pulling oneself up by one's bootstraps (and, apparently, by one's unsevered umbilical cord); demands meritocratic policies; and is teeming with stiff-spined courage. These are the kind of people who hate affirmative action because of how unfair it is, but who thrive on legacy admissions to college and have their mommies and daddies secure them jobs and careers.

Our coddled, cowardly warriors on the Right (with an eager assist from their media enablers) have made masculinity and Tough Guy iconography a central part of their political identity. Here, as but one of countless examples of this core adherence to faux masculinity, is Jonah Goldberg's revealing explanation in October 2003 of his support of the war on Iraq. It is a perverse little exercise that is emblematic of the war-seeking cheerleaders of the Right:

> **Q:** If you're a new sheriff in a really bad town, what's one of the smartest things you can do?
> **A:** Smack the stuffing out of the nearest, biggest bad guy you can.
> **Q:** If you're a new inmate in a rough prison, what's one of the smartest things you can do?
> **A:** Pick a fight with the biggest, meanest cat you can—but make sure you can win.
> **Q:** If you're a kid and you've had enough of the school bullies pants-ing you in the cafeteria, what's one of the smartest things you can do?
> **A:** Punch one of them in the nose as hard as you can and then stand your ground.

Goldberg then approvingly quoted fellow neoconservative war cheerleader Michael Ledeen as follows:

> Well, I've long been an admirer of, if not a full-fledged subscriber to, what I call the "Ledeen Doctrine." I'm not sure my friend Michael Ledeen will thank me for ascribing authorship to him and he may have only been semi-serious when he crafted it, but here is the bedrock tenet of the Ledeen Doctrine in more or less his own words: **"Every ten years or so, the United States needs to pick up some small crappy little country and throw it against the wall, just to show the world we mean business."** That's at least how I remember Michael phrasing it at a speech at the American Enterprise Institute about a decade ago.

Seriously ponder the level of obscenely demented thinking here. Men who have never been near war, who have done everything possible to avoid it, whose lives have been protected and built from the start by their moms and dads to whom they tightly cling, relentlessly urge dropping bombs on other countries and sending their fellow citizens to war so that they can parade around as paragons of strength.

These Faux Tough Guy themes are also unceasingly deployed to demonize liberals and Democrats as cowards and perverts. Behold the chest-beating derision spewed by Goldberg for those who oppose the wars he cheers on:

> I know—from painful experience—that there are lots of people out there who subscribe to the bumper-sticker slogan "peace through strength is like virginity through f**king" . . . **If peace cannot be attained through strength, I invite one of these bespectacled, purse-carrying, rice-paper-skinned sandalistas to walk out into a prison yard.** Let's see how receptive Tiny and Mad Dog are to entreaties over the futility of violence. "Sir, there's no need for fisticuffs, I would be glad to share my Snapple with you. Can't you see this sort of conflict is precisely what the multinational corporations want?"
>
> International relations is much more like a prison yard than like a college seminar at Brown.

Those who are opposed to sending off their fellow citizens to die in one war after another are, in this deranged calculation, "bespectacled, purse-carrying, rice-paper-skinned sandalistas"— in contrast, of course, to the swaggering warrior Goldberg, whose snide, derogatory descriptions of anti-war activists as being "bespectacled"—not to mention bereft of any masculine warrior virtues—rather plainly apply to himself:

Yet Goldberg believes himself to be immune from the accompanying mockery—and even has the audacity to run around talking as though he's George Patton—all because he types from his house about how great wars are and about how "we" (meaning others) must "punch one of them in the nose as hard as you can and then stand your ground" and insists that "the United States needs to pick up some small crappy little country and throw it against the wall, just to show the world we mean business."

War cheerleading is the hallmark of these right-wing tough guys. And indeed, when asked why, despite being of prime fighting age, he never bothered to enlist during the Iraq War, which he claimed to find so important, Goldberg replied,

As for why my sorry a** isn't in the kill zone, lots of people think this is a searingly pertinent question. No answer I could give—I'm 35 years old, my family couldn't afford the lost income, I have a baby daughter, my a** is, er, sorry, are a few—ever seem to suffice.

In other words: I am a full-throated Supporter of the Epic War of Civilizations, but I can't fight in it, because my knee hurts and I need to collect advance checks from Regnery for my books and I want to stay at home and wipe dribble from my baby's chin. But those people over there can and should fight. And in between watching *Star Trek* on television and playing war video games, I will periodically draft articles and posts about how great these wars are and I, too, will therefore be strong and noble, resolute and brave.

Giuliani supporter John Podhoretz of *National Review* and the *New York Post* has trod a life path similar to Goldberg's. He is a reduced version of his father, Norman, and of his mother, Midge Decter—two of the most deeply revered neoconservative figures. In October 2007, it was announced that John had been named editor of *Commentary,* the pro-war neoconservative magazine his father founded and edited for many years.

John Podhoretz's entire career as a tough-guy pundit follows loyally in the path laid out for him by his mommy and daddy. Podhoretz's mother, Midge Decter, previously worked at *Commentary* and has written a whole slew of neoconservative screeds, including *The New Chastity and Other Arguments Against Women's Liberation* and the satire-proof *Donald Rumsfeld: A Personal Portrait*—which, for oozing iconic worship, competes only with her son John's *Bush Country: How George W. Bush Became the First Great Leader of the 21st Century—While Driving Liberals Insane.*

And the nepotistic nurturing of the Podhoretz family extends out beyond its immediate sphere. White House neoconservative (and Iran-Contra convict) Elliott Abrams married Decter's daughter (from her first marriage), and one of his first key jobs in the neoconservative movement was being chosen by Norman to write for *Commentary* (Abrams was also a major contributor to Bill Kristol and Robert Kagan's PNAC).

At the end of 2007, the *New York Times* announced that it had hired Bill Kristol as its new Op-Ed columnist. That announcement provoked widespread bewilderment, given Kristol's lengthy history of pronouncements that were as false as they were banal, as well as his previous vicious attacks on that newspaper. But the process by which Kristol secured his new position was no mystery. Bill's father, Irv, was an old friend of longtime *Times* editor Abe Rosenthal, whose son, Andy, has now succeeded him in that position. Abe was appointed to his position by then-publisher Arthur "Punch" Sulzberger, and Andy was appointed by Punch's son, current publisher "Pinch" Sulzberger. Bill, son of Irv, and Andy, son of Abe, became good friends, just like their dads, and it was Abe's son (Andy) along with Punch's son (Pinch) who together chose Irv's son (Bill) as the new *Times* columnist.

In one sense, this intellectual and career incest reflects a broader and rather damaging aristocratization of our political process. The Bush family photo includes our current President, his brother, the governor of one of our largest states, their father the former President who, in turn, is the son of a former senator. And that clan continuously uses its political power to propagate itself, exploiting its vast power network to strengthen the careers and wealth of its family members while continuously breeding new heirs to the throne.

It is true that neoconservatives and Republicans do not have a monopoly on the political exploitation of family connections. The Kennedys still pervade the political system at all elected levels, and the political careers of Jesse Jackson Jr., Andrew Cuomo, Bill Daley, Senator Bill Casey, Al Gore, and Harold Ford Jr.—to name just a few—clearly benefited from the political accomplishments of their fathers. And Hillary Clinton's status as a leading presidential candidate was derivative, first and foremost, of the fact that she is married to a former president.

But the warmongering neoconservative dependence on parents goes beyond mere exploitation of family ties for political career gain. Many leading neoconservatives end up following in their parents' footsteps—remaining attached to them and becoming carbon copies of them—to an extent that is quite unusual and clearly significant. As a phenomenon, an entire highly influential political movement being so dependent on their parents for their careers and worldview seems, at the very least, to merit some commentary.

Separation from one's parents is a basic rite of passage in becoming an adult. In that regard, rebellion against one's parents is—to invoke an emerging cliché—a feature, not a bug, of adolescence. Repudiating parental control and finding one's own way in life is a critical part of becoming a fully formed adult, and so is an effort to have accomplishments exist independently of Mommy and Daddy. Individuals who travel the exact same career path as their parents, fueled by their parents' friends and accomplishments, and who recite their parents' political views almost uniformly, are people who seem to be reliant on their parents in the extreme.

Rebellion for its own sake—against one's parents or anything else—is adolescent in nature, and is just as mindless as remaining slavishly attached to one's parents. And all of these dynamics exist as generalities with all sorts of exceptions. But in general, choosing to live in the shadows of one's parents—where one copies their path and is shaped and molded by them—would seem to create a very stunted and coddled personality.

Many, perhaps most, of the leading neoconservatives don't seem to have arrived at their political worldview through much intellectual struggle or independence, nor do they seem to have had to make their own way in building their careers. Quite the opposite—they seem to have been bred into their lives, and they just marched, like good little boys, along with their parents' views and plans for them. And they not only willingly accepted, but seem to have eagerly sought, assistance from their parents in building their careers, in exchange for embracing their parents' views almost without deviation.

It's rather ironic (and almost certainly not coincidental) that these same neoconservatives strut around spewing tough-guy warrior rhetoric and sermonizing on the virtues of self-reliance even though they have chosen extremely coddled, privileged lives feeding off the accomplishments and directives of their mothers and fathers. And quite significantly, the political leader they found to represent their belief system, to personify their contrived warrior pose, and to implement their radical agenda— George W. Bush—is as extreme a version of the coddled and father-dependent personality as one could hope to find.

It is glaringly apparent that the twisted and bloodthirsty tenets of neoconservatism that are dominating our country—this insatiable craving for military domination that is as endless as it is pointless, along with the corresponding, equally insatiable desire to expand presidential power—are not rooted in some coherent geopolitical doctrine so much as they are rooted in rotted personality disorders. These neoconservative phenomena are more psychological than political.

This generation's neoconservatives are protected, sheltered recipients of endless nepotistic, parental largesse who never tire of sermonizing to the world about the necessities of self-sufficiency and meritocracy. Further, they insist that their war advocacy demonstrates how resolute and willful they are—self-glorifying announcements they make from positions arranged for them by their mommies and daddies.

Contrast the reality of these playacting men—virtually all of them, at one point or another, contributors to *National Review* or *The Weekly Standard*—with the image the right wing promotes of itself. From a 2004 *National Review* essay on the defining attributes of political conservatism, by John Micklethwait and Adrian Wooldridge:

The heroes of modern American conservatism are **rugged individualists who don't know their place:**

entrepreneurs who build mighty businesses out of nothing, settlers who move out West and, of course, the cowboy. There is a frontier spirit to the Right—unsurprisingly, since so much of its heartland is made up of new towns of one sort or another.

Rugged individualists. Frontier spirit. The cowboy. These are the fantasies our right-wing leaders try to project, precisely because these cartoons mask the ugly reality of what they are and how they lead their coddled, risk-avoiding lives.

Over and over again, those who simply advocate a war in which the lives and limbs of other people will be risked label themselves strong and courageous. *National Review*'s Cliff May—who has never served in the military yet devotes his life to urging more American wars—has actually argued that those who advocate wars by writing and speaking in favor of them (such as himself) are courageous "warriors" every bit as much as those who actually risk their lives in combat.

In 2006, May's colleague Kathryn Jean Lopez wrote that she had seen Oliver Stone's film *World Trade Center* and it reminded her "about why we fight," prompting an e-mailer to remind Lopez: "You do not fight—you never have and, hopefully, never will have to. You are not a member of any of the branches of the armed forces, nor a reservist." In response, May defended Lopez's status as warrior despite steadfastly avoiding anything actually resembling war:

> There is a war of arms. And there is a war of ideas.
>
> They are not just inter-related, they are interdependent. They are equally consequential. . . .
>
> So yes, Kathryn, you are fighting a war. And your e-mailer is ignorant about how wars are fought, about how wars are won and lost, and about the way the world actually works.

One of the nation's most relentless war cheerleaders, Christopher Hitchens, authored a column in the *Boston Globe* celebrating the joys—the "exhilaration"—of watching wars that he cheers on (but does not fight):

> In order to get my own emotions out of the way, I should say briefly that on that day I shared the general register of feeling, from disgust to rage, but was also aware of something that would not quite disclose itself. It only became fully evident quite late that evening. And to my surprise (and pleasure), it was exhilaration. I am not particularly a war lover, and on the occasions when I have seen warfare as a traveling writer, I have tended to shudder.
>
> But here was a direct, unmistakable confrontation between everything I loved and everything I hated. On one side, the ethics of the multicultural, the secular, the skeptical, and the cosmopolitan. (Those are the ones I love, by the way.) On the other, the arid monochrome of dull and vicious theocratic fascism. I am prepared for this war to go on for a very long time. **I will never become tired of waging it,** because it is a fight over essentials. And because it is so **interesting.**

In Hitchens's mind, he is not merely writing about war. He is not merely cheering it on. He is not merely speaking endlessly about it. No. He himself is "waging it." He is a warrior. He is brave, resolute, and strong. In today's pro-war faction in America, war is not merely a means of defending the nation. Zealously advocating for them is the means by which those who lack any acts of real courage in their own lives purport to be warriors, too.

This dynamic demands exposure and criticism because it is so pervasive in the right-wing faction—and so irrational, false, and manipulative. There is nothing courageous or strong about wanting to send other people to war or to keep them in wars that have already been started. And there is nothing weak or cowardly about opposing the commencement of a war in which others will bear the risks. Indeed, to the extent courage and cowardice play any role in war advocacy, one could argue that those who would blithely send other people off to war in order to protect themselves against every potential risk *are driven by fear and weakness.* By the same token, those who are less fearful will require a much higher level of personal threat before finding it just to send fellow citizens off to risk their lives.

It is certainly true that whether someone has fought previously in a war neither proves nor disproves the wisdom of their foreign policy views, nor is prior military service a prerequisite for participating in debates over whether the United States should go to war. But one's views about whether the United States should fight a war that will bring little or no risk to the advocate has nothing to do with personal courage or strength. The phrase "101st Keyboard Brigade"—a term invented to describe the throngs of right-wing bloggers and pro-war pundits who relentlessly cheered on the Iraq War and talked about their resolve and courage as though they themselves were combatants—mocks *not* merely those who support wars but those who strut around as though their support for war means that they are fighting it, and who consequently apply the warrior attributes to themselves.

Clearly, those who will actually incur the risks of war are more likely to think carefully and soberly about whether to start one than are those who urge on wars without any personal interests at stake. It is, for instance, much more difficult for Israelis to urge war with Lebanon than it is for Americans sitting comfortably out of reach of Hezbollah rockets to do so. And it was much more difficult for European monarchs to choose war when their own children would fight on the front lines than it is for American senators and administration officials whose family members won't be doing the fighting to make the same choice. Indeed, the Founders mandated in the Constitution that *only Congress* could declare war because they knew war would be less likely if those who bore the burden (which they assumed would be the nation's citizens) were required to approve of any wars.

One of the most destructive diseases of our political culture is how insulated American war cheerleaders and pundits are from the consequences of the wars they unleash. A remarkably prescient warning of precisely this disease came from Adam Smith in his 1776 *An Inquiry into the Nature and Causes of the Wealth of Nations.* It really is striking how perfectly Smith described our right-wing culture and their war-cheering, establishment media comrades:

> The ordinary expense of the greater part of modern governments in time of peace being equal or nearly equal to their ordinary revenue, when war comes they are both unwilling and unable to increase their revenue in proportion to the increase of their expense. They are unwilling for fear of offending the people, who, by so great and so sudden an increase of taxes, would soon be disgusted with the war; and they are unable from not well knowing what taxes would be sufficient to produce the revenue wanted.
>
> The facility of borrowing delivers them from the embarrassment which this fear and inability would otherwise occasion. By means of borrowing they are enabled, with a very moderate increase of taxes, to raise, from year to year, money sufficient for carrying on the war, and by the practice of perpetually funding they are enabled, with the smallest possible increase of taxes, to raise annually the largest possible sum of money.
>
> **In great empires the people who live in the capital, and in the provinces remote from the scene of action, feel, many of them, scarce any inconveniency from the war; but enjoy, at their ease, the amusement of reading in the newspapers the exploits of their own fleets and armies. To them this amusement compensates the small difference be-**

tween the taxes which they pay on account of the war, and those which they had been accustomed to pay in time of peace. They are commonly dissatisfied with the return of peace, which puts an end to their amusement, and to a thousand visionary hopes of conquest and national glory from a longer continuance of the war.

The right-wing–dominated Republican Party today is even worse than the sickly culture about which Smith warns, since they will not even tolerate mild increases in taxes to fund their war amusements. This is a critical disease in our culture: that all appendages of our political class (other than the military itself) bear no sacrifice whatsoever for the wars they advocate, and hence are "dissatisfied with the return of peace, which puts an end to their amusement, and to a thousand visionary hopes of conquest and national glory from a longer continuance of the war."

More than sixty years ago, George Orwell described this lowly and dangerous mentality perfectly, writing in *Homage to Catalonia:*

The people who write that kind of stuff never fight; possibly they believe that to write it is a substitute for fighting. It is the same in all wars; the soldiers do the fighting, the journalists do the shouting, and **no true patriot ever gets near a front-line trench,** except on the briefest of propaganda-tours.

Sometimes it is a comfort to me to think that the aeroplane is altering the conditions of war. Perhaps when the next great war comes we may see that sight unprecedented in all history, a jingo with a bullet-hole in him.

That is what the Republican Party is filled with, what that party is defined by—a whole slew of John Wayne–like chicken hawks whose lives are devoid of acts of physical courage and warrior virtues pretending to be the soldiers whom they send off to fight. Actual bravery and courageous service to one's country are irrelevant. In their worldview, combat heroes and military veterans such as Carter, McGovern, Wesley Clark, John Kerry, Chuck Hagel, and Jack Murtha are surrender-happy, appeasing, American-hating cowards.

It is the *playacting* that matters, the cheerleading for wars that makes one a Republican "tough guy." Hence, the right-wing "brave warriors" are George W. Bush, Dick Cheney, Newt Gingrich, Sean Hannity, Rush Limbaugh, Bill Kristol, Rudy Giuliani, and Norm and John Podhoretz—people whose lives are devoid of those virtues in reality but who wear the costumes and read the scripts, thus convincing themselves—and their followers in the establishment press—that they embody true warrior virtue.

Shock and Awfulness

Most critically, these tough-guy costumes go beyond mere playacting. This twisted need to prance around as faux courageous warriors has very real—and very destructive—effects in the real world. For our right-wing tough guys and their media fans, it is entirely unfulfilling simply to beat their chests and feel powerful by excitedly threatening war. They want to cheer on the invasions, feel and hear the glorious bombs dropping, behold the devastation that results from their warmongering, wallow in the pulsating sensations of strength and power that it vicariously provides. Starting and cheering for wars becomes the way—the only way—they can maintain the role they are so desperate to play.

The American political press and the right-wing political movement have joined in creating and entrenching a destructive theme that predominates American political discourse—that a politician must prove his leadership and manliness by advocating war. No longer does an American male become a warrior by fighting in a war. Far more important for demonstrating toughness is the willingness to send others off to fight.

Shortly after he took office in 1989, the first President George Bush, plagued by whispers that he was a "wimp" despite his combat heroism during World War II, sent the U.S. military to invade Panama—a country that could not and did not remotely threaten America—and remove its president, Manuel Noriega. On the day of the invasion, writing on the front page of the *New York Times,* political reporter R. W. Apple illustrated how vital war is for an American political leader to prove his "courage" and "strength":

> For George Bush, the United States invasion of Panama early this morning constituted a Presidential initiation rite as well as an attempt to achieve specific goals.
>
> For better or for worse, most American leaders since World War II have felt a need to demonstrate their willingness to shed blood to protect or advance what they construe as the national interest. John F. Kennedy in the Cuban missile crisis, Lyndon B. Johnson and Richard M. Nixon in South Vietnam, Gerald R. Ford in the Mayaguez affair, Ronald Reagan in Grenada and Lebanon, and now Mr. Bush in Panama—all of them acted in the belief that the American political culture required them to show the world promptly that they carried big sticks.
>
> Jimmy Carter did not do it until he sought unsuccessfully to rescue American hostages in Iran late in his term, and politicians of both parties still believe that it cost him dear.
>
> For President Bush—a man widely criticized as recently as a month ago for his purported timidity, a man assailed on Capitol Hill and elsewhere for failing to fully support an attempted coup against General Noriega only in October, a man still portrayed in the Doonesbury

comic strip as the invisible President—showing his steel had a particular significance.

Whatever the other results of this roll of the dice in Panama, it has shown him as a man capable of bold action, especially coming, as it did, on the heels of his Malta summit talks with Mikhail S. Gorbachev and his surprise initiative toward China.

It mattered little that Panama is a tiny country with a tiny military. What mattered was the *display of strength* that, in American political culture, comes from war, no matter how senseless the war, no matter how weak the enemy. And indeed, President Bush's top aides did not emphasize any supposed benefit to American national security from having invaded Panama, but instead celebrated the idea that President Bush showed the world who is boss:

Even though the Panamanian leader was not immediately captured, kept control of his radio station, could remain at large for months and may have left behind mini-Noriegas with disruptive capacities of their own, he appears to have little capacity now to exercise real power.

"We have cut off the head of that government," said Gen. Colin L. Powell, Chairman of the Joint Chiefs of Staff. "Yesterday's 'maximum leader' is today's hunted fugitive," said Secretary of State James A. Baker 3d. Most experts agreed with their assessments. . . .

Last spring, Adm. William J. Crowe Jr., General Powell's predecessor, told a Congressional committee that using military force in a place like Panama could be "a messy, messy business." In the fall, Secretary of Defense Dick Cheney said that direct military intervention would seriously damage United States relations with the other countries of Latin America. Both proved right.

And only last night, Mr. Nixon told a group of senators on Capitol Hill that General Noriega was the sort of man who should be left to fall of his own weight. . . .

The Latin American reaction, even from those nations that have led the way in branding General Noriega an outlaw, was furious. Mexico, for example, said that "fighting international crimes is no excuse for intervention in a sovereign nation." Memories of gunboat diplomacy—a phrase used often today in world capitals—run deep. . . .

Unprepared to scale down the objective—getting rid of General Noriega—Mr. Bush finally decided to scale up the means he would authorize.

Here we find what have become the depressingly familiar constants in virtually every discussion of American war in our mainstream political discourse—the willingness, even eagerness, to wage war against countries that do not and cannot attack us; reflexive support for any war efforts from America's highly technocratic "foreign policy experts"; and the underlying belief that American invasions of other countries are always justifiable because as a country that is inherently good, our invasions and bombs are well-intentioned. Missing entirely from Apple's front-page article were any contrary views from war opponents, any argument that the United States has no right to invade other nations at will, remove their leaders, and then occupy their country.

But far more significant than all of these now-common elements in our discussions of war is the psychological and cultural premise, the way in which wars are equated with strength and toughness. By "cut[ting] off the head of that government" (as Colin Powell put it) and turning its president into a "hunted fugitive" (as James Baker put it), the United States could feel powerful and strong. We showed them—and the world—who was dominant.

As a result, George Bush 41 proved his manhood by invading Panama. Based on this one decision to go to war, the front page of the *New York Times* declared him "capable of bold action." He and his aides "show[ed] the world promptly that they carried big sticks." Bush fulfilled the "Presidential initiation rite" by demonstrating his "willingness to shed blood." Thus, declared Apple, Bush had overcome the perceptions of "timidity" and invisibility by "showing his steel"—all by sitting in the White House and starting a war with a small and weak country.

But as incoherent as this premise is, it is plainly the overriding cultural theme of American politics—that "real men" are leaders who start and prosecute wars. Within this twisted right-wing/media cultural framework, there is no need ever to fight in an actual war or undertake any acts of real courage. That is why combat veterans George H. W. Bush and John Kerry are suspected of being wimps and cowards, while combat avoiders such as Ronald Reagan, George W. Bush, and Rudy Giuliani are deemed tough and courageous.

As Stephen Ducat noted in *The Wimp Factor,* the day after Bush 41 ordered the invasion of Panama, the Associated Press published an article based on the assertions from a "face-reading expert," Laura Rosetree, that trumpeted the manliness of Bush's physical attributes. The headline: "Bush's Chin Proves He's a Macho Guy, Face 'Reader' Says." As usual, "macho" was presented as the antithesis of the empathetic "bleeding heart" liberal man:

> "He doesn't say whatever he's really feeling or thinking," she said. "If you literally read his lips, they are proclaiming, 'I'm not ever going to get sentimental on you. I'm not going to be a bleeding heart.'" . . .

Her conclusion: Bush is a hard-nosed pragmatist and skeptic, a die-hard ideologue, a shrewd negotiator and skilled conciliator, an intellectual who revels in the realm of ideas, a decision-maker who respects facts, disdains feelings and isn't afraid of criticism. . . .

To set the record straight, she says, Bush is a macho man—it's right there in the semicircular knob on his prominent, square-jawed chin.

"That semicircle relates to being very proud of his masculinity, the macho aspect, forcefulness, and being very sensitive to appearing weak in front of other people," she said.

"The wimp image in the presidential campaign must have bothered him excruciatingly," she added.

"His straight chin shows that he makes his major life decisions based on principles and ideology, not on compassion or other people's feelings. This is not the chin of a Santa Claus, it's the chin of a crusader."

The *Time* magazine cover for the issue marking the invasion of Panama and the capture of Noriega depicted bulging biceps covered in the Stars and Stripes.

With a single decision to send the U.S. Marines to invade a small, weak country, Bush 41 transformed himself from effete weakling into macho War President. Adopting the John Wayne template, American leaders—and particularly right-wing political figures—have long been proving their steely manhood via boisterous war cheerleading.

No political leader has ever benefited more from this perverse equation of sending others off to war and personal toughness than his son, George W. Bush. From the moment Bush began exploiting the 9/11 attacks for political gain, his followers—including, as always, our establishment press—depicted this coddled combat-avoider as some sort of MacArthur or Patton.

This deceit found perhaps its most obscene expression in a 2003 Fox News interview conducted by Sean Hannity of Gen.

Tommy Franks, who back then was widely hailed as a war-hero genius, but who today is widely blamed for the failures of the early stages of America's occupation of Iraq. After he retired from active duty, General Franks ran around defending the administration's handling of the Iraq War, all the while insisting that he was nonpartisan and had no allegiance to the Republican Party. But in mid-2004, as the presidential campaign was swinging into full force, Franks released a new book. In conjunction with his book tour, he announced that he was endorsing George W. Bush's reelection.

Franks chose to promote his book, and endorse Bush, on Fox News, in an exclusive interview granted to Hannity during the Republican National Convention. Hannity began the interview by announcing that Franks had the "No. 1 *New York Times* bestseller. It's called *American Soldier.* Congratulations," and then informed his viewers that Franks had decided to announce his endorsement for the presidential election. The following dialogue ensued:

> **FRANKS:** All right. You know, I think about some of the great quotations of history and a lot of them have to do with choice. And the fact of the matter is that there are periods in American history when it's—when it's really important to make a choice.
>
> And that's why Cathy and I are here. That's what this is about. We've made a choice.
> **HANNITY:** And that choice is?
> **FRANKS:** George W. Bush.
> **HANNITY:** You are here to support the president.
> **FRANKS:** Absolutely. I've seen—I've seen this president when it was—when it was dark outside, when the times were hard.
>
> What we've wrestled with is trying to think our way through, how close are we to the end of this threat, to our nation from terrorism? And I've—I've convinced myself that

we're—that we're in this for the long haul. This is not going to be over tomorrow.

And so I thought about things like consistency. I thought about things like persistency. I thought about unswerving, unwavering character. And the longer I thought, and the more Cathy and I talked about it, the more convinced we became that we had to speak up.

HANNITY: You almost sound to me like a guy that's been at war—been in a war with him, like hand in hand. And really, that's really what you have been, in a bunker together, battling . . .

FRANKS: Many, many—sometimes early and sometimes late and sometimes with great frequency. And I—I don't think we have had a period, Sean, in American history, not in my lifetime, when the stakes were as high as they have been.

By that point in the Iraq War, 982 actual American soldiers—people who had, in reality, rather than in Sean Hannity's fantasy, been "in a bunker together, battling"—had been killed in combat in Iraq, and another 8,000 had been wounded. But Bush's followers equated his sending them to fight with Bush himself being a warrior, with his actually being in a "bunker."

The Hannity/Franks interview provides a superb example of the unceasing success of the John Wayne deceit as the central fuel of the Republican Party. In the right-wing world, when it comes to proving one's masculine credentials, cheerleading for a war is not just the equivalent of, but is superior to, actually fighting in one.

But if Hannity/Franks's depiction of Bush as being in a "bunker" was the most obscene example of this twisted equation, perhaps the most explicit was the truly unbelievable discussion that took place on the MSNBC show *Hardball* on the day in May 2003, when Bush flamboyantly dressed up in a fighter pilot costume, landed on an aircraft carrier, and delivered his now-infamous "Mission Accomplished" speech. Establishment media stars and pundits—conservatives and liberals alike—marched forward to pay homage to the triumph and conquest of our great masculine warrior-leader, George W. Bush.

As Bush pranced around in his costume, Matthews literally sounded like a sixth-grade schoolgirl with a crush, hailing Bush as a Real Man, the type of masculine leader America craves—in contrast to the soft and effete Democratic presidents of the past:

> **We're proud of our president. Americans love having a guy as president, a guy who has a little swagger, who's physical,** who's not a complicated guy like Clinton or even like Dukakis or Mondale, all those guys, McGovern. They want a guy who's president.
>
> **Women like a guy who's president. Check it out. The women like this war. I think we like having a hero as our president.** It's simple. We're not like the Brits. We don't want an indoor prime minister type, or the Danes or the Dutch or the Italians, or a Putin. Can you imagine Putin getting elected here? **We want a guy as president.**

And it wasn't just Matthews. As they showed footage of Bush giving his Iraq War victory speech, Matthews was joined in his effusive, drooling praise of Bush's manhood by right-wing pundit Ann Coulter and Democratic pollster Pat Caddell, as they continuously yammered about Bush as some sort of super-male, conquering Roman emperor:

> **MATTHEWS:** What's the importance of the President's **amazing display of leadership tonight?**
>
> [. . .]
>
> **MATTHEWS:** What do you make of the actual visual that people will see on TV and probably, as you know, as well as

I, will remember a lot longer than words spoken tonight? **And that's the President looking very much like a jet, you know, a high-flying jet star. A guy who is a jet pilot. Has been in the past when he was younger, obviously.** What does that image mean to the American people, a guy who can actually get into a supersonic plane and actually fly in an unpressurized cabin like an actual jet pilot?

[. . .]

MATTHEWS: Do you think this role, and I want to talk politically [. . .], the President deserves everything he's doing tonight in terms of his leadership. **He won the war. He was an effective commander. Everybody recognizes that, I believe, except a few critics.** Do you think he is defining the office of the presidency, at least for this time, as basically that of commander in chief? That [. . .] if you're going to run against him, you'd better be ready to take [that] away from him.

[. . .]

MATTHEWS: Let me ask you, Bob Dornan, you were a congressman all those years. **Here's a president who's really nonverbal. He's like Eisenhower. He looks great in a military uniform. He looks great in that cowboy costume he wears when he goes west. I remember him standing at that fence with Colin Powell. Was [that] the best picture in the 2000 campaign?**

[. . .]

MATTHEWS: Ann Coulter, you're the first to speak tonight on the buzz. **The President's performance tonight, redolent of the best of Reagan—what do you think?**

COULTER: It's stunning. It's amazing. I think it's huge. I mean, he's landing on a boat at 150 miles per hour. It's tremendous. It's hard to imagine any Democrat being able to do that. And it doesn't matter if Democrats try to ridicule it. It's stunning, and it speaks for itself.

MATTHEWS: Pat Caddell, the President's performance tonight on television, his arrival on ship?

CADDELL: Well, first of all, Chris, the—I think that—you know, I was—when I first heard about it, I was kind of annoyed. It sounded like the kind of PR stunt that Bill Clinton would pull. But then I saw it. And you know, there's a real—there's a real affection between him and the troops.

[. . .]

MATTHEWS: The President there—look at this guy! We're watching him. He looks like he flew the plane. He only flew it as a passenger, but he's flown—

CADDELL: He looks like a fighter pilot.

MATTHEWS: He looks for real. What is it about the commander in chief role, the hat that he does wear, that makes him—I mean, he seems like—he didn't fight in a war, but he looks like he does.

CADDELL: Yes. It's a—I don't know. You know, it's an internal thing. I don't know if you can put it into words. [. . .] You can see it with him and the troops, the ease with which he talks to them. I was amazed by that, frankly, because as I said, I was originally appalled, particularly when I heard he was going in an F-18. But—on there—but the—but you know, that was—

MATTHEWS: Look at this guy!

CADDELL: —was hard not to be moved by their reaction to him and his reaction to them and—

MATTHEWS: You know, Ann—

CADDELL: —you know, they—**it's a quality. It's an innate quality. It's a real quality.**

MATTHEWS: I know. I think you're right.

The media's hero worship of George Bush—his magical transformation from war avoider into conquering warrior by virtue of his ordering a small, weak country to be invaded—

reached its utterly absurd apogee as Matthews and longtime right-wing tough guy G. Gordon Liddy explicitly admired what they fantasized was the size of George Bush's genitalia:

MATTHEWS: What do you make of this broadside against the USS *Abraham Lincoln* and its chief visitor last week?

LIDDY: Well, I—in the first place, I think it's envy. I mean, after all, Al Gore had to go get some woman to tell him how to be a man. And here comes George Bush. You know, he's in his flight suit, he's striding across the deck, **and he's wearing his parachute harness, you know—and I've worn those because I parachute—and it makes the best of his manly characteristic.** You go run those—run that stuff again of him walking across there with the parachute. **He has just won every woman's vote in the United States of America. You know, all those women who say size doesn't count—they're all liars. Check that out.** I hope the Democrats keep ratting on him and all of this stuff so that they keep showing that tape.

MATTHEWS: You know, it's funny. I shouldn't talk about ratings. I don't always pay attention to them, but last night was a riot because, at the very time [Congressman] Henry Waxman was on—and I do respect him on legislative issues—he was on blasting away, and these pictures were showing last night, and **everybody's tuning in to see these pictures again.**

George Bush had just delivered one of the most absurd speeches in American history—declaring victory in the Iraq War in May 2003 and the glorious "end to major combat operations." The weapons of mass destruction that "justified" his invasion had not been found. Saddam Hussein had not been captured. The insurgency was growing, and no plan for stabilizing Iraq had been formulated. Yet the media was transfixed by Bush's costume—

his dressing up as a conquering warrior—and worshipfully transformed him into the epitome of masculine power and warrior courage, a modern-day Napoleon.

The reverent, besotted depictions of George W. Bush as a swaggering tough guy and warrior—all because he ordered the U.S. military to invade Iraq and then strutted around on an aircraft carrier in a fighter-pilot costume—were ubiquitous among our nation's media stars.

On CNN, Wolf Blitzer excitedly announced "a little bit of history and a lot of drama today when President Bush became the first commander in chief to make a tailhook landing on an aircraft carrier," noting that Bush was "a onetime Fighter Dog himself in the Air National Guard" and that "Bush is no stranger to military aircraft." Brian Williams found Bush almost as attractive as Gordon Liddy did, proclaiming this on his CNBC show:

> And two **immutable truths** about the President that the Democrats can't change: He's a youthful guy. He looked terrific and full of energy in a flight suit. He is a former pilot, so it's not a foreign art farm—art form to him. Not all presidents could have pulled this scene off today.

Fox News's John Scott "reported" that Bush's aircraft landing "was like the Beatles climbed out of that plane, and that's very much what it looked like from here." David Sanger, in the *New York Times,* believed that a better comparison was Tom Cruise:

> But within minutes Mr. Bush emerged for the kind of photographs that other politicians can only dream about. **He hopped out of the plane with a helmet tucked under his arm and walked across the flight deck with a swagger that seemed to suggest he had seen *Top Gun.* Clearly in his element, he was swarmed by cheering members of the *Lincoln*'s crew. . . .**
>
> Never before has a president landed aboard a carrier

at sea, much less taken the controls of the aircraft. **His decision to sleep aboard the ship this evening in the captain's quarters conjured images of the presidency at sea not seen since Franklin D. Roosevelt used to sail to summit meetings.**

That weekend, on CBS's *Face the Nation,* host Bob Schieffer and *Time*'s Joe Klein could barely contain their giddiness and reverence for Bush's stunt:

SCHIEFFER: As far as I'm concerned, that was one of the great pictures of all time. And if you're a political consultant, you can just see "campaign commercial" written all over the pictures of George Bush.

KLEIN: Well, that was probably the coolest presidential image since Bill Pullman played the jet fighter pilot in the movie *Independence Day.* That was the first thing that came to mind for me. And it just shows you how high a mountain these Democrats are going to have to climb. You compare that image, which everybody across the world saw, with this debate last night where you have nine people on a stage and it doesn't air until 11:30 at night, up against *Saturday Night Live,* and you see what a major, major struggle the Democrats are going to have to try and beat a popular incumbent president.

Brit Hume hailed Bush's courage in undertaking this dangerous mission:

But this was risky business. You know, there's grease and oil on the decks of those aircraft carriers. The wind's blowing. All kinds of stuff could have gone wrong. It didn't, he carried it off. Somebody, perhaps he, obviously, believed he could. But this was no slam dunk.

On CNN's *The Capital Gang,* then–*Time* columnist Margaret Carlson described it as "so well done . . . a pretty stirring tableau." On CNN, Laura Ingraham cooed that "speaking as a woman . . . seeing President Bush get out of that plane, carrying his helmet . . . that was a very powerful moment." She pronounced Bush a "real man."

It was not only Bush who benefited from this cartoon equation of cheering for war and thereby becoming a "man." The vast majority of the President's most boisterous pro-war aides—the Doug Feiths and Dick Cheneys and Richard Perles and Paul Wolfowitzes and Elliott Abramses—prattle unceasingly about the need to show resolve, by which they mean support for one war after the next, notwithstanding the fact that they avoided military service and have spent their lives ensconced in think tanks and government jobs. Yet their ranks are virtually devoid of any individuals who have been to war or who served in the military. They specialize in sending other people's sons and daughters to war while shamelessly posturing as brave, Churchillian warriors for freedom.

2008: The Same Script

With the combat-avoiding, war-loving team of Bush and Cheney about to leave the political scene, America's right wing is transparently preparing to have their next leaders read from the same deceitful script. As the Republican Party sought in 2007 to find the successor to George W. Bush, our next "Commander-in-Chief," its entire top tier of candidates and pundits was characterized by tough guys playacting.

More often than not, the GOP primary race resembled some sort of bizarre reality show, where the objective was not to put forth persuasive policy positions but to exude a caricatured version of über-masculinity. As Joe Conason put it in a *Salon* article in July 2007:

Nothing unites the Republican candidates for president or excites the conservative base more than their bellicose barking about war and confrontation. The GOP presidential debates often sound like a tough-man competition, with Rudolph Giuliani denouncing the "cut-and-run" Democrats, Mitt Romney demanding a double-size Guantánamo detention camp, and the rest of the pack struggling to keep pace with the snarling alpha dogs.

Yet while their rhetoric is invariably loud and aggressive, none of these martial orators has seen a day of military service—except for John McCain, whose prospects are rapidly deflating, and Duncan Hunter, whose campaign never got enough air for a single balloon. Unfortunately for those two decorated veterans, their party seems to prefer its hawks to be of the chicken variety.

From the beginning, Rudy Giuliani, the front-runner throughout most of the year, based his entire campaign on his alleged tough-guy status. As *Time* reported in mid-2007, in an article titled "Behind Giuliani's Tough Talk,"

As Giuliani himself put it to the *Detroit News* recently, "The American people are not going to vote for a weakling. They're going to elect someone who will protect them from terrorism for the next four years." It's the same calculus Bush used in 2004.

Right-wing pundits never failed to depict Giuliani as some sort of strong protector and warrior against all that is bad and threatening in the world. John Podhoretz, a Giuliani supporter, gushed: "The Republican Party is the party of strength at home and abroad, and for many, Rudy Giuliani personifies that." His *National Review* colleague Ramesh Ponnuru added: "That [Giuliani] personifies strength 'for many' seems to me to be indisputable."

And our nation's media stars often talked about Giuliani's alleged "toughness" in terms so bizarre, even creepy, that it would make a pornography writer cringe. Here, for instance, was Chris Matthews with *Newsweek*'s Howard Fineman in mid-2007, oozing excitement over Giuliani's paternal protectiveness:

> **FINEMAN:** I mean, "commanding Daddy" is not the phrase I would use because "Daddy" implies some generosity of spirit.
> **MATTHEWS:** Yes.
> **FINEMAN:** What's appealing about Rudy Giuliani is not the generous side, what's appealing about him is the tough-cop side.
> **MATTHEWS:** Right. You just wait until Daddy gets home.
> **FINEMAN:** Yes, that part . . .
> **MATTHEWS:** That Daddy.
> **FINEMAN:** . . . of the daddy. It's the tough-cop side, so . . .
> **MATTHEWS:** Yes. Yes.

They are right in one sense. For the authoritarians comprising the Republican base and the faux-masculine-power-worshiping media pundits, what was appealing about Giuliani was that he conveyed "You just wait until Daddy gets home." Craving a stern daddy as a political leader is the root of the authoritarian mind. Yet these are the warped images that dominate not only their psyches but their political "analysis" as well.

Giuliani himself incessantly milked the happenstance of his proximity to the 9/11 attack in New York by holding himself out as some kind of gladiator who had faced down Islamic terrorists in the arena. He incorporated into his stump speech a passage about terrorism and the Iraq War in which he says, "It is something I understand better than anyone else running for president."

But from beginning to end, Giuliani's self-touted image as a tough guy was pure myth. It had no more substance than did John Wayne's role-playing as a war hero or George Bush's play-acting as a rancher and combat veteran in the bunker with Tommy Franks. When he had the opportunity to fight for his country in Vietnam, Rudy Giuliani hid from military service, engaging in one maneuver after the next to ensure that other, braver American men went off and fought and died in his place. What is "tough" or brave or courageous or resolute about any of that?

Revealingly, Giuliani staffed his campaign with foreign policy advisors who are exactly like him. He was surrounded by men who hold themselves out as brave warriors because they delight in sending other people off to fight one war after the next, yet who never displayed any acts of warrior courage in their lives, uniformly having avoided military service just like their candidate. From the start of his tough-guy campaign, Giuliani's list of foreign policy advisors read like a directory of the nation's most warmongering chicken-hawk neoconservatives—what the *New York Times,* with great understatement, described as "a particularly hawkish group of advisers and neoconservative thinkers":

> Mr. Giuliani's team includes Norman Podhoretz, a prominent neoconservative who advocates bombing Iran "as soon as it is logistically possible"; Daniel Pipes, the director of the Middle East Forum, who has called for profiling Muslims at airports and scrutinizing American Muslims in law enforcement, the military and the diplomatic corps; and Michael Rubin, a scholar at the American Enterprise Institute who has written in favor of revoking the United States' ban on assassination.

This sterling team of combat-avoiding warmongers also included former Bush aide David Frum, who coauthored a book with Richard Perle ambitiously advocating *An End to Evil* through a series of Middle East wars (to be fought by others). Giuliani's team was notable not merely for their insatiable hunger for war but for their particular focus on waging Middle Eastern wars against various enemies of Israel. As *Harper's* Ken Silverstein wrote:

> There's also Martin Kramer, who spent 25 years at Tel Aviv University and whose Middle East policy can basically be summarized as "What's Good for Israel," and former Senator Robert Kasten of Wisconsin, whose career was best known for his loopy attacks on the United Nations and for being arrested for drunk driving after running a red light and driving down the wrong side of the road.
>
> I asked Augustus Richard Norton of Boston University, an expert adviser to the Iraq Study Group, for his take on Giuliani's crew. He dubbed the group "AIPAC's Dream Team."
>
> "What I find fascinating," he said, "is how skewed this team seems to be in terms of the regional focus. Most of the members are well known as Israel advocates. There is no real expertise on Africa, Asia, Latin America, or much of Europe."

Here again, with Giuliani, we found the most common and defining attribute of the would-be right-wing male leader: the toxic combination of a life devoid of physical courage and warrior virtues, combined with a drooling desire to send others off to war in order to feel and be perceived as powerful and brave.

What is most striking about the mind-set of the right-wing chicken hawk is its stark contrast with the way in which actual war veterans think. To fake right-wing tough guys, war is exactly like a video game—some distant, abstract battle where one can feel pulsating sensations of excitement and toughness from winning, but suffer no real consequences by losing. It is risk-free fun, and thus easily cheered on.

Senator Joe Lieberman has become one of the nation's most tenacious war advocates, not only steadfastly supporting the endless occupation of Iraq but also becoming one of the first figures of any national significance to call overtly for an attack on Iran. He never stops talking about "resolve" and "strength" and "Churchill" and "toughness"—as though he is the embodiment of those attributes by virtue of his glee in sending others off to fight wars and bomb other countries.

Lieberman's cheap warmongering is directly the by-product of his complete lack of connection to any real wars. Like most of his fellow war-cheerleading neoconservatives, Lieberman was of prime fighting age during the Vietnam War yet steadfastly avoided service. As a result, Lieberman—like most of the right-wing pro-war contingent in America—views war the way an adolescent does. As Jeffrey Goldberg recounted in his 2007 *New Yorker* profile:

> Lieberman likes expressions of American power. A few years ago, I was in a movie theatre in Washington when I noticed Lieberman and his wife, Hadassah, a few seats down. The film was *Behind Enemy Lines,* in which Owen Wilson plays a U.S. pilot shot down in Bosnia. Whenever the American military scored an onscreen hit, Lieberman pumped his fist and said, "Yeah!" and "All right!"

That is about as vivid a profile of the neoconservative warrior mentality as one can get: paranoid and frightened guys who derive personal and emotional fulfillment by giddily cheering on military destruction from a safe and comfortable distance. As an actual warrior—Gen. Wesley Clark—pointed out in mid-2007, the sort of chest-beating, casual war threats that come spewing forth from the likes of Joe Lieberman could only be made by someone completely unfamiliar with war, and would rarely be made by any real military officer:

> Senator Lieberman's saber rattling does nothing to help dissuade Iran from aiding Shia militias in Iraq, or trying to obtain nuclear capabilities. In fact, it's highly irresponsible and counterproductive, and I urge him to stop. . . .
>
> The Iranians are very much aware of U.S. military capabilities. They don't need Joe Lieberman to remind them that we are the militarily dominant power in the world today.
>
> **Only someone who never wore the uniform or thought seriously about national security would make threats at this point.** What our soldiers need is responsible strategy, not a further escalation of tensions in the region. Senator Lieberman must act more responsibly and tone down his threat machine.

Clark's criticism applies to virtually the entire top level of the American right. Its loudest, most flamboyant warriors—beginning with George Bush, Dick Cheney, Rudy Giuliani, Newt Gingrich, Rush Limbaugh, and on down—are not only individuals who never went anywhere near the military but are people who actively avoided combat when their country was at war. And real warriors are beginning, with increasing clarity, to make that point. From *New York Magazine* in 2007:

> "If Giuliani is the nominee, we're going to hammer him with ads, and it's going to be easy because the issue is simple: He's a draft dodger," says Jon Soltz, an Iraq vet who served as a captain and runs VoteVets.org, a left-leaning version of Swift Boat Veterans for Truth. "Giuliani gets a zero-zero," says General Wesley Clark, an adviser to the group. "He wasn't willing to risk his life for his

country, and he has no relevant experience that's in any way useful to be commander-in-chief. He hosted the U.N. and had a large police force."

Giuliani was born in 1944, which placed him at prime fighting age throughout the mid-1960s and into the early 1970s as the Vietnam War raged on. Yet this supreme Tough Guy obtained one deferment after the next—including one under highly questionable circumstances—to ensure that he did not have to fight for his country, instead sending other Americans off to die. As Joe Conason reported in *Salon,*

> During his years as an undergraduate at Manhattan College and then at New York University Law School, Giuliani qualified for a student deferment. Upon graduation from law school in 1968, he lost that temporary deferment and his draft status reverted to 1-A, the designation awarded to those most qualified for induction into the Army.
>
> At the same time, Giuliani won a clerkship with federal Judge Lloyd McMahon in the fabled Southern District of New York, where he would become the United States attorney. He naturally had no desire to trade his ticket on the legal profession's fast track for latrine duty in the jungle. So he quickly applied for another deferment based on his judicial clerkship. This time the Selective Service System denied his claim.
>
> That was when **the desperate Giuliani prevailed upon his boss to write to the draft board, asking them to grant him a fresh deferment and reclassification as an "essential" civilian employee.** As the great tabloid columnist Jimmy Breslin noted 20 years later, during the former prosecutor's first campaign for mayor: "Giuliani did not attend the war in Vietnam because federal Judge Lloyd MacMahon [*sic*] wrote a letter to the draft board in 1969 and got him out. Giuliani was

a law clerk for MacMahon, who at the time was hearing Selective Service cases. MacMahon's letter to Giuliani's draft board stated that Giuliani was so necessary as a law clerk that he could not be allowed to get shot at in Vietnam."

The very idea that a law clerk for a federal judge—fresh out of law school—is "essential" in any way is absurd on its face. Yet Giuliani was so desperate to avoid fighting for his country that he invoked this rationale in order to ensure that someone else was sent in his place.

What makes Giuliani's evasion of military service all the more galling is that—like so many of his right-wing comrades— the cultural and political divide illustrated by the war in Vietnam was the centerpiece of his right-wing appeal. Indeed, in September 2007, Giuliani published a lengthy article in *Foreign Affairs* intended to outline his overall approach to foreign policy, and this Vietnam-era draft dodger had the audacity to cite America's lack of resolve in finishing that war as a major cause of weakness. Giuliani wrote,

> America must remember one of the lessons of the Vietnam War. Then, as now, we fought a war with the wrong strategy for several years. And then, as now, we corrected course and began to show real progress. Many historians today believe that by about 1972 we and our South Vietnamese partners had succeeded in defeating the Vietcong insurgency and in setting South Vietnam on a path to political self-sufficiency.
> **But America then withdrew its support, allowing the communist North to conquer the South. The consequences were dire, and not only in Vietnam:** numerous deaths in places such as the killing fields of Cambodia, a newly energized and expansionist Soviet Union, and **a weaker America.**

If fighting and winning in Vietnam were such a critical prong in protecting America's national security—as he contends now—where was Giuliani when the war was being waged? Why did he hide and avoid the fight? And what possible excuse is there for allowing him, in light of this behavior, to parade around as some sort of Father-Warrior-Protector while demeaning others as weak and cowardly and without the resolve to fight for the United States?

With the exception of John McCain, who was revealingly attacked by most of the Hard Right, the same can and should be said for the other leading GOP presidential candidates in 2007—Mitt Romney and Fred Thompson, and briefly, Newt Gingrich. They pranced around as tough guys, sounding as bellicose as possible, even though the reality of their own lives when it comes to war is indistinguishable from Giuliani's. All were of prime fighting age during the Vietnam War, and all engaged in one maneuver after another to ensure that they did not fight.

In November 2007, a *New York Times* profile detailed what Mitt Romney was doing during the Vietnam War. Although the article reflects quite poorly on his character, it demonstrates why his candidacy began to resonate among our country's right-wing war-cheerleading faction. Romney's life mirrors that faction's perverse "values" perfectly.

While many of his fellow citizens from 1966 to 1969 were being killed in Vietnam, Romney—"a sheltered child of privilege," as the article put it—spent those years in Paris and other cities in France trying to convert the French to Mormonism, which enabled him to obtain a "missionary" deferment. When Romney and his fellow Mormon missionaries encountered anti-American sentiment from war opponents, they decided that the French—unlike Romney and his war-supporting, war-avoiding friends—were "weak":

The missionaries had often met with hostility over the Vietnam War. "Are you an American?" was a common greeting, Mr. Romney recalled, followed by, " 'Get out of Vietnam!' Bang!" The door would slam. **But such opposition only hardened their hawkish views. "We felt the French were pretty weak-kneed,"** [Romney's fellow missionary Byron] Hansen said.

So early on, Romney shared one of the defining values of the political movement he sought to lead: namely, the belief that those who want to send other people off to fight wars are "strong" and "courageous," while those who oppose sending others off to war are "weak." As Romney's co-missionary put it, perfectly encapsulating the right-wing war cheerleaders of both then and now,

> Most of the missionaries, though, were also relieved that their service meant a draft deferment. "I am sorry, but no one was excited to go and get killed in Vietnam," Mr. Hansen said, acknowledging, "In hindsight, **it is easy to be for the war when you don't have to worry about going to Vietnam."**

What's particularly reprehensible about all of this is that so much of the Republican Party spent years mauling Bill Clinton for avoiding service in a war *that he opposed.* But for years, Romney emphatically supported the Vietnam War yet actively avoided service and never enlisted:

> Many church leaders considered the war a godly cause, and Mr. Romney said at the time he thought that it was essential to holding back Communism. . . .
> Eventually, the great debates of the day intruded even at Brigham Young. In the fall of 1970, the student government president and others distributed a pamphlet encouraging opposition to the Vietnam conflict by quot-

ing past Mormon leaders on the evils of war, stirring a predictable campus fury.

Mr. Romney wanted no part of such things. "If we had asked Mitt to sign that pamphlet, he would have had a heart attack," said Terrell E. Hunt, a fellow Cougar who signed it.

Mitt Romney, then and now: showing what a supertough patriot he is by cheering on wars that other people—but never he or his family—risk their lives to fight. What makes it all the more repellent is that while many Mormons did enlist—Brigham Young University was one of the few campuses that was a hotbed of *pro-war activism*—Romney actively avoided service, first with his missionary deferment and then by obtaining a student deferment once he got back from France.

And now he has the audacity to claim that he wanted to fight, but cites his high lottery number as a reason why his supposed desire was never fulfilled—as though there was no such thing as voluntary enlistment:

> Mr. Romney, though, said that he sometimes had wished he were in Vietnam instead of France. "There were surely times on my mission when I was having a particularly difficult time accomplishing very little when I would have longed for the chance to be serving in the military," he said in an interview, "but that was not to be."

Note the lack of agency that he tries to insinuate—military service "was not to be," as though he so desperately wanted to fight but it was just a matter of bad luck, having nothing to do with his own actions, that he never managed to make it to the glorious combat fields of Vietnam. It's exactly the same deceitful little act that we heard in 2007 from our brave, combat-avoiding

Warrior-in-Chief whom Romney wants to replace. As the *Washington Post*'s Dan Froomkin reported:

> President Bush wishes that he could be alongside the troops in Iraq—except that he's too old.
>
> At least that's what he reportedly told a blogger embedded with U.S. troops in Iraq. . . . "N. Z. Bear," one of the eight guests sitting around a table with Bush at the White House, reported: "Responding to one of the bloggers in Iraq he expressed envy that they could be there, and said he'd like to be there but 'One, I'm too old to be out there, and two, they would notice me.' "

Poor Mitt Romney and George Bush—such frustrated would-be warriors, wanting so badly to fight in combat but thwarted at every turn by circumstances beyond their control. So what exactly was it that prevented Romney from fulfilling his wishes to fight? A video narration that accompanied the *New York Times* article contained an interview with one of Romney's fellow missionaries at the time. He playfully explains how he and Romney had found zany costumes, dressed up in them, and formed a group that had a "fun time doing little Vaudeville routines"—all while Romney's fellow citizens were being slaughtered in the Vietnam War that he so believed in.

More repugnantly still, both the *Times* article and the video accompanying that article contain all sorts of quotes from Romney and his co-missionaries complaining about how very hard life was for them in France because it was so difficult to convert people, without any sense of how that "hardship" compared to their fellow citizens' fighting and dying in the Vietnam jungle. It's hard to put into words what twisted self-absorption and lack of empathy are required to wallow in such self-pity—exactly the same strain that led Romney, at a candidates' forum in Iowa in 2007, to respond to a question about his five sheltered sons' lack of military service by equating their work on his presidential campaign with other Americans' sons and daughters who are in the Iraq War that Romney so loves and exploits for political gain:

> **QUESTION:** How many of your five sons are currently serving in the U.S. military, and if none of them are, how do they claim to support this War on Terrorism, by enlisting in our U.S. military?
>
> **ROMNEY:** Well, the good news is we have a volunteer army and that's the way we're going to keep it. . . . They've chosen not to serve in the military, in active duty. I respect their decision in that regard. . . .
>
> One of the ways my sons are showing support for our nation is by helping me get elected because they think I'd be a great President. My son Josh brought the family Winnebago and has visited ninety-nine counties, most of them with his three kids and his wife, and I respect that and all of those who serve this great country.

Although Romney claimed he was ultimately convinced by his presidential-candidate-and-senator father that the Vietnam War was wrong, he spent most of those years cheering it on—from the same safe and sheltered distance where one finds most of our right-wing tough-guy warriors today, the ones who understandably recognize themselves in both Romney and Giuliani. Needless to say, a centerpiece of both of their campaigns was how "tough" and courageously pro-war they are.

This reality, however, never prevents the media from oozing with admiration over the alleged masculine prowess of Republican leaders. After one GOP presidential debate in June, *Newsweek*'s Howard Fineman went on MSNBC News and—as the GOP candidates paraded through the Reagan Library, the site of the debate—declared Republicans to be the Party of Real Men, something that voters find "reassuring":

[I]f you look at that picture and took away all of the writing and all of the words, and just had the image, could the American people tell that those were Republicans? I think the answer is yes. There is a hierarchical, there is, **dare I say it, male, there is an old-line quality to them that some voters, indeed a lot of voters, find reassuring.** And this is something that the Democrats need to understand. The Democrats are the "we are family" party, which is great, but this is the other side of the conversation and this is their home here. We really are in Reagan country.

This is how our political pundits routinely speak of Republican males whose lives are devoid of anything to justify it. The adoration is so excessive that it frequently is embarrassing to hear, and truly borders on bizarre homoerotic worship. Anyone who believes that to be hyperbole ought to consider the following:

In a June 2007 column, *The Politico*'s Roger Simon actually said that Romney is "[s]trong, clear, gives good soundbite, and *has shoulders you could land a 737 on.*" Simon had previously swooned that Romney has "chiseled-out-of-granite features, a full, dark head of hair going a distinguished gray at the temples, and a barrel chest," adding, "On the morning that he announced for president, I bumped into him in the lounge of the Marriott and up close he is almost overpowering. He radiates vigor."

National Review's Ramesh Ponnuru pointed out "that Mitt Romney is good-looking—an observation by John J. Miller that draws TNR's ridicule—has been observed by many political commentators." And MSNBC's Chris Matthews virtually declared Romney to be the Ultimate Male. From the August 13, 2007, edition of MSNBC's *Hardball with Chris Matthews:*

MATTHEWS: Let me ask you about Mitt Romney. You know, I watched him on the *Today* show this morning. **He looks like a million bucks. Everything is perfect. Everything**

about him is perfect—his look, his manner, everything, the shirt, never rolled-up sleeves, the tie always tied. That perfection—is that the Republican Party of the twenty-first century?

On the January 19th edition of *Hardball,* Matthews said of Romney: "He has the perfect chin, the perfect hair, he looks right." On February 13, Matthews said Romney has "got a great chin, I've noticed." And while Matthews and others have questioned whether Romney is just an empty vessel of presidential imagery, he is endlessly discussed in terms of his chiseled strength. What drives all of this is that Romney has fed every crumb of war-seeking rhetoric to the Republican base that they crave. And in return, the media dutifully depicts him as tough and manly.

The media's swooning over the masculine magnetism of the draft-avoiding Washington lobbyist Fred Thompson was even more embarrassing, even more cringe-inducing. In May 2007, the aforementioned Howard Fineman went on Chris Matthews's show and said: "Thompson not only is 'tough on defense,' but *he himself is 'a tough guy.'* " In June, Matthews—while speaking with his guest, *Time*'s Ana Marie Cox—unleashed this truly bizarre rant about Thompson's manly sexiness:

> Does [Fred Thompson] have sex appeal? I'm looking at this guy and I'm trying to find out the new order of things, and what works for women and what doesn't. Does this guy have some sort of thing going for him that I should notice? . . .
>
> Gene, do you think there's a sex appeal for this guy, this sort of mature, older man, you know? He looks sort of seasoned and in charge of himself. What is this appeal? Because I keep star quality. You were throwing the word out, shining star, Ana Marie, before I checked you on it. . . .
>
> **Can you smell the English Leather on this guy,**

the Aqua Velva, the sort of mature man's shaving cream, or whatever, you know, after he shaved? Do you smell that sort of—a little bit of cigar smoke? You know, whatever.

What can even be said about that? And nobody really seems to find this odd or disturbing or objectionable at all—that night after night, one of the featured "journalists" of a major news network goes on television and, with some of our most prestigious journalists assembled with him, speaks admiringly about the smells and arousing masculinity and the "daddy" qualities of various political officials, and that this metric is, more or less, the full extent of his political analysis.

Beyond its sheer weirdness, such a description is extremely difficult to understand, even when observing Thompson's own campaign biography. Thompson has been a government lawyer, an actor, and a senator. Though Thompson does not mention it, he was also—for two decades—what a 1996 profile in *Washington Monthly* described as "a high-paid Washington lobbyist for both foreign and domestic interests." This folksy, down-home, regular guy has spent his entire adult life as a lawyer and lobbyist in Washington, except when he was an actor in Hollywood, and—of course—evaded combat.

So what exactly, in Fineman's eyes, made Thompson such a "tough guy"? Fineman clone Mark Halperin, in a fawning piece in *Time* the week prior—hailing Thompson's "magnetism" and praising him as "poised and compelling" and exuding "bold self-confidence"—provided the answer:

> Even before his *Law & Order* depiction of district attorney Arthur Branch, Thompson nearly always played variations on the same character—a straight-talking, tough-minded, wise Southerner—basically a version of what his supporters say is his true political self.
>
> And he is often cast as a person in power—a military

official, the White House chief of staff, the head of the CIA, a Senator or even the President of the U.S. It could be called the Cary Grant approach to politics. As the legendary actor once explained his own style and success, "I pretended to be somebody I wanted to be, and I finally became that person."

The only thing that made Thompson a "tough guy" is that he pretends to be one; he playacts as one. There is nothing real about it.

The same week, in response to Michael Moore's request that Thompson debate him over health care, Thompson—showing what a tough guy he really is—filmed a forty-second YouTube video where he chomped on a cigar and told Moore to check into a mental hospital. Chris Matthews had *Time*'s Mark Halperin on his show to giggle with him like sixth-grade boys high-fiving each other after the cool kid they are desperate to be near (played by Thompson) unleashed some adolescent prank on the nerdy kid in the corner:

> **MATTHEWS:** Wait till you catch this. . . .
>
> Mark Halperin, is Thompson's cigar-chomping chide a sign that he's serious about getting in this race?
>
> **HALPERIN:** Chris, I've got to see your "Ha ha"!
>
> **MATTHEWS:** I have to tell you, Mark, it's for real. I can't fake it. But let me ask you this . . .
>
> **HALPERIN:** I agree.
>
> **MATTHEWS:** Is this the kind of winning performance that the avuncular Fred Thompson needs to win this thing?
>
> **HALPERIN:** I echo your "Ha ha." Mega "ha ha" to you, Chris. Because that is exactly what this kind of campaign is going to have to be. He said he has said he's going to run in an unorthodox campaign.
>
> That kind of video gets the net roots totally in a lather. They hate Michael Moore. They like the jab. They like the cigar. It's a total winner.

MATTHEWS: So there is a right-wing net roots as well as a left-wing net roots?

HALPERIN: Look, it shows that this guy has the flair for the dramatic. He understands what the net roots cares about. He was aggressive on immigration. I think right now that this guy is poised to come in and be a key player in this.

MATTHEWS: He's also brilliant, because the attack from a defensive position is one of the smartest moves in politics. There you go again. He posed as if he was defending himself against Michael Moore and took his head off.

Chewing on a cigar in front of a camera and telling someone to go to a mental hospital is, to them, what makes someone a tough guy—"aggressive" and "avuncular." It is the John Wayne syndrome—costumes and scripts supplanting reality.

The same is true of Fineman's mindless claim that Thompson is "tough on defense." What does that even mean? Marvel at this quote from Thompson, from CNN on March 1, 2003, when he was urging the invasion of Iraq:

Can we afford to appease Saddam, kick the can down the road? Thank goodness we have a president with the courage to protect our country. **And when people ask what has Saddam done to us, I ask, what had the 9/11 hijackers done to us—before 9/11?**

That is quite an incredible mentality, and it has applicability for all sorts of situations. One can easily extend it:

THOMPSON: I think we should invade and bomb Uruguay.
QUESTION: What has Uruguay done to us?
THOMPSON: When people ask what has Uruguay done to us, I ask, what had the 9/11 hijackers done to us—before 9/11?

That mind-set can be described by many adjectives, but "tough" is not one of them. "Toughness" can be demonstrated by actually fighting in a war. Toughness is demonstrated when a political candidate tells people what they do not want to hear. Toughness is *not* demonstrated by sending other people to war. But people like Fineman (i.e., media purveyors of Beltway conventional wisdom) reflexively, and incoherently, equate blind militarism and warmongering with toughness even though it is anything but. The illusion of manliness clichés, tough-guy poses, and empty gestures of "cultural conservatism" are what the Republican base seeks, and media simpletons like Fineman, Halperin, and Matthews eat it all up just as hungrily.

Chicken-Hawk History

Few articles captured the right-wing pretense of toughness as well as the June 2007 cover story in *The Weekly Standard* by Dean Barnett, titled "The 9/11 Generation." Barnett's article contended that America's current youthful generation is courageous and noble because it has answered the call of military service, in contrast to the cowardly Vietnam-era baby boomers who chose protest instead. Its reasoning highlighted (unintentionally) exactly what is so corrupt, ignoble, and deceitful about the manufactured image created by the right-wing political movement that has come to dominate the Republican Party.

The crux of Barnett's homage is expressed as follows:

In the 1960s, history called the Baby Boomers. They didn't answer the phone.

Confronted with a generation-defining conflict, the cold war, the Boomers—those, at any rate, who came to be emblematic of their generation—took the opposite path from their parents during World War II. Sadly, the excesses of Woodstock became the face of the Boomers' response to their moment of challenge. War protests where agitated youths derided American soldiers as baby-killers added no luster to their image.

Few of the leading lights of that generation joined the military. Most calculated how they could avoid military service, and their attitude rippled through the rest of the century. In the 1970s, '80s, and '90s, military service didn't occur to most young people as an option, let alone a duty.

But now, once again, history is calling. Fortunately, the present generation appears more reminiscent of their grandparents than their parents.

Within these four paragraphs, one finds myths laid on top of more myths. To begin with, while Barnett contrasts two signifi-cant groups of the Vietnam era—those who bravely volunteered for combat and/or who were drafted (Jim Webb and John Mc-Cain and Chuck Hagel and John Kerry) and those who protested the war—he revealingly whitewashes from history the other major group, the most ignoble one, the one that happens to in-clude virtually all of the individuals who lead Barnett's political movement: namely, those who claimed to support the war but did everything possible to evade military service.

Most revealingly, Barnett condemns those who refused to fight because *they opposed the war and chose instead to work against it,* but ignores completely those who *favored the war but sent others to fight and die in it.* Barnett has to ignore this group. He has no choice. He cannot possibly criticize such indi-viduals, because this group includes the editors and writers of the magazine in which he is writing and virtually the entire lead-ership of the political movement that he follows.

Back in 2005, the political blogger Digby wrote a seminal post that comprehensively described all three "baby boomer" groups of the Vietnam era—including the one Barnett understandably wants to delete from history—as follows:

> We are dealing with a group of right wing glory seekers who chose long ago to eschew putting themselves on the line in favor of tough talk and empty posturing—the Vietnam chickenhawks and their recently hatched offspring of the new Global War On Terrorism. These are men (mostly) driven by the desire to prove their manhood but who refuse to actually test their physical courage. Neither are they able to prove their virility as they are held hostage by prudish theocrats and their own shortcomings. So they adopt the pose of warrior but never actually place themselves under fire. This is a psychologically difficult position to uphold.
>
> The [Vietnam] war provided two very distinct tribal pathways to manhood. One was to join "the revolution" which included the perk of having equally revolutionary women at their sides, freely joining in sexual as well as political adventure as part of the broader cultural revolution.
>
> (The 60's leftist got laid. A lot.) And he was also deeply engaged in the major issue of his age, the war in Vietnam, in a way that was not, at the time, seen as cowardly, but rather quite threatening. His masculine image encompassed both sides of the male archetypal coin—he was both virile and heroic.
>
> The other pathway to prove your manhood was to test your physical courage in battle. There was an actual bloody fight going on in Vietnam, after all. Plenty of young men volunteered and plenty more were drafted. And despite the fact that it may be illogical on some level to say that if you support a war you must fight it, certainly if your self-image is that of a warrior, tradition

requires that you put yourself in the line of fire to prove your courage if the opportunity presents itself. You simply cannot be a warrior if you are not willing to fight. . . . Men who went to Vietnam and faced their fears of killing and dying, whether voluntarily or involuntarily, put themselves to this test.

And then there were the chickenhawks. They were neither part of the revolution nor did they take the obvious step of volunteering to fight the war they supported. Indeed, due to the draft, they allowed others to fight and die in their place despite the fact that they believed heartily that the best response to communism was to aggressively fight it "over there" so we wouldn't have to fight it here.

These were empty boys, unwilling to put themselves on the line at the moment of truth, yet they held the masculine virtues as the highest form of human experience and have portrayed themselves ever since as tough, uncompromising manly men while portraying liberals as weak and effeminate.

In this regard, the "9/11 Generation" is no different from its predecessor. One group is composed of an extremely small percentage of young Americans who volunteer to fight in combat. Contrary to Barnett's attempt to hold them up as the symbolic prop of the "9/11 Generation," they actually represent—as noted in the first chapter—a tiny percentage of Americans in this age group. A far larger percentage of Americans actually fought in the Vietnam War than fought in the "9/11 era."

Then there is the much larger percentage of young Americans who vigorously oppose the 9/11-era warmongering. And finally there is the tragically sizable portion—much larger than was true of the hated "baby boomer" generation—characterized by that most contemptible attribute: vocal war-cheerleading and a self-image of resolute strength combined with a refusal to fight, *even though the war missions they cheer on are suffering due to a lack of volunteers.*

Contrary to the military heroism with which Barnett tries to cloak his political movement, it is this lowliest group—the "empty boys," the war cheerleaders who send others to fight in their wars—that leads the country's right wing and has led the country for the last seven militarized years; which publishes *The Weekly Standard* and edits *National Review* and broadcasts the most popular right-wing talk-radio shows and Fox News programs; and that has been responsible for the series of liberty-abridging policies implemented, the wars the United States has fought, and the new ones it threatens to fight, ever since the 9/11 attacks. The political movement of which Barnett is a part and off which *The Weekly Standard* feeds is led by the very group of Vietnam-era baby boomers who failed "to answer the phone."

It is no surprise, then, that the younger generation of the political movement led by the Vietnam-era chicken hawks largely emulates their cowardly and principle-free behavior. The defining attribute of the *Weekly Standard* strain of the "9/11 Generation"—led by Rush Limbaugh and Newt Gingrich and Sean Hannity and Dick Cheney and George W. Bush—is the unprecedented ease with which one can cheer on endless wars without having to make even the most minimal sacrifices to sustain them. *That* is the unique and defining attribute of the Republican Party strain of the 9/11 Generation.

Toughness isn't measured by how willing one is to order the U.S. military—the most powerful in the world—to start wars. Strength isn't a function of how willing someone is to torture or otherwise abuse helpless detainees in captivity. And manliness certainly isn't demonstrated by being as bellicose and antagonistic as possible when doing so entails absolutely no risk.

Quite the contrary, swaggering faux-masculinity, mindless militarism, and an excessive fear-driven willingness to use force are unmistakable signs of profound weakness, almost always leading to worthless devastation. As Albert Camus said of the widespread willingness to send others off to die, "Mistaken ideas always end in bloodshed, but in every case it is someone else's blood. That is why some of our thinkers feel free to say just about anything."

Imagine someone who lies in bed at night, clutching a rifle, and leaping out of bed upon hearing every noise, guns blazing, petrified that there is an intruder after them. Such an image conjures real weakness, even hysteria—not strength, and certainly not traditional masculine warrior virtues. That is even truer of the person who lies in bed and dispatches someone else to do the shooting upon hearing every noise. One can debate whether that behavior is prudent or wise. But what it plainly is not is tough and strong.

While the Great American Hypocrites on the Right now prioritize their tough-guy costumes and warrior playacting, this is far from the only deceitful role they play. This process of prancing around, pretending to be the opposite of what they actually are, is what they do. It is who they are, particularly when it comes to winning elections.

Just as was true of their pioneer, John Wayne, playacting as a warrior while running away from war is not enough. Piled onto their pretenses of toughness are a whole array of other disguises, all of them designed to mask the ugly reality of what they are. Principal among these—as examined in the following chapter—are their endless efforts to masquerade as wholesome and moral family men.

That's how twice- and thrice-divorced and draft-avoiding individuals like Newt Gingrich and Rush Limbaugh become media symbols of the Christian values voters and tough-on-defense stalwarts. And it's how a lifelong Beltway lobbyist and lawyer like Thompson, who avoided Vietnam, standing next to his twenty-five-years-younger second wife, was held up by our media as a good Baptist, a Regular Guy symbol of piety, and a no-nonsense, tough-guy, super-masculine warrior who will protect us all. It's what enables the serial adulterer with the incomparably wrecked family life, tough-guy Rudy Giuliani, to proclaim with a straight face that he opposes same-sex marriage because he believes that it is vital to preserve the "sanctity of marriage."

To perpetuate that sham, the same pattern repeats itself time and again. Just as our right-wing tough guys exploit advocacy of endless wars to mask their lack of actual courage and strength, so, too, do they exploit their purported belief in "traditional morality" to obscure the fact that their lives are bereft of such morality. But because their mindless, vapid media allies eagerly swallow and digest all of these manipulative images, Americans are continuously presented with personality images of these right-wing political leaders that are the very opposite of reality.

CHAPTER FOUR

Wholesome Family Men

SERIAL DIVORCES, THIRD WIVES, GAY PROSTITUTES, DRUG ADDICTIONS, AND MISTRESSES

The Republican Party has become so dependent on pretending that its leaders are morally superior, wholesome family men that they have invented numerous slogans designed to stake a claim to this moral high ground: The Moral Majority. Family Values. The Values Voter. Traditional Marriage. Yet time and again, the politicians parading around under these moralistic banners have lived their lives in complete contradiction of them. Just as they do with tough-guy war-cheerleading, the country's right-wing leaders, in order to deceive the American voter, have cynically dressed up in moralistic costumes to hide what Great American Hypocrites they actually are.

Throughout the 1990s, America's right wing and our nation's media stars were driven mad by an endless obsession with moralizing about every detail of the sex life of Bill Clinton, including—literally—explicit discussions on our television news programs and in our nation's newspapers about whether the President's penis was marked by unique spots. That bizarre obsession plummeted to previously unthinkable depths when the GOP-led Congress actually impeached the twice-elected, highly popular President of the United States who had presided over national prosperity and relative peace.

Since then, sexual moralism has taken center stage along with mindless militarism in the electoral strategy of the right wing of the Republican Party. But the leaders whom this party puts forth as the Beacons of traditional morality are the very living and breathing embodiments of that which they claim to condemn. In their actual lives, right-wing leaders personify the sexual sleaze and amoral hedonism against which they endlessly sermonize. Sexual morality and traditional marriages are campaign props that they trot out to disguise themselves and win elections. But those props disappear completely when it is time for them to live their actual lives.

Indeed, throughout 2006 and 2007, evidence continued to emerge that "Family Values" and "Traditional Marriage"—particularly for those who had crusaded for Bill Clinton's impeachment in the late 1990s—were nothing but manipulative lip service. The evidence has now piled up sky high demonstrating that the very moral crusaders leading the witch hunt against Bill Clinton were living the most decadent private lives imaginable. Indeed, huge numbers of their key leaders during the impeachment spectacle were themselves engaged—not once or twice but *chronically*—in behavior that was equal to, and often far more extreme than, that which led them to exploit the President's sex life as an election issue and make condemnations of his private life their most compulsive pastime.

Former GOP House Speaker and Christian Conservative Newt Gingrich has a long history of adultery in Washington, beginning in the 1970s while he was married to his first wife. As *Salon*'s Stephen Talbot reported in 1998, Gingrich "has admitted sexual indiscretions during his first marriage." As Talbot put it, Gingrich demanded a divorce from his first wife "in her hospital room where she was recovering from uterine cancer surgery," and then,

> Shortly after that infamous encounter, Gingrich refused to pay his alimony and child-support payments. The First Baptist Church in his hometown had to take up a collection to support the family Gingrich had deserted.

Six months after divorcing his first wife, Gingrich married his second, one of several women with whom he had been cheating during his first marriage. And in short order, Gingrich began again searching for and having sex with other women, eventually finding the new woman whom he wanted to be his third wife. In 1999, in the midst of the GOP inquisition into Clinton's sexual improprieties, Gingrich—who was fifty-six years old at the time—was having adulterous sex with his own congressional aide Callista Bisek, who was twenty-four years younger. In 2000, Gingrich dumped his second wife and married the young, pretty Bisek.

Gingrich firmly believes that the law must preserve the sanctity of marriage. As CNN reported in 2007, when Gingrich was considering running for president,

> Former House speaker and potential presidential candidate Newt Gingrich has confessed, telling conservative Christian leader James Dobson that he was cheating on his wife at around the same time the House was impeaching President Bill Clinton over his White House affair with Monica Lewinsky.

In this same hypocritical regard, GOP representative Bob Barr is a virtual clone of Gingrich. Barr was the House manager for Clinton's impeachment and was also lead sponsor of the "Defense of Marriage Act," a law that prohibits the federal government from recognizing same-sex unions. That law has the effect, among other things, of rendering the United States one of the very few countries in the Western world not to grant immigration rights to the same-sex partners of its own citizens, thus forcing gay Americans who have a foreign spouse to make the hideous choice between residing outside of their own country or being separated from the person with whom they want to spend their lives. To justify this law, Barr roared,

> The flames of hedonism, the flames of narcissism, the flames of self-centered morality are licking at the very foundation of our society, the family unit.

This righteous defender of "the family unit" and crusading enemy of hedonism has—like Gingrich and Rudy Giuliani—had three wives. The second wife of the pro-life Barr filed an affidavit during their divorce proceeding attesting that she had had an abortion with his approval, because he believed she had cheated on him. Barr's former wives have twice had to take him to court to complain about his failure to pay child support. And a 1999 article in *American Journalism Review* reported, Barr "invoked a legal privilege during his 1985 divorce proceeding so he could refuse to answer questions on whether he'd cheated on his second wife with the woman who is now his third."

Powerful GOP congressman Dan Burton, a staunch social conservative, supported Clinton's impeachment, used his position as chairman of the Government Reform and Oversight Committee to investigate Clinton's personal life relentlessly, and publicly called the President a "scumbag." Burton was one of the first of the righteous GOP congressmen to insist that Bill Clinton's sex life was a matter of grave public concern, rising on the floor of the House as early as 1995 to compare Clinton to Bob Packwood as he thundered,

> But why, I ask, are we excusing or ignoring similar behavior? **No one, regardless of what party they serve,**

no one, regardless of what branch of government they serve, should be allowed to get away with these alleged sexual improprieties, and yet it is obvious to me . . . that a double standard does exist.

In 1998, Burton learned that *Vanity Fair* was preparing a lengthy article on his sleazy and adulterous behavior. To preempt the article, Burton—according to a 1999 *Salon* article— "startled the country by suddenly admitting that he had fathered a child out of wedlock." While he made payments to the woman who had stayed silent all those years, he never had any involvement in his son's life. In a tone so impersonal that Burton might as well have been talking about a piece of furniture, rather than his own son, he coolly stated during an interview: "The boy and the mother and my wife and my family and I have all reached an agreement about this a long time ago."

During the Clinton impeachment proceedings, Matthew Glavin was the president of the socially conservative Southeastern Legal Foundation, which ultimately led the efforts to have Clinton disbarred. According to *Time* in 2000, Glavin was "charged with public indecency for allegedly fondling himself and an undercover park ranger in May in Georgia's Chattahoochee River National Recreation Area."

When GOP Louisiana congressman (and impeachment supporter) Bob Livingston was named Speaker of the House in 1998 to succeed the adulterous Gingrich, he quickly resigned before being inaugurated when it was revealed that *Hustler* magazine was about to publish documented reports of his own lengthy and numerous adulterous affairs. Livingston was succeeded in Congress by the prostitute patron, adulterer, and staunch social conservative David Vitter.

During the Clinton impeachment, the GOP chairman of the House Judiciary Committee (also a House impeachment manager) was Henry Hyde. This social conservative was exposed by *Salon*'s David Talbot as having engaged in behavior for years that—even for this Values Voters crowd—was quite astonishing:

> Fred Snodgrass, a 76-year-old Florida retiree, says he gets so upset when he watches Rep. Henry Hyde on TV that "I nearly jump out of my chair" . . . "These politicians were going on about how he should have been on the Supreme Court, what a great man he is, how we're lucky to have him in Congress in charge of the impeachment case. And all I can think of is here is this man, this hypocrite who broke up my family."
>
> Snodgrass says Hyde carried on a five-year sexual relationship with his then-wife, Cherie, that shattered his family. Hyde admitted to *Salon* Wednesday that he had been involved with Cherie Snodgrass, and that the relationship ended after Hyde's wife found out about it. At the time of the affair, which lasted from 1965 to 1969, Fred Snodgrass was a furniture salesman in Chicago, and his wife was a beauty stylist. They had three small children, two girls and a boy. Hyde, then 41 years old, was a lawyer and rising star in Republican state politics. In 1966, he was elected for the first time to the Illinois House. Hyde was married and the father of four sons. (His wife, Jeanne Hyde, died of breast cancer in 1992, after a 45-year marriage.)
>
> "Cherie was young and naive at the time," said a Snodgrass family intimate. "She was a glamour queen with three young kids, stuck at home. Then this Prince Charming guy, Hyde, comes along. She was very impressed with him. He was 12 years older, he was a hotshot, he knew everyone downtown. She had nothing, and he comes along, shows her off, she was young and beautiful."

Hyde was forty-one years old at the time, but he dismissed the accusations as mere "youthful indiscretions," and the Family Values congressman vowed,

> The statute of limitations has long since passed on my youthful indiscretions. . . . The only purpose for this being dredged up now is an obvious attempt to intimidate me and it won't work. I intend to fulfill my constitutional duty and deal judiciously with the serious felony allegations presented to Congress in the Starr report.

In the world of GOP hypocrisy, there was no reason at all to allow the House Manager's serial adultery with a married woman and mother of young children to interfere with the important work of impeaching a popular president over the sexual improprieties detailed in the Starr Report.

Louis Beres, the chairman of the Christian Coalition of Oregon during the Clinton impeachment proceedings, was accused by three female family members of molesting them repeatedly during their preteen years. Beres first lied and denied the accusations, only to confess once the police investigation intensified, blaming it—according to police reports obtained by the *Portland Mercury*—on the fact that he was "experiencing a great deal of stress at the time . . . he was millions of dollars in debt and facing bankruptcy." No charges could be filed because the statute of limitations had elapsed.

And on and on and on. The individuals who never tire of making public displays of how concerned they are with our national moral fabric—the crusading right-wing moralists who found Bill Clinton's sex life cause for condemnation—are well aware that their party is filled to the brim with sleazy, corrupt hedonists.

But as long as they help keep the party in power, they are not just tolerated but embraced. That dynamic is a core operating principle of the Bush-led Republican Party, and it is why Newt

Gingrich, Rush Limbaugh, David Vitter, and so many others were able to rise within it despite the fact that their dalliances were an "open secret" in Washington GOP power circles. For our country's Great American Hypocrites, reality is irrelevant. Those who can maintain deceitful appearances are revered.

Paging Republican Scandal

As hypocritical as that wholesome 1990s bunch was, they are no match for the Great American Hypocrites who now dominate the "Values Voters" faction of the Republican Party. The sexual-morality crusaders of today evince such a huge gap between their rhetoric and their actions that the term "hypocrisy" is inadequate to describe them. It is some form of hypocrisy cubed. The same people who endlessly snow the American people into voting for them by exploiting wedge themes of sexual morality and staking claim to sexual normalcy now stand revealed (using their standards) as some of the most sexually depraved people in the country.

In September 2006, GOP House Speaker Denny Hastert was smack in the middle of one of the tawdriest sex scandals in American political history. News had just erupted that a GOP senior congressman and a leader of its anti-online-pornography campaigns, Representative Mark Foley, had for years been engaging in lewd and highly inappropriate behavior with underage congressional pages. Far worse, compelling evidence emerged that the entire top level of the GOP House leadership—including Speaker Hastert—were long aware of these improprieties and did nothing, thus allowing Foley unfettered access to the pages.

As a result, Hastert became the target of intense criticism and was desperately battling to keep his job. In need of absolution and support from a moral authority among his upstanding Republican base, to whom did Hastert turn? A priest or respected reverend? An older, wise political statesman with a reputation for integrity and dignity? No, there was only one person with sufficient credibility among the pious Republican base to give Hastert the blessing he needed: Rush Limbaugh. And so that is where Hastert went hat in hand in order to obtain the Decree That He Had Done Nothing Wrong. In September 2006, Hastert was a guest on Limbaugh's radio show, where the two men agreed that Hastert had done nothing immoral. To show his support, Limbaugh posted a photograph of himself and Hastert on his website.

As much as one tries, it is exceedingly difficult to expunge that photograph of Limbaugh and Hastert from one's mind because, in all its visceral hideousness, it really illustrates the principal reason why the Mark Foley scandal resonated so strongly. *That* is the real face of the ruling Republican Party, and it had been unmasked—violently—by the exposure of the gay underage-page predator Representative Mark Foley and his social conservative allies who long protected and harbored him.

After all, if the phrase "moral degenerate" can be fairly applied to anyone, there are few people who merit it more than Rush Limbaugh. He is the living and breathing embodiment of moral turpitude, with his countless overlapping sexual affairs; his series of shattered, dissolved, childless marriages; his hedonistic and illegal drug abuse; his jaunts—with fistfuls of unprescribed Viagra (but no wife)—to the Dominican Republic. By contrast, Rush Limbaugh makes the serial adulterer and thrice-married John Wayne look like the Paragon of Family Virtue.

Yet Limbaugh is whom Hastert chose as the High Priest of the Values Voters, to whom he made his pilgrimage, and from whom he received his benediction. The difference between Rush Limbaugh and Mark Foley, to the extent there is one, was one of hedonistic tastes, not rectitude. Yet Rush is inarguably the leader of the conservative movement's most righteous wing.

Over the course of the next year, a seemingly endless stream of Mark Foleys emerged from under the rocks of the Values Voters leadership. Larry Craig, longtime conservative Idaho senator and co-chairman of the Mitt Romney presidential campaign, took his 100 percent Christian Coalition voting record with him into a Minneapolis airport men's room searching for anonymous gay sex, and thereafter pled guilty to disorderly conduct charges.

Social conservative senator David Vitter of Louisiana was revealed to be a regular customer of a Washington, D.C., whorehouse, while his wife was at home raising their small children. Indeed, this mid-2007 scandal involving Vitter's appetite for high-priced hookers, followed closely by the Larry Craig bathroom sex-solicitation episode, brought the ugly soul of the GOP's social conservative pretense into full, unadorned view.

The Louisiana senator was one of the chief sponsors of the GOP's 2006 proposed constitutional amendment to protect the sanctity of traditional marriage by banning same-sex marriages. This is what he said during the debate over that amendment: "I don't believe there's any issue that's more important than this one."

To Vitter, there was not a single issue more important than amending the Constitution to ban same-sex marriages. Not a single one. *That* is the most important issue there is in the United States. Whatever one's views are on same-sex marriages and the like, just imagine the internal universe of a person who seriously believes banning them is the Most Important Issue in the United States.

Same-sex marriages are, to Vitter, no different from natural disasters that destroy the lives of thousands of his constituents. As the Human Rights Campaign reported:

> Louisiana Senator David Vitter, speaking at a Lafayette Parish Republican Executive Committee luncheon, referred to hurricanes Katrina and Rita coming through the same areas as a same-sex marriage.
>
> In his statements at the luncheon, Vitter referred to the impact of both hurricanes on the Lafayette area. "Unfortunately, it's the crossroads where Katrina meets Rita,"

said Vitter. "I always knew I was against same-sex unions."

Vitter's moral center is not something he developed only recently. No. It is rock solid, something he "always knew." Once the amendment failed to pass, Vitter solemnly observed:

> Eventually, Congress is going to have to catch up to the wisdom of the American people or the American people will change Congress for the better.

Senator David Vitter, Fighter for the Moral Wisdom of the American People. The Religious Freedom Coalition declared about Vitter in December 2003, when he announced he was running for the Senate:

> A good friend of social conservatives, Republican Congressman David Vitter of Louisiana has announced he will run for the seat being vacated by Senator Breaux. Congressman Vitter is pro-life and a **true social conservative.**

Vitter's desire to use the law to impose his rock-solid traditional morality is not confined to marriage. Proclaimed the Religious Freedom Coalition: In general, Vitter "[was] one of the most conservative Republicans in the House," as he also "loathes gambling and rarely votes against his party or the president." (Vitter's deeply moral opposition to gambling may be as authentic as his commitment to traditional marriage: His anti-gambling crusades were fueled in part by some Jack Abramoff money designed to attack certain gaming interests in order to help Abramoff's other gambling casino clients.)

When Vitter was elected to the Senate, James Dobson's Focus on the Family celebrated his victory in its newsletter to its members, announcing: "David Vitter, the Christian Conservative, became the first Republican to win a Louisiana Senate seat since Reconstruction."

And as with so many of the pious stalwarts of the Republican Party, Vitter injected his personal life into his campaign by parading around as the Wholesome Man of Family Values, a real salt-of-the-earth moralist. One of the most revealing stories ever written about Vitter was a lengthy profile by Mary Jacoby in *Salon* when Vitter's election to the Senate in 2004 appeared certain:

> A family-values far-right conservative named David Vitter appears headed for victory on Tuesday in the U.S. Senate race in Louisiana. . . . He presents himself as a morally righteous, clean-cut family man, and his wife and three young children have become virtual campaign props.

As for Vitter's background, she noted:

> In Congress, Vitter became a reliable vote for the extreme right, earning a 100 percent rating from the American Conservative Union in 2002. He vowed to outlaw abortion in almost all cases, even when pregnancy results from rape or incest; his only exception was to save the life of the mother. And—with an eye on the governor's office—he continued the crusade against gambling that he'd started in 1993 with the ethics complaint against Gov. Edwin Edwards.

But most amazing of all is this charming incident that occurred back in 1999, when Bill Clinton's adultery was on the minds of all righteous Southern Republican Christian Values Voters:

> As Vitter geared up in 2002 to run for governor, his bitter race against Treen came back to haunt him. A Treen

supporter, local Republican Party official Vincent Bruno, blurted out on a radio show that he believed Vitter had once had an extramarital affair.

The *Louisiana Weekly* newspaper followed up. Bruno told the paper that **the young woman had contacted the Treen campaign in 1999 because she was upset that Vitter was portraying himself as a family-values conservative and trotting out his wife and children for campaign photo ops.** Bruno, who declined to comment for this story, and John Treen interviewed the woman, who said she had worked under the name "Leah."

But **after nearly a year of regular paid assignations with Vitter,** the lawmaker asked her to divulge her real name, according to Treen, citing the account he said she gave him. Her name was Wendy Cortez, Treen said. She said Vitter's response was electric. "He said, 'Oh, my God! I can't see you anymore,'" John Treen told me, citing the woman's account to him and noting that Vitter's wife is also named Wendy. And Wendy Vitter does not appear to be the indulgent type.

Asked by an interviewer in 2000 whether she could forgive her husband if she learned he'd had an extramarital affair, as Hillary Clinton and Bob Livingston's wife had done, Wendy Vitter told the *Times-Picayune*: "I'm a lot more like Lorena Bobbitt than Hillary. If he does something like that, I'm walking away with one thing, and it's not alimony, trust me."

Jacoby also noted this in her article:

Vitter, Bruno and others interviewed the alleged prostitute several times in 1999. She also met with a respected local television reporter, Richard Angelico, the *Louisiana*

Weekly said. But Angelico declined to run with the story after she would not agree to go on camera, the paper said. Vitter denied the allegations.

But shortly before the *Louisiana Weekly* was set to publish its story, he dropped out of the governor's race, saying he needed to deal with marital problems. "Our [marriage] counseling sessions have . . . led us to the rather obvious conclusion that it's not time to run for governor," Vitter said at the time.

So, to recap: In Louisiana, Vitter carried on a yearlong affair with a prostitute in 1999. Then he ran for the House as a hardcore social conservative, traipsing around with his wife and kids as props, leading the public crusade in defense of traditional marriage.

Once in Washington, he became a client of Madame Deborah Palfrey's "escort service," even as he announced that amending the Constitution to protect traditional marriage was the most important political priority the country faces. People such as Rush Limbaugh, Fred Thompson, and Newt Gingrich—with their second, third, and fourth wives in tow—supported the same amendment.

Revealingly, while Senate Republicans demanded that Larry Craig resign his Senate seat in the wake of his gay bathroom sex scandal—claiming that their doing so showed their fervent belief in the need for high moral standards for elected officials—they did nothing of the kind with regard to Vitter. Quite the contrary, they vigorously supported Vitter. In the midst of the Craig scandal, as Republicans were demanding Craig's resignation, *Roll Call*'s Emily Heil appeared on MSNBC and reported:

If you look at David Vitter, I couldn't find anyone to talk to me about him in the days after his scandal. No one would talk to me about it—they said this is a private matter, this is a family member. **And when [Vitter] eventually met with Republicans behind closed doors, they gave him a hearty round of applause,** as I was told. I don't think Senator Craig is going to get that kind of reception.

That report was consistent with articles in the immediate aftermath of the Vitter disclosures, such as one from Louisiana's *News Star* titled "GOP Leaders Support Vitter":

Republican leaders generally are circling the wagons around embattled U.S. Sen. David Vitter, Louisiana Republican Party Chairman Roger Villere said Thursday.

"The consensus is they don't want him to resign," Villere said after spending hours in phone consultation with Republicans for the past three days.

What wretched and transparent hypocrisy. If Craig had resigned, his replacement would have been chosen by the Republican governor of Idaho, but Vitter's replacement would be selected by Louisiana's Democratic governor. Moreover, Vitter's adultery was merely of the heterosexual (albeit illegal, prostitute-hiring) variety, whereas Craig attempted to have sex with a man. Hence, Senate Republicans sought to push Craig out while protecting Vitter. One would think we could at least dispense with the fiction that the Moral Values Senate caucus trying to oust Larry Craig was motivated by anything resembling actual principles, in view of the fact that it was simultaneously giving rousing applause to David Vitter.

It goes without saying that no gay candidate would stand a chance of receiving the presidential nomination from the party that stands for traditional marriage. Indeed, the Idaho Family Values Association, in the wake of the Larry Craig scandal, issued a statement calling—explicitly—for the GOP to purge all gay politicians from the party:

The Party, in the wake of the Mark Foley incident in particular, can no longer straddle the fence on the issue of homosexual behavior. Even setting Senator Craig's situation aside, **the Party should regard participation in the self-destructive homosexual lifestyle as incompatible with public service on behalf of the GOP.**

But they would never call for excluding political figures who dumped their wives and are on their second or third marriages—actions at least as deviant from principles of traditional marriage as anything Senator Craig did—because so many of their pious supporters engage in the same behavior, as Idaho's traditionally high divorce rates demonstrate. Indeed, statistics compiled by the Nationwide Center for Health Statistics have long placed Idaho in the top 10 of the highest divorce rates nationwide—along with such gay-marriage-banning states as Tennessee, Arkansas, Alabama, Kentucky, and Wyoming. These righteous crusaders for "moral principles" apply their dictates only when there is political gain to be had, and routinely overlook, suspend, and violate these "principles" to ensure that their leaders and followers are never limited in their own behavior.

Beyond this, a virtual army of prominent GOP Values Voters leaders—who parade around as Paragons of Traditional Marriage Virtue and who unceasingly attempt to pass or enforce laws to coerce moral behavior and punish those who deviate—were exposed as wallowing in the sleazy mire of Foley, Craig, and Vitter. *In just a one-year period beginning in November 2006,* the nation was subjected to these GOP moral leaders:

- Social conservative televangelist Ted Haggard (bought crystal methamphetamine from the male prostitutes he hired for sex)

- GOP Washington State representative Richard Curtis (was involved in a payment dispute with a male prostitute he met in a gay bookstore while wearing women's undergarments)
- Giuliani campaign co-chair for South Carolina and state treasurer Thomas Ravenel (arrested for cocaine trafficking)
- McCain campaign co-chair for Florida, GOP state representative Bob Allen (arrested for paying $20 to a male undercover officer for oral sex in a Titusville city park)
- Pro-war and anti-gay-rights pundit Matt Sanchez (exposed as a former gay prostitute and porn star)
- Right-wing Denver talk-radio host Scott Eller Cortelyou (arrested on suspicion of using the Internet to lure a child into a sexual relationship)
- Former GOP South Dakota representative Ted A. Klaudt (arrested on charges of rape and other offenses against two girls who were his foster children)
- Michael Flory, head of the Michigan Federation of Young Republicans and speaker at the 1992 Republican National Convention (pleaded guilty to sexual battery for abusing a twenty-two-year-old fellow member during a Federation of Young Republicans national convention; when he was falsely denying the accusations, Flory—according to the prosecutor—had "been running around telling everybody what a piece of trash [the victim] is")
- Glenn Murphy, chairman of Indiana's Clark County Republican Party and the Young Republican National Federation (resigned in the wake of a criminal investigation alleging that the thirty-three-year-old social conservative performed unwanted oral sex on a sleeping twenty-two-year-old male relative)
- Defense contractor Brent Wilkes (convicted of bribing the married, GOP Family Values congressman Randy "Duke" Cunningham, now a convicted felon himself, with cash and prostitutes)

Beyond this impressive pile of recent GOP social conservative sex scandals was one of the most revealing: the Mark Foley scandal of 2006. When that story broke, it had been mentioned that Foley was involved in enacting some of the recent Republican-sponsored laws aimed at pornography and the Internet. But it really went far beyond that.

As he spent his spare time sending overtly sexual IM messages and e-mails to underage male pages, Representative Foley was at the center of promoting virtually every law and program of the last ten years ostensibly designed to battle the evils of Internet sex and minors. It is not an exaggeration to say that Foley devoted his whole congressional career to adding decades of imprisonment to the mandatory punishments for those who use the Internet to talk about sex with minors. He did not merely condemn that which he was doing—he made the crusade against it his life's work. That's why, all over the Internet, one finds things such as this:

STATEMENT OF ATTORNEY GENERAL JOHN ASHCROFT ON THE PASSAGE OF THE SMITH-POMEROY-FOLEY CHILD OBSCENITY AND PORNOGRAPHY PREVENTION ACT

I am pleased that the House of Representatives passed the Child Obscenity and Pornography Prevention Act, a bill that will strengthen the ability of law enforcement to protect children from abuse and exploitation. I urge the Senate to bring this important legislation to the floor as soon as possible.

I want to thank Chairman Sensenbrenner for guiding this important legislation through the Judiciary Commitee [sic], **and Congressmen Lamar Smith, Mark Foley, and Earl Pomeroy for their leadership on this bill.** They have worked tirelessly to protect the health and safety of children.

The Department of Justice remains solid in its commitment to identify, investigate, and prosecute those who sexually exploit children. I look forward to working with Congress to see to it that this legislation becomes law, so that we may continue in our efforts to eliminate child pornography and prosecute offenders.

And Foley is not an isolated case of shocking hypocrisy. The hordes of those—the David Vitters and Rush Limbaughs and Newt Gingrichs and Jim Bakkers and Mark Foleys of the world—who have publicly crusaded against other people's moral behavior, and who seek to use the power of the government to enforce their obsessions, are in many cases fighting their own demons. They have no other way to cleanse themselves.

We have been barraged with laws, programs, and sermons from a political movement whose most powerful pundit is a multiple-times-divorced drug addict who flamboyantly cavorts around with a new girlfriend every few months in between Viagra-fueled jaunts to the Dominican Republic. It is a political movement whose legacy will be torture, waterboarding, and naked, sadomasochistic games in Iraqi dungeons (or, to Limbaugh, "blowing off steam"), propped up by a facade of moralism and dependent on the support of those who have been propagandized into believing that they are voting for the Party of Values and Morals.

Cheap Lip Service

Even in the face of this unrelenting record of rank hypocrisy, chronic adultery, and sexual sleaze, the GOP continues to deceive Americans into believing that it is the party of Sexual Virtue and Traditional Marriage, and that its leaders are the wholesome Family Men that America urgently requires to reset its moral compass. And our establishment media continues to ingest and disseminate these ludicrous themes.

As recently as October 2006, right before the midterm elections, the thrice-married serial adulterer Newt Gingrich insisted that the GOP's political salvation rests on its continuing exploitation of these sexual and cultural themes. Writing in *Human Events,* Gingrich contended that Republicans should remind the electorate that "Republicans are right to favor traditional American conservative social values, and the left is completely wrong to put San Francisco left-wing values third in line to be President by electing Nancy Pelosi (Calif.) to speaker of the House."

Indeed. Compare the dirty San Francisco values of Pelosi (from her official biography) to the Christian Traditional Marriage Values embraced by Gingrich:

Nancy Pelosi's "San Francisco left-wing values"

Upon graduation in 1962, she married Georgetown University graduate Paul Pelosi. Pelosi and her husband, Paul Pelosi, a native of San Francisco, have five children: Nancy Corinne, Christine, Jacqueline, Paul and Alexandra, and five grandchildren.

Newt Gingrich's
"traditional American conservative social values"

In 1981, Newt dumped his first wife, Jackie Battley, for Marianne, wife number 2, while Jackie was in the hospital undergoing cancer treatment. He famously visited Jackie in the hospital where she was recovering from surgery for uterine cancer to discuss details of the divorce. He later resisted paying alimony and child support for his two daughters, causing a church to take up a collection. For all of his talk of religious faith and the importance of God, Gingrich left his congregation over the pastor's criticism of his divorce.

Marianne and Newt divorced in December 1999 after

Marianne found out about Newt's long-running affair with Callista Bisek, his one-time congressional aide. According to *The New York Post,* Gingrich asked Marianne for the divorce by phoning her on Mother's Day 1999. Newt (57) and Callista (34) were married in a private ceremony in a hotel courtyard in Alexandria, Va., in August 2000. . . .

So those who repeatedly dump their wives for new and better versions are stalwart defenders of traditional American and Christian values. Those who stay married to their original spouse for their entire lives and raise a family together are godless, radical heathens who seek to undermine the country's moral fiber and Christian traditions.

The extreme contrast between GOP "values" rhetoric and reality goes far beyond Pelosi and Gingrich. The leading contenders for the Democratic presidential nomination throughout 2007—Hillary Clinton, Barack Obama, John Edwards—remain married to their first spouses, thereby shielding their children from the trauma of divorce and remarriage. But with the exception of Mitt Romney, the leading GOP contenders—Rudy Giuliani, John McCain, and Fred Thompson—behaved like Gingrich, dumping their spouses and bringing new women, step-mothers, into the lives of their children.

One of the very few GOP social conservatives to speak honestly about the transparent deceit characterizing the Republicans' exploitation of Values Voters issues is Governor Mike Huckabee. As he put it in 2007, in warning against the unbridled hatred directed by many Republicans at the Clintons:

The second thing, and this'll really wrangle, again, some of my Republican colleagues. Bill Clinton and Hillary went through some horrible experiences in their marriage, because of some of the reckless behavior that he has admitted he had. I'm not defending him on that—it's indefensible. But they kept their marriage together. **And a lot of the Republicans who have condemned them, and who talk about their platform of family values, interestingly didn't keep their own families together.**

It was the Values Voters of the morally upstanding Republican Party that gave America its first divorced president, as Ronald Reagan moved into the White House with his second wife, Nancy. Reagan's highly dysfunctional and quite untraditional family was composed of children with different mothers who were often not even on speaking terms with their Moral Majority dad.

During the MSNBC discussion about Fred Thompson between Chris Matthews and *Newsweek*'s Howard Fineman, detailed in the prior chapter, they classified Thompson not merely as an exemplar of masculine virtues but also as a true "cultural conservative." Fineman assured the audience that Thompson has "a strong record on cultural issues **as a cultural conservative from the South.**" But in what conceivable way could Thompson be said to be a "cultural conservative"?

Unlike the leading Democratic contenders of 2007—all of whom are still married to their first spouse—Thompson divorced his wife (and the mother of his two children) after twenty-five years of marriage and proceeded, at the age of fifty-nine, to marry a woman twenty-five years younger than he. In 2002, the *Washington Post*'s Lloyd Grove wrote:

> Fred Thompson and Jeri Kehn met six years ago on the Fourth of July in Nashville. . . .
>
> "Hollywood Fred"—as the divorced Thompson was nicknamed because of his successful movie career—has been linked to a variety of women, including country singer Lorrie Morgan, pundit-pollster Kellyanne Fitzpatrick, *Time* magazine writer Margaret Carlson, Nathans

restaurant owner Carol Joynt and Washington PR executive Sydney Ferguson.

Revealingly, in the very same show where Thompson was
hailed as a "cultural conservative," Chris Matthews again held
forth obsessively on the Clintons' marriage, and one of his guests
referred to "the incredible fascination that the American public
has . . . on the private lives of the Clintons." Matthews dredged it
all up again: Gennifer Flowers; Kathleen Willey; the *Weekly Standard* cover story from that week that "calls the Clintons 'a rivet-
ing saga of lust and ambition'"; "the women who want us to
know about the relationships with Bill"; and—as Matthews put
it—the "pair of new books [that] exquisitely expose Bill and
Hillary Clinton as a couple of soap opera characters."

But Fred Thompson? Fineman: "He's got a strong record on
cultural issues as a cultural conservative from the South."
Matthews: "He fits the need for a Bible Belt candidate." And the
week before, Matthews provoked this exchange with social conservative leader Ken Blackwell, the failed GOP gubernatorial
candidate from Ohio:

> **MATTHEWS:** Let me ask you about your party and the cul-
> tural right. I noticed that there is no cultural conservative
> southern Baptist type running this time. The President isn't
> quite in that category, but people are very comfortable with
> this president, in terms of his beliefs, his Christian beliefs, his
> cultural values. Is there a candidate out there now **that
> shares the President's cultural values?**
> **KEN BLACKWELL, FORMER OHIO SECRETARY OF
> STATE:** It seems as if Fred Thompson, who has yet to de-
> clare, is starting to build a momentum among social conser-
> vatives. But I will tell you—
> **MATTHEWS:** Well, he's from Tennessee. He's from the
> buckle of the Bible Belt. I believe he is Baptist. He fits. He is

pro-life. He has been for many years. He fits all of the categories. There's nobody else like him.

Social-Christian conservative Fred Thompson, who proclaims to be "pro–traditional marriage," has a current wife (his second) who is not only twenty-five years younger than he, but, as mentioned earlier, is *four years younger than his own daughter* (from his first marriage).

When explaining his profound and solemn opposition to same-sex marriages (Thompson voted for laws prohibiting same-sex marriages and against laws banning discrimination against gays), he said: "Marriage is between a man and a woman, and judges shouldn't be allowed to change that." But according to *The Politico*'s Mike Allen, this is how Thompson jocularly describes his own romantic life:

> During a question-and-answer session with House members on April 18, Thompson was asked about his colorful dating history from 1985 to 2002, while he was divorced.
>
> "I was single for a long time, and, yep, I chased a lot of women," Thompson replied, chuckling, according to an attendee who took notes. "And a lot of women chased me. And those that chased me tended to catch me."
>
> The remark drew laughter from men and grins from women, according to witnesses.

Mystifying indeed, is that people who are on their second or third marriages, with children from each union, can with a straight face proclaim themselves believers in traditional marriage. And—more curiously still—insist that the laws be structured so as to recognize their own highly untraditional and un-Christian sexual exploits and serial marriages, while so avidly concerning themselves with prohibiting or denouncing the sexual behaviors and unions of certain other citizens. And it's even more of a mystery that such hypocritical moralizers are taken seriously.

But Beltway pundits are eager to be so easily fooled. Their thought processes and emotional reactions are dominated by these shallow and inauthentic symbols of masculinity and piety, notwithstanding the wholesale departure from reality by the GOP leaders who purvey these illusions. The pundits find two-dimensional, cartoon images that are just clichéd archetypes—really, caricatures—deeply satisfying.

The issue is not that these Traditional Marriage proponents sometimes stray from their own standards. People are imperfect. Many people will inevitably falter. The point is that they apply these supposed principles because it is expedient to do so, in ways that are politically comfortable, thus revealing the complete inauthenticity of their alleged convictions. And nothing illustrates this inauthenticity more starkly than the GOP's endless though patently insincere exploitation of the so-called sanctity of marriage and anti-gay laws for their own political gain.

Cost-Free Moralizing Only

It would be one thing if Republicans were consistent and honest in how they preach of the need for government and law to enforce moral standards and defend "traditional marriage." That would still be an abuse of the proper role of law, but at least one could say that they were expressing their views honestly. But that is the opposite of what they do. There is nothing at all consistent about the moral positions they espouse. Quite the contrary, they espouse only those moral positions that are politically beneficial to them, that demand moral concessions from small minorities while overlooking and even endorsing the moral deviations of the majority of voters at whom their manipulative claims are aimed.

In November 2005, Texas became the latest state to approve a referendum to incorporate into its state constitution a ban on same-sex marriages. When Texas's GOP governor, Rick Perry, signed the bill to hold the referendum, he did so at a Christian evangelical school alongside what he called his pro-family "Christian friends." When asked why he supported the ban, he replied, simply enough: "I am a Christian and this is about values."

But if Christian values, along with a desire to promote a pro-family agenda, were really the motivations behind the gay-marriage ban, one would expect that these same advocates would be working unceasingly for a ban on divorce and remarriage as well, institutions at least as un-Christian as same-sex marriages. And yet, while more than twenty states have now approved referendums enacting gay-marriage bans into their state constitutions, none of them has voted to prohibit divorce and remarriage, or even to make divorce laws more restrictive.

Quite the contrary, Texas has one of the most permissive divorce laws in the nation. No-fault divorces and second and third marriages—concepts as foreign to Christianity as are same-sex marriages—are not just common but accepted, both socially and under the law. How can Christians possibly allow, and enthusiastically take advantage of, the continuation of permissive divorce laws that plainly violate Christian beliefs?

After all, there is little doubt that Christianity prohibits most divorces every bit as much as it does same-sex marriages. As Dr. Kah-Jin Jeffrey Kuan, a Methodist minister and associate professor of theology, put it during a 2004 speech on divorce:

> Jesus himself explicitly prohibits divorce and remarriage in the New Testament (in Matthew 5:31–32, 19:3–9; Mark 10:11–12; Luke 16:18). For Jesus, remarrying a divorced person constitutes adultery, a serious sin which the entire Bible has much to say about.

Samuele Bacchiocchi, Ph.D., of Andrews University, has written that while some liberal Christians claim there is a narrow exception in the Gospels allowing divorce on the grounds of adultery, there is no question that

> The teaching of Jesus is fundamental to the study of the Biblical view of divorce and remarriage because Jesus clarifies the reason for the Old Testament concession (Deut. 24:1) and reaffirms **God's creational design for marriage to be a permanent, indissoluble covenant. . . .**
>
> God's original plan consists of a man and a woman being united in a marriage bond so strong that the two actually become one flesh (Gen. 2:26; Matt 19:6; Mark 10:8). The "one flesh" unity of the couple is reflected especially in their offspring who partake of the genetic characteristics of father and mother, and the two are absolutely inseparable. Jesus affirms that it is God Himself who actually joins together a couple in marriage and **what God has joined together no human being has the right to separate.**

The permanence of the marital union is every bit as fundamental to the Christian concept of traditional marriage as is the requirement of the spouses being of opposite gender. Christians are required, of course, to vow to God to remain with their spouse "till death do us part" and "for as long as we both shall live." Christian ministers routinely proclaim: "That which God has brought together, let no one put asunder."

And yet the divorce laws of Texas could not deviate more dramatically from this Christian teaching on marriage. Obtaining a divorce in Rick Perry's Texas is shockingly easy. Texas law allows no-fault divorce. Under that law, to obtain a divorce, one need merely be able to demonstrate one of two very permissive grounds:

(1) the marriage has become insupportable because of discord or conflict of personalities that has destroyed the legitimate ends of the marriage relationship and prevents any reasonable expectation of reconciliation; or this no-fault ground (2) living separate and apart without cohabitation for 3 years.

That's all there is to it. If you are a Texas citizen who wants to violate the marital vows you made before God by tearing apart your marital union—a union that, according to Christian doctrine, God has mandated be permanent and indissoluble—all you have to do is claim that you have irreconcilable differences with your spouse, or live apart for three years, and the divorce is yours.

And Texans, like citizens in every state that has banned gay marriages, are taking advantage of these anti-Christian divorce laws with great gusto. While the lowest divorce rate in the country belongs to the first state to legalize gay marriages (Massachusetts, at 2.4 per 1,000 population), Texas is in the top half of states in this respect, with a divorce rate of 4.1. The highest divorce rates, almost uniformly, are in the Bible Belt. Those states that make a flamboyant show of banning gay marriages continue to allow themselves the luxury of divorcing whenever the mood strikes.

Worse, permissive divorce is not only undeniably anti-Christian but, as numerous studies have demonstrated, it is a phenomenon that can shatter the lives of our nation's children. And yet not only do most pro-family activists focus on gay marriages to the almost complete exclusion of talking about the epidemic of divorce, many of them are themselves divorced and remarried.

It is not difficult to understand what accounts for this transparent gap in consistency when it comes to applying so-called traditional marriage values. The congregations frequented by the likes of Governor Perry are filled with divorced and remarried churchgoers, as are the voting blocs he and the Republican Party need to win elections, as are the mailing lists of the pro-family groups that are most vocal in their opposition to same-sex marriage. When Governor Perry condemns same-sex marriage on the grounds that it violates Christianity, he is condemning very few of his constituents and political allies, since, presumably, very few of them want to enter such a marriage.

Hence we have scads of people sitting around opposing same-sex marriage on the basis of Christianity while their third husbands and multiple stepchildren and live-in girlfriends sit next to them on the couch. And that includes, most prominently, the leadership of the GOP's Values Voters movement.

Social conservative Ross Douthat of *The Atlantic Monthly* is, like Mike Huckabee, one of the very few voices in that movement to address this hypocrisy and manipulation honestly. In a session he recorded in mid-2007 for BloggingheadsTV, he perfectly explained this important (though almost always overlooked) dynamic in the context of discussing the disparity in the GOP's treatment of the disgraced gay adulterer Larry Craig (demanding his resignation) and its treatment of the disgraced straight adulterer and prostitute-patronizer David Vitter (supporting him):

> The reason that gay rights became a political issue in a way that various other frankly **more important issues having to do with marriage and family life did not—particularly issues about divorce and heterosexual divorce rates** and single parenthood—is that, clearly, it is easier to demonize gay people. And it is much more of an electoral winner.
>
> Obviously, I think the broader conservative concern about family values in American life is correct. I think the way it has manifested itself in our political life is that **nobody wants to be the guy out there telling people—**

hey, you know, your heterosexual marriage or your out-of-wedlock children are the problem. It's much easier to say—here is this particular manifestation that you can easily set aside and say I'm not gay.

The blatantly self-interested, manipulative use of moral issues is rampant in GOP politics, and virtually every national Republican candidate shamelessly milks it for political gain. In late August 2007, a low-level Iowa state court declared unconstitutional that state's recognition of only opposite-sex marriages. Quite predictably, the GOP presidential candidates fell all over themselves to denounce the decision in the name of traditional marriage.

Here was John McCain the day following the decision:

> Today was **a loss for the traditional family,** and I am disappointed that a judge would thwart the will of the people. I have always supported **the traditional definition of marriage** as between one man and one woman.

By contrast, this is John McCain's real-life defense of marriage, from *Washington Monthly*'s Steve Benen:

> McCain was still married and living with his wife in 1979 while, according to *The New York Times'* Nicholas Kristof, "aggressively courting a 25-year-old woman who was as beautiful as she was rich." McCain divorced his wife, who had raised their three children while he was imprisoned in Vietnam, then launched his political career with his new wife's family money.

And as detailed in *Biography:*

> McCain married Carol Shepp, his first wife, in 1965. He adopted her two children from a previous marriage, and

they have a daughter, born in 1966. The couple divorced in 1980. He and his second wife, Cindy, have four children.

How can John McCain claim to believe that the law should recognize only "traditional marriages" while simultaneously demanding that the law recognize his own second marriage—also known as an adulterous relationship under the precepts of Christianity (Mark 10:11—"And he said to them, 'Whoever divorces his wife and marries another, commits adultery against her' ")? Whatever else McCain's own family is, "traditional" it is not.

And perhaps most ludicrous of all was the spectacle of Rudy Giuliani keeping a straight face as he spent 2007 touting the sanctity of marriage. In September, he made a pilgrimage to the so-called Values Voters Summit in Washington, D.C., where he spoke privately to social conservative leaders and solemnly pontificated on the importance of marriage and the vital social role it plays. Giuliani's campaign website explained that he emphatically opposed same-sex marriage because—and this is really what he said—he believes in "preserving the *sanctity of marriage* between a man and a woman."

Rudy Giuliani—the front-runner throughout 2007 for the Party of Traditional Marriage—is a testament to how pervasively moral issues are so sleazily abused by the Republican Party. Giuliani began his long, winding, varied life of Traditional Marriage by doing something that is illegal in many states: He married his own second cousin, Regina Peruggi. After fourteen years of marriage—the last several years of which they lived apart—Giuliani divorced her and obtained an annulment from the Catholic Church on the ground that he had not received the dispensation required from the Church when its members wish to marry their own cousins.

Next up in the Giuliani sanctity-of-marriage carousel was television news anchor Donna Hanover, whom Giuliani met, began dating, and then moved in with while he was still married to his first wife. Hanover herself had been married and divorced by the time she met Giuliani. Although they had two children together, news reports began surfacing in New York during Giuliani's tenure as mayor that he was carrying on an adulterous affair with one of his aides, Cristyne Lategano, who is twenty-one years his junior.

As CBS News reported in 2000, in an article titled "The Women in Giuliani's Life: Donna . . . Judith . . . Cristyne . . ."

> The woman Hanover blames for seriously damaging her 16-year marriage to the mayor is former City Hall communications director Cristyne Lategano.
>
> At her news conference, Hanover didn't mention Lategano by name, but said, "For several years, it was difficult to participate in Rudy's public life because of his relationship with one staff member."
>
> Hanover's spokeswoman, Joannie Danielides, later said her boss was referring to Lategano.
>
> In 1997, *Vanity Fair* magazine reported there was a romantic link between Lategano and Giuliani.

Giuliani had long denied the reports of his adulterous affair with his young aide. But in response to Hanover's statement blaming Lategano and her lengthy affair with the mayor for the breakup of Hanover's marriage, Lategano did not bother to deny the accusations, instead simply saying: "I have no desire to speculate why Donna Hanover decided to issue the statement that she did. Understandably, this is a difficult time. I wish both the mayor and Donna Hanover a successful resolution."

But the most proximate cause of the breakup of Giuliani's second marriage—the one to the mother of his children—was his adulterous affair with an altogether different mistress, latest wife Judith Nathan Giuliani, who herself was also previously married to another man (with whom she has a child). And the method Giuliani chose for leaving his second wife makes Newt Gingrich's cancer-bedside-divorce-negotiations look almost humane by comparison. As Steve Benen reported in *Washington Monthly*:

> Giuliani informed his second wife, Donna Hanover, of his intention to seek a separation in a 2000 press conference. The announcement was precipitated by a tabloid frenzy after Giuliani marched with his then-mistress, Judith Nathan, in New York's St. Patrick's Day parade, an acknowledgement of infidelity so audacious that *Daily News* columnist Jim Dwyer compared it with "groping in the window at Macy's." In the acrid divorce proceedings that followed, Hanover accused Giuliani of serial adultery, alleging that Nathan was just the latest in a string of mistresses, following an affair the mayor had had with his former communications director.

It bears repeating that Giuliani believes the law should continue to bar gay people from marrying because of what he calls "the sanctity of marriage." And the thrice-married individual—like Gingrich and Limbaugh—was perfectly acceptable to huge swaths of Republican voters who have adopted so-called traditional morality as a governing political view.

Although one wouldn't know it from listening to pro-family groups and Republican politicians, there are actually other mandates of Christianity beyond prohibitions on homosexuality. Most of the divorces they are getting and the multiple "remarriages" they are enjoying are as sinful under Christianity as same-sex marriages are.

Moralizing is easy—and worthless—when the moralizer does not have to sacrifice anything or restrain himself. Thus, the Republican faithful and their media enablers approve of bans on same-sex marriage. It does not cost them anything. But they do want to divorce and find new spouses, often more than once.

Consistent application of their claimed belief in traditional marriage would entail that our secular marriage laws must comport to Christian doctrine by excluding any marriages that are not biblical. Once they are married, they have to stay married, or at least are certainly barred from remarrying.

But the GOP will not be mounting a campaign for our marriage laws to reflect Christian norms regarding divorce and remarriage, because there is no sincerity to their moralistic movement. When it comes time to win elections, the Republican Party holds itself out as the vanguard of traditional morality, even as many of its leaders, as a matter of enduring lifestyle, engage in the sleaziest and most untraditional sexual and moral behavior. They advocate politically popular moralistic laws that restrain small minorities, while ensuring their own freedom to indulge a pathology of sexual excesses and marital infidelity that would make John Wayne proud, if not envious.

CHAPTER FIVE

Small-Government Tyrants

Ever since Ronald Reagan famously declared in his 1980 inaugural address that "government is not the solution to our problems; government is the problem," Republicans have masqueraded as the party of limited government. Its leaders reflexively pledge to keep government off the backs of regular, hardworking Americans. Homage is paid to the wisdom and insight of the American people, which, Republicans endlessly insist, is far superior to the judgment of government officials. As Reagan proclaimed after delivering his famous line,

> From time to time we've been tempted to believe that society has become too complex to be managed by self-rule, that government by an elite group is superior to government for, by, and of the people. Well, if no one among us is capable of governing himself, then who among us has the capacity to govern someone else?

This political battle cry is, in reality, grounded in a populist cultural argument—namely, that the Republican Party takes the side of ordinary Americans against the faceless, power-hungry, freedom-abridging Washington bureaucrat. In this rendition of America's culture war, which pits normal folks against D.C. politicians, right-wing leaders are on our side, doing everything in their power to keep government out of our lives.

Throughout the 1990s, large swaths of the right-wing movement were motivated by extreme versions of this anti-government mythology. Right-wing leaders endlessly peddled the narrative that Bill Clinton and the rest of the Washington liberal establishment had targeted the core freedoms of the heartland. Clinton's attorney general, Janet Reno, was one face of this federal tyranny, as she sent what they called "jackbooted thugs" into David Koresh's Branch Davidian compound and Elian Gonzales's bedroom. Hillary Clinton was coming to take over health care. The Clintons wanted to control the lives of ordinary Americans, everything from our churches to our businesses to our schools. Liberty-defending weekend militias were the new symbols of the stalwart right-wing defense against invasive federal government power.

With Clinton gone from the political scene, the Bush administration ushered in truly unprecedented expansions of federal power—including virtually unlimited detention and surveillance powers aimed at American citizens even on U.S. soil. Yet all but a handful of right-wing Republican ideologues immediately shed their small-government pretenses as they cheered on almost every one of these power grabs, transforming themselves almost overnight from liberty-defending warriors to loyal authoritarian followers.

In light of this transformation, it is easy to forget how central were these small-government themes for decades in the right-wing movement, and how central they are certain to be once again in the 2008 election. Election time is when the right-wing movement dusts off its manipulative, plainly insincere ideals, and no ideal is more insincere than its alleged belief in individual liberty secured by limited federal power. Ever since the successful campaign of Ronald Reagan in 1980, the Republicans have claimed that their leaders would courageously protect regular Americans from the big, bad government in Washington.

Throughout the 1990s, conservatism was defined by its fear of expansive powers seized by the federal government—particularly domestic law-enforcement and surveillance powers. Conservatives vigorously opposed every proposal to expand the government's investigative and surveillance authority on the grounds that such powers posed intolerable threats to our liberties. More than specific policies, the right-wing ideology was grounded in warnings against the dangers of unchecked government power. Illustrating this ideology was the speech delivered by Ronald Reagan in accepting his party's nomination at the 1980 GOP Convention:

> "Trust me" government asks that we concentrate our hopes and dreams on one man; that we trust him to do what's best for us. My view of government places trust not in one person or one party, but in those values that transcend persons and parties. The trust is where it belongs—in the people.

Following this path, conservatives have endlessly claimed that they stand for limitations on government intrusion into the lives of Americans. One article in 2000 on the right-wing website Free Republic actually decried the dangerous loss of liberty and privacy as a result of what it alarmingly described as the Clinton administration's use of a "secret court" (something called the "FISA court") that actually enables the federal government to *eavesdrop on American citizens!* Worse, warned the article, the judicial approval that the government obtains for this eavesdropping is in secret, so we don't even know who is being eavesdropped on! As Philip Colangelo insisted when

Clinton was President in an article prominently posted on Free Republic,

The Secret FISA Court: Rubber Stamping Our Rights

Seven judges on a secret court have authorized all but one of over 7,500 requests to spy in the name of National Security. They meet in secret, with no published orders, opinions, or public record. Those spied on may never know of the intrusion. Now, Clinton has expanded the powers to include not only electronic, but physical searches.

The aftershock of the Oklahoma City bombing sent Congress scurrying to trade off civil liberties for an illusion of public safety. A good ten weeks before that terrible attack, however with a barely noticed pen stroke President Bill Clinton virtually killed off the Fourth Amendment when he approved a law to expand the already extraordinary powers of the strangest creation in the history of the federal judiciary. . . .

With the FISA court now able to authorize physical searches as well as electronic surveillance simply by citing national security concerns the elite legal circle is nearly complete. The act is a triumph for our constitutional system of checks and balances, former Indiana Sen. Birch Bayh explained in the twilight of the Cold War. It establishes that the authority to conduct foreign intelligence surveillance in this country will be shared by all three branches of government.

In the aftermath of the Oklahoma City bombing, Democrats and Republicans are competing to come up with more ingenious ways to erode civil liberties. . . . Given the current political atmosphere, the Clinton administration's past support for expanding the FISA court's authority, as well as a long, sorry history of abuse, the

elite legal posse will no longer need to strain very hard
to pull the noose right around the Bill of Rights.

The conservative commenters at Free Republic—having
been fed a steady diet of anti-government rhetoric for decades—
predictably reacted to news of expanded eavesdropping powers
under FISA with such liberty-minded sentiments as "This is
beyond frightening"; "This does not bode well for continued
freedom"; "Franz Kafka would have judged this too wild to fic-
tionalize. But for us—it's real." One worried right-wing com-
mentator wondered: "Any chance of Bush rolling some of this
back? It sounds amazing on its face." Another pointed out—
quite rationally—the severe dangers of allowing the government
to exercise power in secret and with little oversight:

> This is one of those ideas that has a valid purpose be-
> hind it, but is wide open to terrible abuse. And there's no
> way to check to see if it is abused.
>
> Like all things that don't have the light of day shining
> on them, you can be sure that it is being twisted to suit
> the purposes of those who hold the power.

Conservatives thus used to claim that they considered things
such as unchecked surveillance powers to be quite disturbing
and bad—and the secret eavesdropping about which they were
complaining back then was at least conducted with judicial
oversight. But with a Republican president in office, all of the
distrust conservatives claimed to have of the federal government
evaporated. Because they trust in George W. Bush and he
knows what's best for us, he should have not just those powers
but many more, and he should exercise all of them in secret,
too, with no interference from the courts or Congress.

Few things are more striking than the gap between the actual power-expanding behavior of Republicans when in office
and the manipulative limited-government rhetoric they spew

when they want to win elections or attack Democrats. What Republicans claim to despise when they are out of power is exactly what they do when they are in power.

Indeed, if one goes back and actually reads the statements made by GOP leaders throughout the 1990s, the complete and total reversal of all their views upon taking over the government in 2001 is truly mind-boggling. Such a trip down memory lane shows how boisterously conservatives used to pretend that they believed in principles of limited government powers, the need for investigations into lawbreaking accusations, and the preference for individual liberty over increased security.

Let us begin with then-senator John Ashcroft, one of the architects of the wild expansions of secret federal surveillance powers in the early years of the Bush administration. Back in July 1997, Ashcroft was warning of the profound dangers posed by far less invasive government powers than the ones he would go on to implement.

Specifically, Ashcroft was sounding the alarm bells over the Clinton administration's proposals for the federal government to overcome encryption technology in order to enable the government to monitor international computer communications—powers that were justified by the Clinton administration on the ground that terrorists use such communications. Ashcroft—who as Bush's attorney general would go on to approve wholly unprecedented *warrantless* spying on Americans' telephone calls and e-mails—wrote, in an article titled "Keep Feds' Nose Out of the Net":

> J. Edgar Hoover would have loved this. The Clinton administration wants government to be able to read international computer communications—financial transactions, personal e-mail and proprietary information sent abroad—**all in the name of national security.**
>
> In a proposal that raises obvious concerns about Americans' privacy, President Clinton wants to give

agencies the keys for decoding all exported U.S. software and Internet communications. . . .

Not only would Big Brother be looming over the shoulders of international cybersurfers, he also threatens to render our state-of-the-art computer software engineers obsolete and unemployed.

Granted, the Internet could be used to commit crimes, and advanced encryption could disguise such activity. However, we do not provide the government with phone jacks outside our homes for unlimited wiretaps. Why, then, should we grant government the Orwellian capability to listen at will and in real time to our communications across the Web?

The protections of the Fourth Amendment are clear. The right to protection from unlawful searches is an indivisible American value. . . .

Every medium by which people communicate can be exploited by those with illegal or immoral intentions. Nevertheless, **this is no reason to hand Big Brother the keys to unlock our e-mail diaries, open our ATM records or translate our international communications.**

Those who made such arguments in 1997 when Democrats were in power were deemed by the right wing to be great patriots defending core American liberties. But once Bush was ensconced in the White House, anyone who urged limits on government power was an ally of the Terrorists working subversively to destroy America. In fact, in 2002, then–Attorney General John Ashcroft went before the Senate and told them that anyone who expressed concerns about the unchecked, vast surveillance powers bestowed by the Patriot Act was aiding the Terrorists:

We need honest, reasoned debate, and not fearmongering. To those who pit Americans against immigrants and citizens against non-citizens, to those who scare peace-loving people with phantoms of lost liberty, my message is this: Your tactics only aid terrorists, for they erode our national unity and diminish our resolve. They give ammunition to America's enemies, and pause to America's friends. They encourage people of goodwill to remain silent in the face of evil.

Thus, the very same "small-government" right-wing leader who warned that Clinton was becoming "Big Brother," compared him to J. Edgar Hoover, and accused him of eviscerating the Fourth Amendment transformed almost overnight into a Great American Hypocrite. With John Ashcroft and his fellow conservatives in charge of the federal government, it actually became a patriotic duty not to question their power or to oppose their domestic spying efforts, as such questioning was "fearmongering" that "aid[s] terrorists" and "give[s] ammunition to America's enemies."

If there was one idea that could be said to be predominant in the right-wing movement during the 1990s, it was that Real Americans should not and do not trust the federal government. The defining feature of America, they claimed relentlessly, was that Americans want strong limits on governmental power, especially powers that could be aimed at Americans on U.S. soil.

The single most influential Republican leader of that era, Newt Gingrich, actually went on *Meet the Press* in 1995 and explained how those rugged cowboys and individualist conservatives feared the federal government and insisted on limiting its intrusion into our lives *even if it meant giving up some security.* He dramatically pronounced that fear of the federal government is part of the core American character. As the May 11, 1995, issue of *Roll Call* recounted,

When asked on NBC's "Meet the Press" about Rep. Helen Chenoweth's (R-Idaho) outrageous proposal to force federal law enforcement agents to check with local sheriffs before making an arrest, Gingrich finally got around to opposing it, but not before cautioning that **"Easterners . . . and people who live in big cities ought to understand that there is, across the West, a genuine sense of fear of the federal government. This is not an extremist position in much of the West."**

As a result of the federal assault on the Branch Davidian complex in Waco, Texas, and a shoot-out at a white supremacist's cabin in Idaho, Gingrich repeated, "There is in rural America a genuine—and particularly in the West—a genuine fear of the federal government and of Washington, DC."

That was the glorious era of the Weekend Militias, whereby suburban and rural American dads dressed up in soldier costumes and, rather than going golfing or fishing, marched around in formation ready to defend their freedoms from the incursions of the federal government and the New World Order, in the threatening form of black U.N. helicopters, Janet Reno, and Hillary Clinton. That was when conservatives were fond of claiming that ingrained in the American spirit is a fear and distrust of federal power that the government ignored at its peril.

With George Bush occupying the Oval Office, those who express distrust over the federal government's having unlimited powers to detain and engage in surveillance against citizens are paranoid, anti-American freaks. Back then, though, they were rugged, salt-of-the-earth patriots who represented the Real America. From the *Los Angeles Times* on May 15, 1995:

Shedding an earlier caution, many Republican politicians have been speaking out with increasing boldness to support positions taken by right-wing militia groups.

Even as President Clinton has attacked the groups' claims to patriotism, House Speaker Newt Gingrich (R-Ga.) and a growing corps of allies from Western states have recently **expressed sympathy for some citizens' fears of encroaching government, called for new scrutiny of federal law officers** and rejected demands for investigations of the militias themselves.

While none are defending the Oklahoma City bombing or anti-government violence, they are seeking to focus the policy debate stirred by the attack not on the militias but on the government agencies that militia members and their sympathizers consider the enemy. . . .

Last week, Gingrich declared that **Sen. Craig Thomas (R-Wyo.) has declared his sympathy for Westerners angry at government, saying: "I don't disagree with their arguments." And Rep. Helen Chenoweth (R-Ida.) has said plainly that citizens "have a reason to be afraid of their government."**

The leading right-wing journals were filled to the brim with this sort of government-fearing rhetoric. Bush supporter Ramesh Ponnuru wrote in the May 8, 2000, edition of *National Review* of the dangers of federal government "storm troopers," as illustrated by the seizure of Elian Gonzales. Ponnuru specifically protested the way in which such law-enforcement powers are justified with claims that they are exercised for our own good, for our protection:

At every step of this drama, we have been invited to ponder how administration officials feel. Network anchors said that the standoff must be "tearing Reno up," given her deep concern for children; her deputy, Eric Holder, told us that he held her as she cried. Afterward, there was endless talk about the patient, compassionate attorney general. The INS agents who did the dirty work were also available to the press. They said they had never encountered such resistance before, citing the couch that had been placed against the door.

Let us hope this administration's mercy is never deployed against us. If that happens, we will be reassured that we are being pummeled and jailed for our own good. Our punishers may be psychiatrists, as Elian's are likely to be. For now, though, the style of government licensed by our carelessness does not touch us. . . . **Like Winston Smith, we weep and realize that we love Big Brother.**

Throughout his presidency, we have been bombarded with tales of George Bush's devotion to protect us all. We should therefore be grateful to him for his spying on us and his detention policies and his use of torture as he struggles to defend us. Like Winston Smith, we weep and realize that we love Big Brother.

And then we come to Deroy Murdock, writing on April 13, 2001, in *National Review* of the grave dangers to our country from allowing political officials to act in violation of the law with no accountability and without so much as an investigation:

[The Cato Institute's Timothy] Lynch exposes a maddening culture of impunity in which few officials face serious consequences for violating the law. **This double standard, in which federal badges become licenses for lawlessness, typified the Clinton-Reno years.** The Bush-Ashcroft team should end this intolerable situation by prosecuting those federal officials who apparently broke the law at Waco and thereby contributed to the injury and deaths of scores of innocent American citizens. . . .

"Because numerous crimes at Waco have gone unpunished," Lynch states, "the people serving in our federal police agencies may well have come to the conclusion that it is permissible to recklessly endanger the lives of innocent people, lie to newspapers, obstruct congressional subpoenas, and give misleading testimony in our courtrooms."

While it is ugly but legal to lie to reporters, these other acts clearly are criminal. **Private citizens are jailed for less. Unless "equal justice under law" is a slogan as hollow as a spent bullet casing, federal prosecutors must indict and try the law enforcement officials who, as Timothy Lynch convincingly argues, set the U.S. Code ablaze eight Aprils ago.**

Convicted criminal (pardoned by Bush 41) and current Bush official Elliott Abrams also spoke so very eloquently in *National Review*—specifically, the September 1997 issue—of the need in our system of government to have objective oversight and investigation, not politicized and friendly rubber-stamping from the Justice Department, when our highest government officials are accused of breaking the law. This, he insisted, was a core principle of the right-wing political ideology:

For conservatives, Waco is in large part a quis custodiet problem: Who guards the guardians? Whatever faith we may wish to place in the professionals of the FBI, who guards them from error? Who looks over their shoulder? Who punishes their abuses?

This is a problem only in practice, not in theory. In theory, the answer is easy: the professionals of the Department of Justice. Distinguished practitioners of the law who are presidentially appointed to the department work together with Justice's career staff to provide a check on the FBI and other federal law-enforcement agencies. This is critical, because the balance between energetic law enforcement and limits on excessive government power will not be maintained if the Justice Department does not seek vigorously to maintain it.

The right-wing political movement spent all of the 1990s claiming to distrust governmental power and even printing bumper stickers like this to prove it:

I Love My Country
BUT FEAR MY GOVERNMENT

These are the same people who continue to publish screeds like this one—from *National Review* in 2004—still pretending to believe in these conservative principles:

> Yet in the long run, Goldwater had an extraordinary influence on the Republican Party. . . . He did as much as anyone to redefine Republicanism **as an antigovernment philosophy: "I fear Washington and centralized government more than I do Moscow,"** he said—and this from a cold warrior who had once suggested lobbing a nuclear bomb into the men's room at the Kremlin. . . .
>
> But, in philosophical terms at least, **classical conservatism does mean something.** The creed of Edmund Burke, its most eloquent proponent, might be crudely reduced to six principles: **a deep suspicion of the power of the state;** a preference for liberty over equality; patriotism; a belief in established institutions and hierarchies; skepticism about the idea of progress; and elitism. . . .
>
> **The American Right exhibits a far deeper hostil-**

ity toward the state than any other modern conservative party. How many European conservatives would display bumper stickers saying "I love my country but I hate my government"?

How many would argue that we need to make government so small that it can be drowned in a bathtub? **The American Right is also more obsessed with personal liberty than any other conservative party. . . .**

The heroes of modern American conservatism are not paternalist squires but **rugged individualists who don't know their place:** entrepreneurs who build mighty businesses out of nothing, settlers who move out West and, of course, the cowboy. There is a frontier spirit to the Right—unsurprisingly, since so much of its heartland is made up of new towns of one sort or another.

These "rugged individualists" of the frontier, these swaggering skeptics and despisers of government power, these Burkean defenders of individual liberty who hate "centralized government" and—above all else—are guided by "a deep suspicion of the power of the state," now want to vest virtually unlimited secret power in the President to detain, interrogate, and spy on Americans. When George Bush was caught breaking the law by spying on Americans without warrants, they insisted that he had the right to do so, that it was for our own good, for our protection, and that we ought to be grateful. Has there ever been a political movement more antithetical to the political values they pompously espouse than the right-wing movement—those "small-government" authoritarians—epitomized by *National Review* editors?

Once securely in power, these small-government conservatives churned out brand-new theories that enabled some of the most severe expansions of federal power in our nation's history. They insisted that congressional investigations and judicial oversight of the activities of the President are all unnecessary, that they are merely partisan obstructionism. We could and should place blind faith in the Leader to exercise power for our own Good, said the limited-government deceivers.

As but one illustrative example, consider the 2007 debate over legislation demanded by the Bush administration to expand drastically the scope of the President's power under FISA to eavesdrop on the conversations and read the e-mails of Americans *with no warrants of any kind*. In October, *National Review* published an editorial on FISA and eavesdropping that described perfectly the conservative movement's view of America today (at least with one of their own in power):

> A sensible FISA fix would set a low threshold for the executive branch to commence monitoring. There should be **no restrictions** when targets are non-citizens outside the United States, even if they contact people **inside the United States.**

So: The President and those under his command should be completely free to eavesdrop on every one of the international calls you make to, or receive from, any foreign "target"—with no oversight or restrictions of any kind. And since the designation of foreign "target" is within the discretion of the executive, *National Review*—following along with the official position of the Republican Party—is advocating that the President possess virtually absolute and unchecked power to eavesdrop on any international calls made or received by Americans. And that's not all:

> Reasonable suspicion should be the standard **when an American citizen or permanent resident alien is targeted. . . .** As federal judge Richard Posner has observed, probable cause allows us to monitor known dangers, whereas the security challenge today is to figure out who is a danger.

So even when the President wants to eavesdrop on calls and other communications (such as e-mails) of *American citizens inside the United States,* there should be no more "probable cause" requirement. That standard, imposed by the Founders as a central check on federal power, is now too burdensome—so sayeth the conservative advocates of restrained government power and adherents to the original intent of the Founders. And they all but admit that their vision is barred by the Constitution—not that they care, as they proceed to argue:

> It is irrational to give non-Americans within our borders probable-cause protection: The Fourth Amendment does not require it, and experience shows that most foreign terrorists who infiltrate the U.S. are either illegal aliens or temporary legal immigrants.

They argue for the elimination of "probable-cause protection" for *"non-Americans"* by asserting that the "Fourth Amendment does not require it." Presumably, then, based on their own argument, the Fourth Amendment *does* guarantee "probable-cause protection" for eavesdropping on American citizens—yet *National Review* nonetheless expressly argues that this protection, even for Americans, ought to be abolished ("Reasonable suspicion should be the standard when an American citizen . . . is targeted"). Even by the premises of their own argument, then, they are expressly advocating the abolition of the core Fourth Amendment protection for American citizens—the right to be free from government searches in the absence of probable cause.

In fact, the United States has managed under every president from Carter to Clinton to defend itself in compliance with the probable-cause burden under FISA. Every U.S. president was able *simultaneously* to defend the national security of the United States and honor the requirement that American citizens not be spied on by their government in the absence of probable cause. That was true even as Ronald Reagan—as the *National Review* folklore goes—heroically vanquished the Soviet Empire.

But according to *NR,* that all happened before the Greatest and Most Sophisticated Threat Ever Known to Mankind—small roving bands of stateless and army-less Islamic Terrorists—Changed the World Forever:

> International terrorist networks are different from the Communist threat that FISA's Cold War–era authors had in mind. They are less predictable, more likely to strike, and more adept at exploiting new technologies which allow them to remain in contact with their operatives.

When Communists were the Enemy du Jour—when we faced the grave threat posed by what Reagan called the "Evil Empire"—they were the root of all Evil, the Soul-less, God-less Machiavellian Warriors with designs on World Domination who posed a grave, imminent, and existential threat to our nation, to everything we held dear. Back then, in the Era of the Communist Enemy, even to suggest that there was anything restrained or unthreatening or at least rational about the Evil Communists would subject one to all sorts of invective—involving allegations of anti-Americanism and treason and moral relativism and the like—from the *National Review*s of the worlds.

But no longer. Now that the Communist supervillains of yesteryear have been replaced by Islamic Terrorists as today's Prime Enemy, Communists have undergone a radical, retroactive makeover. According to *National Review,* back then we could afford laws like FISA and we could expect our government to abide by annoying constitutional guarantees (such as the Fourth Amendment) because those Communist simpletons were rational, sensible, even honorable enemies—and not very sophisticated. By contrast the Enemies we now face are so cunning, so Evil, so fanatical, so scary that we must change the very nature of our country. Constitutional and other restrictions on government power are literally obsolete, argues *National Review,* because the people who insisted on those safeguards were unaware of the unprecedented Evil posed by the Islamic Terrorist.

Hence, the modern conservative movement embodied by *National Review* expressly calls for the complete abolition of restrictions on the President's power to eavesdrop on virtually all of our international calls, and the abolition of probable-cause protections for when the federal government can monitor our communications. After all, if we don't submit to all of this, we might lose our freedoms.

A belief in endless expansions of government power is—along with endless wars—now the defining feature of today's Republican Party, at least its dominant right-wing faction. In April 2007, *The Weekly Standard*'s Michael Goldfarb participated in a conference call with former senator George Mitchell, during which Mitchell advocated a timetable for withdrawal from Iraq. The following day, this is what Goldfarb wrote about that call:

> Pam Hess, the UPI reporter who gave us this extremely moving and persuasive glimpse of the liberal case for the war in Iraq, asked if timetables for withdrawal "somehow infringe on the president's powers as commander in chief?" Mitchell's less than persuasive answer: "Congress is a coequal branch of government . . . the framers did not want to have one branch in charge of the government."
>
> True enough, but they sought an energetic executive with **near dictatorial power** in pursuing foreign policy and war. So no, the Constitution does not put Congress on an equal footing with the executive in matters of national security.

So according to our nation's right-wing liberty warriors, the American Founders risked their lives and fortunes in order to wage war against Great Britain and declare independence from the King, all in order to vest "near dictatorial power" in the American President in all matters of foreign policy and national security. And, of course, for the Michael Goldfarbs of the world, war and national security—and the near-dictatorial power vested in the President in those areas—now encompass virtually every government action, since scary and dangerous Muslims are lurking on every corner and the entire world, including American soil, is one big battlefield in the War on Terrorism.

Until the Bill Kristols, Dick Cheneys, John Yoos, and other authoritarians of that right-wing strain that define today's Republican Party entered the political mainstream, one never heard of prominent Americans who describe the power that they *want* to vest in our political leaders as "near dictatorial." Anyone with even a passing belief in American political values would consider the word "dictatorial"—at least rhetorically, if not substantively—to define that which we avoid at all costs, not something that we seek, embrace, and celebrate. If there is any political principle that was previously common to Americans regardless of partisan orientation, it was that belief.

One of the principal purposes of *The Federalist Papers* was to assuage widespread concerns that the President would be, in essence, a new British king. That fear was not eliminated or even diminished, but instead was *particularly pronounced,* with regard to the President's role as Commander-in-Chief, which is why there are so many safeguards in the form of congressional powers designed to limit that role. All of this is excruciatingly basic and obvious, really not much beyond what seventh-grade civics students are taught about what distinguishes a republic from a dictatorship.

What the actual Americans who founded the country feared (as opposed to "hoped for and craved") was that the President would wield "near-dictatorial power." Anyone with doubts should simply read Article II—defining the powers of the President—and see how limited those powers are. Even the glorious-sounding Commander-in-Chief's power is nothing more than the power, *when Congress decides to fund a military and when it authorizes the use of military force,* to act as top general directing troop movements and the like. In all other respects, those powers are checked, regulated, and limited by the people through their Congress.

In October 2007, Bill O'Reilly devoted the beginning of his *Fox News* show to warning Americans about the dangerous radicalism of John Edwards, proclaiming that "John Edwards has no chance to become president because he's simply too Far-Left for most Americans." After highlighting all the scary, fringe positions Edwards holds, O'Reilly summarized what Far Left America would look like once John Edwards got done with it:

> Would you support President John Edwards? Remember, no coerced interrogation, civilian lawyers in courts for captured overseas terrorists, no branding the Iranian guards terrorists, and no phone surveillance without a specific warrant.

Just consider what this says about our modern conservative. In the current right-wing worldview, one cannot even fathom an America plagued by habeas corpus, search warrants, and a military that fails to torture its detainees.

O'Reilly has aptly highlighted here the new ideological divide in our political culture—one is now on the "Left," even the "Far Left," if one supports what were previously the defining attributes of basic American liberties. Conversely, one is Serious and Responsible and Centrist/Right only if one is too sophisticated and "tough" to actually think that such effete and abstract things matter. Under the cover of darkness, late at night, John Edwards must be reading filthy leftist tracts, like Federalist No. 84 by Alexander Hamilton:

> The observations of the judicious Blackstone, in reference to the latter, are well worthy of recital: "To bereave a man

of life, [says he] or by violence to confiscate his estate, **without accusation or trial, would be so gross and notorious an act of despotism, as must at once convey the alarm of tyranny throughout the whole nation;** but confinement of the person, by **secretly hurrying him to jail, where his sufferings are unknown or forgotten, is a less public, a less striking, and therefore a more dangerous engine of arbitrary government.**

And Edwards, along with the Far Left minions he leads, seems to be following in the footsteps of the subversive American-hater Thomas Jefferson, who wrote this:

The Habeas Corpus secures every man here, alien or citizen, against everything which is not law, whatever shape it may assume. . . . Freedom of the person under the protection of the habeas corpus I deem [one of the] essential principles of our government.

What Republican stalwarts now call the "Far Left" was not, of course, the first "un-American" political faction trying to subvert freedom with their "un-American" warrant fixation. What today's right wing now deems to be subversive radicalism was actually the centerpiece of America before it was even born.

In 1972, the U.S. Supreme Court unanimously ruled that the warrantless eavesdropping on American citizens perpetrated by Richard Nixon was unconstitutional. Nixon appointee Justice Lewis Powell wrote for the Court that the ideas which the Bill O'Reillys and Dick Cheneys today consider to be "left-wing radicalism"—namely, judicial warrants and strict oversight on government power—are the very ideas that lie at the core of American liberty dating back to British common law:

Over two centuries ago, Lord Mansfield held that common-law principles prohibited warrants that ordered the arrest of unnamed individuals who the officer might conclude were guilty of seditious libel. "It is not fit," said Mansfield, "that the receiving or judging of the information should be left to the discretion of the officer. **The magistrate ought to judge; and should give certain directions to the officer.**" Leach v. Three of the King's Messengers, 19 How. St. Tr. 1001, 1027 (1765).

Lord Mansfield's formulation touches the very heart of the Fourth Amendment directive: that, where practical, a governmental search and seizure should represent both the efforts of the officer to gather evidence of wrongful acts and **the judgment of the magistrate that the collected evidence is sufficient to justify invasion of a citizen's private premises or conversation.** Inherent in the concept of a warrant is its issuance by a "neutral and detached magistrate." Coolidge v. New Hampshire, supra, at 453; Katz v. United States, supra, at 356. The further requirement of "probable cause" instructs the magistrate that baseless searches shall not proceed.

These Fourth Amendment freedoms cannot properly be guaranteed if domestic security surveillances may be conducted solely within the discretion of the Executive [407 U.S. 297, 317] Branch. The Fourth Amendment does not contemplate the executive officers of Government as neutral and disinterested magistrates. Their duty and responsibility are to enforce the laws, to investigate, and to prosecute. Katz v. United States, supra, at 359–360 (Douglas, J., concurring).

But those charged with this investigative and prosecutorial duty should not be the sole judges of when to utilize constitutionally sensitive means in pursuing their tasks. The historical judgment, which the Fourth Amendment accepts, is that unreviewed executive discretion may yield too readily to pressures to obtain incriminating evidence and overlook potential invasions of privacy and protected speech. . . .

The Fourth Amendment contemplates a prior judicial judgment, not the risk that executive discretion may be reasonably exercised. This judicial role accords with our basic constitutional doctrine that individual freedoms will best be preserved through a separation of powers and division of functions among the different branches and levels of Government. Harlan, Thoughts at a Dedication: Keeping the Judicial Function in Balance, 49 A.B.A.J. 943–944 (1963). The independent check upon executive discretion is not [407 U.S. 297, 318] satisfied, as the Government argues, by "extremely limited" post-surveillance judicial review. Indeed, post-surveillance review would never reach the surveillances which failed to result in prosecutions. **Prior review by a neutral and detached magistrate is the time-tested means of effectuating Fourth Amendment rights.** Beck v. Ohio, 379 U.S. 89, 96 (1964).

And America—from its founding—has also been defined not by the creativity of our torture techniques or by the merciless interrogation tactics we use, but by the humane treatment we accorded even our most inhumane enemies. Throughout our history, our distrust of political leaders meant that we did not want to vest them with the power to abuse prisoners, nor did we want such conduct to define who we are. Historian David Hackett Fischer, in his book *Washington's Crossing,* recounted the treatment of British and Hessian prisoners of war by George Washington's Continental Army:

> Washington and his officers set a high standard in their treatment of Hessian captives at Trenton. He issued instructions that "the officers and men should be separated. I wish the former may be well treated, and that the

latter may have such principles instilled in them during their confinement, that when they return, they may open the Eyes of their Countrymen."

Not all Americans wanted to do these things. Always some dark spirits wished to visit the same cruelties on the British and Hessians that had been inflicted on American captives. But Washington's example carried growing weight, more so than his written orders and prohibitions. He often reminded his men that they were an army of liberty and freedom, and that the rights of humanity for which they were fighting should extend even to their enemies. . . . Even in the most urgent moments of the war, these men were concerned about ethical questions in the Revolution.

It was George Washington's values, not those of the medieval torturer glorified by Bill O'Reilly and Sean Hannity and embodied by Dick Cheney, that defined America's political identity. In 2007, the *Washington Post* published a lengthy article reporting on the elite American Army unit responsible for interrogating Nazi prisoners of war during World War II. These American warriors had become disgusted by the reporting of torture and other abuses perpetrated by the Bush administration and cheered on by the Republican Party, and they spoke out:

> For six decades, they held their silence.
>
> The group of World War II veterans kept a military code and the decorum of their generation, telling virtually no one of their top-secret work interrogating Nazi prisoners of war at Fort Hunt.
>
> When about two dozen veterans got together yesterday for the first time since the 1940s, many of the proud men lamented the chasm between the way they conducted interrogations during the war and the harsh measures used today in questioning terrorism suspects.

Back then, they and their commanders wrestled with the morality of bugging prisoners' cells with listening devices. They felt bad about censoring letters. They took prisoners out for steak dinners to soften them up. They played games with them. . . .

Blunt criticism of modern enemy interrogations was a common refrain at the ceremonies held beside the Potomac River near Alexandria. . . .

Several of the veterans, all men in their 80s and 90s, denounced the controversial techniques . . . The interrogators had standards that remain a source of pride and honor.

"During the many interrogations, I never laid hands on anyone," said George Frenkel, 87, of Kensington. "We extracted information in a battle of the wits. I'm proud to say I never compromised my humanity."

Being an American who believed in the core political principles of the country always meant adhering to these standards and embracing these values. Today's Republican Party, acting contrary to its election rhetoric of conservatism and limited government power, has repudiated, trampled upon, and made a mockery of the core principles defining our country.

Today in the right-wing world, the very ideas that they spent the last several decades loudly touting and that long defined America have become the hallmarks of leftist radicalism. And the media has dutifully ingested this new framework. Thus, our Beltway establishment first looked the other way, then acted to protect the President of the United States once it was revealed that he was spying on the communications of American citizens in violation of the leftist doctrine called "law."

And, to be sure, none of this is specific to John Edwards. As O'Reilly warned, all Democrats who believe in radical theories such as search warrants and prohibitions on torture are of suspect loyalties:

"Talking Points" believes most Americans reject that fool-
ishness. And it has become a problem for both Barack
Obama and Hillary Clinton. Senator Obama is much
closer to the Edwards view than Senator Clinton is, but
the Democratic party can easily be branded as soft on
terrorism. It's tough to make distinctions in this area.

Indeed, under the rule of the "love-my-country-but-fear-
my-government" party, it is no exaggeration to say that the
United States has turned into a lawless surveillance state. If
that sounds hyperbolic, just review the disclosures over the
course of recent years concerning what databases the federal
government has created and maintained—everything from
records of all domestic telephone calls we make and receive,
to the content of our international calls, to risk-assessment
records based on our travel activities, to all sorts of new categories of information about our activities obtainable by the FBI
through the use of so-called National Security Letters. And
none of that includes, obviously, the as-yet-undisclosed surveillance programs undertaken by the most secretive administration in history.

This endless expansion of federal government power by the
small-government, states-rights wing of the Republican Party is
no longer even news. They barely bother to espouse these principles *except when it comes time to win elections.* In April 2007,
leading conservatives Andy McCarthy, David Frum, and John
Yoo participated in an event to argue for this Orwellian proposi-
tion: "Better More Surveillance Than Another 9/11." In the right-
wing mind, there is the ultimate irony: We need to empower the
federal government to maintain comprehensive dossiers on all
Americans; otherwise, our freedoms might be at risk from The
Terrorists.

The results of this complete abandonment of alleged small-
government principles by the Republican Party are as predictable as they are dangerous. This November 11, 2007, report

from the Associated Press is extraordinary, yet barely caused a ripple:

> As Congress debates new rules for government eavesdropping, a top intelligence official says it is time that people in the United States change their definition of privacy.
>
> The central witness in a California lawsuit against AT&T says **the government is vacuuming up billions of e-mails and phone calls as they pass through an AT&T switching station in San Francisco, California.**
>
> Mark Klein, a retired AT&T technician, helped connect a device in 2003 that he says diverted and copied onto a government supercomputer every call, e-mail, and Internet site access on AT&T lines. . . .
>
> "Anonymity has been important since the Federalist Papers were written under pseudonyms," [privacy lawyer Kurt] Opsahl said. "The government has tremendous power: the police power, the ability to arrest, to detain, to take away rights. . . .
>
> "There is something fundamentally different from the government having information about you than private parties," he said. "We shouldn't have to give people the choice between taking advantage of modern communication tools and sacrificing their privacy."
>
> **"It's just another 'trust us, we're the government,' " he said.**

At the end of 2007, the nonpartisan groups, Privacy International and Electronic Privacy Information Center, released their annual survey of worldwide privacy rights. The United States had been downgraded from its 2006 ranking of "Extensive Surveillance Society" to "Endemic Surveillance Society," the worst possible category there is for privacy protections, the category also occupied by countries such as China, Russia, Singapore, and Malaysia. The survey uses a variety of objective factors to determine the extent of privacy protections citizens enjoy from their government, and the United States now finishes at the bottom for obvious reasons, including the vastly expanded domestic surveillance and data-collection powers ushered in during the Bush presidency, all exercised with virtually no oversight.

The same political party that spent decades tricking Americans into believing that they stood for limited government has now ushered in a virtually limitless framework of government spying and unchecked power. Its top officials are telling Americans that we must fundamentally redefine what we understand privacy to mean when it comes to the power of our own government to spy on us. The right-wing faction that formed weekend militias to guard against a tyrannical government it claimed to hate and distrust now meekly and submissively cheers on every expansion of power, including powers completely anathema to core American freedoms.

Despite all of that, this same party will deceive Americans by giving lip service to these limited-government principles in order to win in 2008. In November 2007, Rudy Giuliani spoke to the Federalist Society, where he repeatedly invoked Reagan's limited-government principles and railed against Democrats "because they want to impose and give more and more responsibility to the central government." Fred Thompson's campaign website proclaimed that "we must allow individuals to lead their lives with minimal government interference." Every Republican candidate has repeatedly paid homage to these ideals. As it always does, the GOP will endlessly claim throughout 2008 that its newly selected Leader is the Guardian of Limited Government and the protector of Real Americans against power-hungry politicians.

Compassionate Authoritarians

Yet again, one finds that GOP leaders do not merely fail to adhere to their claimed principles and the images they strive to project. They are, in reality, the very opposite of those principles, the antithesis of their campaign images.

In April 2007, various Republican presidential candidates attended a meeting of the conservative economics group Club for Growth. Afterward, *National Review*'s Ramesh Ponnuru spoke to the Cato Institute's president, Ed Crane, about what the candidates said. The brief report filed by Ponnuru is simply extraordinary:

> Crane asked if Romney believed the president should have the authority to arrest U.S. citizens with no review. Romney said he would want to hear the pros and cons from smart lawyers before he made up his mind.

Mitt Romney could not say—at least not until he engaged in a careful and solemn debate with a team of "smart lawyers"—whether, in the United States of America, the President has the power to imprison American citizens without any opportunity for review of any kind. But in today's Republican Party, Romney's openness to this definitively tyrannical power is the moderate position. Ponnuru goes on to note,

> Crane said that he had asked Giuliani the same question a few weeks ago. The mayor said that he would want to use this authority infrequently.

It was almost as though Giuliani was positioning himself in this race as the "compassionate authoritarian"—"Yes, of course I have the power to imprison you without charges or review of any kind, but as President, I commit to you that I intend (no promises) to 'use this authority infrequently.' "

The leading Republican candidates for president either embraced or were open to embracing the idea that the President can imprison Americans without any review, based solely on the unchecked decree of the President. And, of course, that is nothing new, since the current Republican President, George Bush, not only believes he has that power but has exercised it against U.S. citizens and legal residents—including those arrested not on the battlefield but on American soil.

What kind of American isn't just instinctively repulsed by the notion that the President has the power to imprison citizens with no charges? And what does it say about the current state of our political culture that one of the two political parties has all but adopted as a plank in its platform a view of presidential powers and the federal government that is—literally—the exact opposite of the principles on which this country was founded? Even that renowned "liberal" Justice of the Supreme Court, Antonin Scalia, has pointed out how very un-American such powers are: "The very core of liberty secured by our Anglo-Saxon system of separated powers has been freedom from indefinite imprisonment at the will of the Executive."

At around the same time Giuliani and Romney were providing their extraordinary answers, *The Atlantic*'s Andrew Sullivan cited the views on this matter of Winston Churchill, whom Republicans love to trot out as their prop to symbolize "resolute strength":

> The power of the executive to cast a man into prison without formulating any charge known to the law, and particularly to deny him judgment by his peers for an indefinite period, is in the highest degree odious, and is the foundation of all totalitarian governments whether Nazi or Communist.

The extent to which the Great American Hypocrites of the Republican Party are hostile to our most basic constitutional traditions and defining political principles of limited government really cannot be overstated. They simply do not believe in them.

Indeed, Rudy Giuliani expressly does not believe in what

Antonin Scalia described as the "very core of liberty secured by our Anglo-Saxon system." And Mitt Romney has to convene a team of lawyers before he can decide whether he does. And Ramesh Ponnuru can pass along these views as though they are the most unremarkable things in the world, nothing that warrants comment, just the latest position of the Republican candidates, like whether they believe in adjustments to the capital gains tax or employer mandates.

Ponnuru's report would be akin to an item in a leading liberal magazine along these lines:

> Spoke to both Clinton and Obama today and asked whether they intended to seize and nationalize all American industries after they are inaugurated. Clinton said she would have to consult first with lawyers and decide only after a full debate, and Obama said he would likely only nationalize some industries, perhaps not all.

Or:

> Spoke to both Edwards and Clinton today and asked whether they intended to shut down conservative Christian churches. Edwards said he would want to hear the pros and cons from smart lawyers before he made up his mind, and Clinton said that she would want to use this authority infrequently.

Ponnuru's report must be viewed in its context—the context being that the hero and icon of the Republican Party over the last seven years, George W. Bush, has, in fact, imprisoned U.S. citizens and insisted that he has the power to throw Americans into black holes indefinitely with no charges or review of any kind. That is the modern Republican Party. Its base, its ruling factions, simply do not believe in our most basic constitutional guarantees. For anyone who wants to dispute that, how is it possible to reconcile the above with any claim to the contrary?

Indeed, at this point, it is doubtful that any Republican candidate *could* simply stand up and emphatically oppose this grotesque idea without creating real problems for himself among Republican voters—not even so much because executive, due-process-less imprisonment is important to the Republican base, but rather because it has become a symbol of the Bush presidency, and one shows loyalty to the Movement by defending it (and is guilty of the worst sin—disloyalty—by opposing it). These days, it's only those despicable liberals who whine about quaint "terrorist rights" like due process.

Hypocrites with Bad Credit

The Republican Party's complete betrayal of its own alleged small-government principles is hardly confined to powers of detention, interrogation, spying, and lawbreaking. Quite the contrary, it extends into every realm of governance.

It has long been clear that there is nothing remotely limited about Republican governance in any area, nor do Republicans have an iota of mistrust of government when they are in power. There has been a long line of decidedly unconservative actions by the Bush administration that have been almost uniformly cheered on by the right wing—from exploding discretionary domestic spending to record deficits, to an emergency convening of the federal government to intervene in one woman's end-of-life decisions, to attempts to federalize marriage and medical laws—all of which could not be any more alien to what has been meant by conservatism for the past forty years.

It is now inescapably clear that the Republican Party is anything but the party of limited government—more like the party of fiscal gluttony and recklessness. As an October 2007 article from McClatchy News Service documented,

Bush Is the Biggest Spender since LBJ

WASHINGTON—George W. Bush, despite all his recent bravado about being an apostle of small government and budget-slashing, is the biggest spending president since Lyndon B. Johnson. In fact, he's arguably an even bigger spender than LBJ.

"He's a big government guy," said Stephen Slivinski, the director of budget studies at Cato Institute, a libertarian research group.

The numbers are clear, credible and conclusive, added David Keating, the executive director of the Club for Growth, a budget-watchdog group. . . .

Take almost any yardstick and Bush generally exceeds the spending of his predecessors. . . .

Discretionary spending went up in Bush's first term by 48.5 percent, not adjusted for inflation, **more than twice as much as Bill Clinton did** (21.6 percent) in two full terms, Slivinski reports.

Indeed, ever since President Bush was inaugurated, discretionary, domestic spending has skyrocketed, both in absolute terms and when compared with the budget-balancing Clinton administration. In 2003, the libertarian Cato Institute published a detailed assessment of federal government spending over the last thirty years—titled *"Conservative" Bush Spends More Than "Liberal" Presidents Clinton, Carter.* Its conclusion:

But the real truth is that national defense is far from being responsible for all of the spending increases. According to the new numbers, defense spending will have risen by about 34 percent since Bush came into office. But, at the same time, non-defense discretionary spending will have skyrocketed by almost 28 percent. Government agencies that Republicans were calling to be abolished less than 10 years ago, such as education and labor, have enjoyed jaw-dropping spending increases under Bush of 70 percent and 65 percent respectively. . . .

After all, in inflation-adjusted terms, Clinton had overseen a total spending increase of only 3.5 percent at the same point in his administration. More importantly, after his first three years in office, non-defense discretionary spending actually went down by 0.7 percent. This is contrasted by Bush's three-year total spending increase of 15.6 percent and a 20.8 percent explosion in non-defense discretionary spending.

Those profligate spending patterns only worsened as the Bush presidency proceeded. In 2005, the right-wing American Enterprise Institute published a study by its own Veronique de Rugy and *Reason* magazine's Nick Gillespie. The report was titled *Bush the Budget Basher,* and it concluded, "After five years of Republican reign, it's time for small-government conservatives to acknowledge that the GOP has forfeited its credibility when it comes to spending restraint."

Not only has President Bush violated every claimed tenet of conservatism when it comes to restraints on federal spending, he ranks among the most fiscally reckless presidents in modern times—so insists the pro-Bush AEI:

"After 11 years of Republican majority we've pared [the budget] down pretty good," Rep. Tom DeLay (R-Texas) crowed a few weeks back during ongoing budget deliberations. But nothing could be farther from the truth, at least since the GOP gained the White House in 2001.

During his five years at the helm of the nation's budget, the president has expanded a wide array of "compassionate" welfare-state, defense, and nondefense programs. When it comes to spending, Bush is no Reagan. Alas, he is also no Clinton and not even Nixon. The recent president he most resembles is in fact fellow Texan and legendary spendthrift Lyndon Baines Johnson—except that Bush is in many ways even more profligate with the public till.

These massive spending increases are entirely independent of any 9/11-related or defense-based expenditures: "When homeland security spending is separated out, the increase in discretionary spending is still huge: 36 percent on Bush's watch." During the Bush presidency, total real discretionary outlays increased by 35.8 percent. By comparison, the same figure increased by only 11.2 percent during the deficit-plagued Reagan administration, and during the budget-balancing Clinton administration, it *decreased by 8.2 percent.* All of this led the AEI report to conclude: **"It seems incontestable that we should conclude that the country's purse is worse off when Republicans are in power."**

Compare that profligate, deficit-spawning behavior to the pretty words of Ronald Reagan at the 1980 RNC Convention:

> The head of a government which has utterly refused to live within its means and which has, in the last few days, told us that this year's deficit will be $60 billion, dares to point the finger of blame at business and labor, both of which have been engaged in a losing struggle just trying to stay even. . . . [I]t is time for our government to go on a diet.

And in his 1984 convention speech, Reagan mocked the Democrats' propensity to spend into deficits and scoffed, "About a decade ago, they said federal spending was out of control, so they passed a budget-control act and, in the next five years, ran up deficits of $260 billion. Some control." Yet the same party that claims to revere Reagan and be guided by his principles of fiscal restraint converted Bill Clinton's multibillion-dollar surplus into a multibillion-dollar deficit almost overnight.

While the GOP runs time and again on a platform of limited government, its leaders seek to extend the tentacles of government into virtually every area of Americans' lives. This was the promise made by Ronald Reagan in 1980: "I pledge to restore to the federal government the capacity to do the people's work without dominating their lives." Yet the reality of the Republican Party has been precisely the opposite.

With the bulk of the nation's political attention devoted to the Bush administration's radical terrorism and war policies, the relentless domestic invasions into the private realm of adult Americans usually go unnoticed. But underneath the media radar, the administration and its right-wing congressional allies have been actively placating the religious conservative wing of the Republican Party through all sorts of liberty-infringing and highly invasive measures. On every level, it is difficult to envision a political party more hostile to individual liberty than the current Bush-led Republicans.

One of the leading items on the agenda of religious conservatives is their desire to prevent adult citizens who want to gamble from doing so—not by persuading them of the evils of gambling, but by abusing the power of the federal government and making it a criminal offense for those adults to choose to gamble. In 2006, congressional Republicans, led by senators Bill Frist and John Kyl, attached a broad anti-gambling provision onto a bill designed to *enhance port security,* which meant that nobody could vote against it.

That provision "prohibit[s] gamblers [i.e., adults] from using credit cards, checks and electronic fund transfers to settle their online wagers," and it also dramatically enhances the enforcement powers of the federal government to arrest and imprison adults who choose to spend the money they earn by sitting in their homes and gambling online.

As reflected by the observations at *National Review*'s Corner of Andrew Stuttaford (one of the few remaining conservative genuine believers in individual liberty), Republicans have now almost completely abandoned any belief in limitations on the power and reach of the federal government to regulate every aspect of our lives, while Democrats, imperfect though they are, have taken the role of insisting upon the right of citizens to be free from unwarranted federal government intervention. Here is Stuttaford, quoting Democratic representative Barney Frank:

> [Frank]: "If an adult in this country, with his or her own money, wants to engage in an activity that harms no one, how dare we prohibit it because it doesn't add to the GDP or it has no macroeconomic benefit. Are we all to take home calculators and, until we have satisfied the gentleman from Iowa that we are being socially useful, we abstain from recreational activities that we choose? . . .
>
> "People have said, What is the value of gambling? Here is the value. Some human beings enjoy doing it. Shouldn't that be our principle? If individuals like doing something and they harm no one, we will allow them to do it, even if other people disapprove of what they do."
>
> [Stuttaford]: Barney Frank talking sense, Senator Frist not. Draw your own conclusions.

Barney Frank is typically held up (for less than noble reasons) as the face of contemporary big-government liberalism, yet Frank's formulation here—"If individuals like doing something and they harm no one, we will allow them to do it, even if other people disapprove of what they do"—is an expression of the core, defining *limited-government* principle, which previously defined (at least ostensibly) small-government conservative ideology. Those principles are ones that the Republican Party, under power-crazed authoritarians like Bill Frist, not only clearly reject but have actively worked to undermine in virtually every realm.

The Bush administration and its GOP congressional allies have been waging a similar war against the evils of adult pornography. The Mark Foley–sponsored "Adam Walsh Child Protection and Safety Act of 2006" has as one of its principal, hidden purposes the imposition of a regulatory scheme designed to make it as prohibitively expensive and burdensome as possible to produce and distribute adult pornographic products or to maintain adult websites.

The First Amendment bars them from doing what they really want to do, which is criminalize the production and distribution of any material they consider to be pornographic (just as they have criminalized gambling). As a result, they are attempting to accomplish the same objective via the indirect strategy of imposing so many record-keeping and other bureaucratic requirements on companies that produce pornography—compliance is virtually impossible without hiring attorneys and new employees strictly to work on record keeping—that companies can no longer afford to do so and are scared out of operating or are driven out of business.

During the Senate confirmation hearings of Michael Mukasey as attorney general, longtime GOP senator Orrin Hatch of Utah, in questioning Mukasey, made clear that when it comes to policies of the Justice Department, his primary concern is that the DOJ is not doing enough to battle the evils of what even he calls **"mainstream, adult pornography."**

Hatch argued that "pornography and obscenity consumption harms individuals, families, communities." Unfortunately, Hatch said, the DOJ has a "terrible record enforcing adult obscenity law"—such enforcement stopped during the Clinton administration, and while it increased substantially during the Bush administration, it has not been enough to satisfy Hatch.

The problem, Hatch contended, is that the DOJ is prosecuting only "extreme" obscenity—not what he calls "mainstream obscenity." Since most consumers access only "mainstream obscenity," not "extreme obscenity," this strategy is misguided—it prosecutes "too narrow a range of obscenity." Also, warned Hatch, there are far too few FBI resources being devoted to what he called "mainstream obscenity prosecutions."

In response, Mukasey promised to review the policy of prosecuting only "extreme" rather than "mainstream" pornography, and intoned, "I recognize that mainstream materials can have an effect of cheapening a society, objectifying women, and endangering children in a way that we can't tolerate." And virtually every time Bush's previous attorney general, Alberto Gonzales, appeared before the Senate Judiciary Committee, Senator Hatch demanded—even in the midst of what his party claims is the Epic War Against Islamic Terrorism—that more FBI agents and DOJ resources be devoted to prosecuting and imprisoning Americans who consume and produce consensual, adult pornography.

This desire to exert government control over virtually every facet of the private lives of Americans is now a defining trait of the limited-government Republican Party. Even today, the official platform of the Republican Party of Texas—the party of George Bush and the most influential state Republican Party in the country—explicitly opposes "the legalization of sodomy." They want it to be a *criminal offense* for gay adult Americans to have consensual sex in the privacy of their own homes. They want governmental power to extend into adults' bedrooms and, with the awesome force of criminal law, regulate and control the type of sex they have and with whom they have it. Those are the same people who, come election time, prance around paying homage to the need to keep politicians out of people's lives.

The Texas Republican Party also opposes "custody of children to homosexuals." They want the government, through the powers exercised by its courts, to take away from gay parents their own children. Numerous other state GOP platforms contain similar provisions.

In the face of this endless expansion of government power over the last seven years, even some on the Right are now tacitly acknowledging that their movement no longer has anything to do with limited government power. In 2006, fervent Bush supporter Fred Barnes wrote a Bush-revering book titled *Rebel-in-Chief.* In that book, Barnes actually *celebrates* the fact that George Bush has dispensed with any notions of a restrained federal government and has, instead, converted the federal government into an instrument for imposing a "conservative" vision on America. This transformation was described in a review of Barnes's book by Christopher Wilcox in the *New York Sun,* who expressed oozing admiration for both Barnes and his book:

> One of Mr. Barnes's most important points is how unhappy many conservatives are with Mr. Bush's big-spending ways. This certainly has been reported elsewhere, but Mr. Barnes goes further, claiming that **Mr. Bush is deliberately transforming the conservative movement from its small-government orientation to a more activist approach.**

What does it even mean to say that Bush is "transforming the conservative movement from its small-government orientation to a more activist approach"? What is left of "the conservative movement" if one guts from it its "small-government orientation"? Isn't that somewhat like transforming the peace movement away from its opposition to war or the environmental movement away from its opposition to pollution?

It is virtually impossible to imagine a political party that has less to do with principles of limited government than today's Republican Party. Every time they are in power, these Great

American Hypocrites greedily expand the control that the federal government exerts over the lives of American citizens in literally every area. And while a few rare souls on the Right have begun honestly acknowledging that their movement no longer has anything to do with such principles, the campaign tactic of the GOP is still grounded in the deceitful effort to persuade Americans that Republicans are devoted to protecting the average American against the ever-expending power of political officials.

CHAPTER SIX

John McCain

THE SAME OLD PRODUCT WRAPPED
IN THE SAME OLD PACKAGING

The GOP nominee for 2008—John McCain—is, in virtually every important respect, a completely typical Republican presidential candidate. He relies upon character mythology far more than substantive positions on issues to sustain his appeal. He endlessly claims to uphold personal values that he has chronically violated in reality—including his vaunted apolitical, truth-telling independence; his devotion to "traditional family values"; his Regular Guy credentials; his supposed hostility to the prerogatives of the elite; his honor-bound integrity; and his commitment to limited government and individual liberty. One finds, in McCain's actual life, rather than in his rhetoric and media-sustained mythology, one act after the next that directly violates each of these relentlessly touted principles, and in that regard, he is a standard, run-of-the-mill Republican hypocrite.

The electoral dynamic discussed in this book applies to McCain most vividly when it comes to the reverence that most of our nation's establishment political journalists harbor for him. The vast bulk of the establishment press, as many unashamedly admit, are blindly enamored of McCain and swoon in his presence—

probably more so than any modern political candidate in many years, if not decades. As a result, just as was true for Ronald Reagan and George W. Bush before him, McCain has been permitted to construct a public image that is unscathed by any critical scrutiny from an adoring, even intimidated political press corps.

There is, of course, one sense in which McCain is quite atypical for a modern Republican politician: Rather than strutting around as a pretend warrior, he actually did volunteer to serve in combat. By all accounts, his behavior once he was captured by the North Vietnamese forty years ago was both brave and honorable.

Thus, while McCain is as casually receptive to war as any other politician in the American mainstream—perhaps more so—that thirst for war does not seem to be grounded in a perceived lack of actual courage. When viewed in the context of his conduct forty years ago, McCain's personal "toughness" is beyond question. His love of war, though, must have some other motive, and whatever that is, it is both destructive and dangerous.

It is difficult to imagine how McCain's war service four decades ago could or should play much of a role in the outcome of the 2008 election. After all, he is the nominee of a party that, in the last two elections, vigorously supported a President who avoided combat service and a Vice President who avoided military service altogether while viciously demonizing two consecutive Democratic nominees who volunteered to serve in Vietnam. The GOP even depicted the combat-avoiders as conquering war-hero, tough guys while depicting the actual military veterans as effete and subversive cowards. Having spent the last eight years insisting, along with our press corps, that one's war service (or war avoidance) is irrelevant in one's fitness to serve as President, it is hard to imagine how they will suddenly elevate McCain's war record into a vital issue of "character"—though they will undoubtedly try.

Revealingly, once McCain's nomination seemed increasingly likely in 2007 and early 2008, the dominant right-wing, war-loving faction of the Republican Party began expressing intense opposition, even contempt, for McCain—not merely *despite* his status as a war hero, but in part, *because* of it. Unceasingly, the leading right-wing pundits and political leaders have demonstrated they value the *mirage* of the traditional masculine warrior virtues far more than the reality.

The leaders in their party who actually have fought in combat, and who thus seem to have a *genuine appreciation for the horrors of war,* are often considered unreliable heretics (Chuck Hagel, Colin Powell, and even Bob Dole and Bush 41 are excellent examples). And the most vicious Republican contempt is reserved for those Democratic politicians who have exemplary records of military service, such as Jack Murtha, Wes Clark, George McGovern, and Jimmy Carter.

All of those individuals, Republican and Democrat alike, having been exposed to the realities of combat, exhibit a reluctance and even hatred for war that is completely anathema to the chicken-hawk, war-seeking faction of that party. That faction views war as a harmless video game and believes that only those who are weak-willed or lacking in character would be the slightest bit hesitant to send others off to foreign lands to fight and die. A reluctance to wage wars is, in this twisted perspective, a sign of Chamberlain-like cowardice. Churchillian courage is demonstrated only by the belief that war is a glorious and honorable instrument for securing one's interests. Thus, those who view war with dread—as actual veterans of combat typically do—are considered suspect among this strain on the war-loving Right.

Despite this, one can expect the hard-core, war-crazed Limbaugh-Kristol-Coulter wing of the Republican Party to fall into line behind McCain. That's because John McCain exhibits virtually none of the reluctance over wars that most real warriors do. Quite the contrary, McCain has become one of the most relentlessly war-advocating American political officials over the last decade. And ultimately, what the modern GOP Right cares about more than anything else is that their Leader be willing to wage new American wars, and there is no question that John McCain fits that bill completely.

John McCain has merrily sung in public about bombing Iran, to the tune of the Beach Boys' famous classic *Barbara Ann* ("Bomb, bomb, bomb—bomb, bomb Iran . . ."). When most of the Republican Party was beginning to accept the necessity of following the will of the American people and bringing about an end to the disaster in Iraq, McCain vehemently argued that we should send still more combat troops, go hundreds of billions of dollars more into debt, and indefinitely prolong the war. When asked how long he envisioned the U.S. occupation of Iraq continuing, he replied that he would find fifty years acceptable, or even one hundred years, assuming that the United States was not sustaining "significant casualties," whatever that might mean.

McCain's America is one where we manage, run, and rule the world with our superior military force; endlessly occupy and interfere in countless other countries; and, whenever we perceive it as vaguely desirable, commence new wars. Like the post-9/11 George Bush, McCain is at the very far end of the militaristic spectrum, viewing the use of American force not as a "last resort" but as a preferred instrument in achieving U.S. goals. In short, the vision that John McCain has of the United States is entirely alien to our constitutional traditions and the warnings of the Founders: not a Republic, but an Empire waging Endless War.

Former *Los Angeles Times* editor Matt Welch, author of *McCain: The Myth of a Maverick,* delivered a speech at the Cato Institute in January 2008 in which he explained that McCain's "whole career, his life, his training, his family background has been to be a member of . . . the Imperial Class"; that McCain is motivated by an "inspiring trust of America's governance of the world"; and that "he would be the **most imperial-oriented President, most militaristic President, since Teddy Roo-**

sevelt, at least." McCain himself has acknowledged that the war-loving Teddy Roosevelt is his role model, remarking, "I return to kind of the Teddy Roosevelt outlook toward things." As a February 2008 *USA Today* article noted, "McCain has long identified Roosevelt, president from 1901 to 1909, as a political idol."

After five years of a failed and discredited war in Iraq, and an even longer period in a protracted and increasingly unsuccessful occupation of Afghanistan, the American public is war-weary. The U.S. military is dangerously overstretched, and American resources simply can no longer sustain the Bush/Cheney course of U.S. military domination of the world, which McCain plainly wants not merely to maintain, but to *escalate.*

The Iraq War is one of the most unpopular wars in American history, if not the most unpopular. By itself, that war has all but destroyed the Bush presidency, rendering the President both disliked and distrusted across the political spectrum. In a minimally rational world, McCain's front-and-center advocacy for that war—and his desire that America remain in Iraq *indefinitely*—would be a devastating, even fatal, flaw for his candidacy.

Beyond Iraq, McCain is as pure a warmonger as it gets in the American political mainstream. He is supported by the most extreme neoconservative ideologues, such as Bill Kristol, John Bolton, and Joe Lieberman, precisely because they perceive, correctly, that he would be the candidate most likely to enable their paramount dreams of unending Middle East war. The virtual certainty that McCain will ensure the endless occupation of Iraq and, worse, will inevitably provoke more wars, ought to be considered his greatest political liability, not his strongest asset.

But our establishment media is anything but rational. In U.S. national elections, eagerness to wage war is equated with "character" and "toughness." There is no such thing as being excessively militaristic. Quite the opposite, there exists a direct relationship between a candidate's willingness to support and threaten wars and the respect the candidate merits from the establishment press as a serious and tough foreign-policy hawk. And thus, while McCain would pay a substantial price for his war support in a rational world, in our Beltway Media World, it becomes a reflection of his strength and seriousness. And the media, with a straight face, depicts McCain as a moderate and an independent, notwithstanding his loyal support for the most radical and destructive Bush/Cheney policies.

In this regard, and so many others, John McCain's candidacy is similar to that of George W. Bush. In 2000, the dominant media theme was that likeability—choosing the candidate with whom one would "most want to have a beer"—was the key determining factor in selecting a President. As is now amply documented, the 2000 media corps revered George Bush the way hordes of insecure high school freshmen revere the star quarterback, while they despised and mocked Al Gore just as the overly earnest school nerd is taunted.

Evidence demonstrating the influence exerted by the 2000 media's Bush-love and Gore-hatred is far too abundant to chronicle here. But perhaps the most vivid account reflecting the press corps' love affair with George Bush was the 2003 book by *Time* magazine's Margaret Carlson, titled *Anyone Can Grow Up: How George Bush and I Made It to the White House,* in which she reminisces about the tight and affectionate bond between her fellow journalistic colleagues and candidate Bush:

> I miss George Bush. Sure, I see him every day up on a podium, breezing into a fund-raiser, or walking across the South Lawn to Marine One. True, I was only a few dinner plates away from him at Katharine Graham's house and within joking distance at the White House Christmas party, where he charmed my goddaughter.
>
> But once a man is president, he changes, you change, and the situation changes. He's Mr. President ("Trailblazer" to the Secret Service). Anyplace you might see Bush up close is now off-limits. He's sur-

rounded by men in black talking into their wrists and driving armored Chevy Suburbans with gunwales. He travels on Air Force One. You travel on the press charter behind him. . . .

The campaign, or specifically the campaign plane, is the last time the press gets to see the man who would be president more closely than an attentive viewer of C-SPAN. Bush didn't like campaigning, so he treated the time on the press like recess, **a chance to kick back between math and chemistry classes. He was seductive, playful, and most of all, himself. It's a failure of some in the press—well, a failure for me—that we are susceptible to a politician directing the high beams of his charm at us.** That Al Gore couldn't catch a break had something to do with how he was when his hair was down. Only it never was.

Carlson added that the media hated the earnest Gore as much as it loved the playful Bush because Gore was "intent on proving he was the smartest kid on the planet." She continued at length in that same vein—invoking seemingly every high school cliché to explain the 2000 election dynamic as one driven by the press's petty personality obsessions. As *The Daily Howler*'s Bob Somerby wrote in reviewing Carlson's book:

Carlson goes on, at considerable length, about how Bush "bond[ed] with the goof-off in all of us" on that plane. Persistently, she portrays the press corps—and herself— as if they were feckless teen-agers. On the plane, "[Bush's] inner child hovers near the surface," she writes. And not only that; "Bush knows how to push the buttons of your high school insecurity." But then, **"a campaign is as close as an adult can get to duplicating college life."**

Bush "wasn't just any old breezy frat brother with

mediocre grades . . . He was proud of it," Carlson writes, approvingly. This seems to explain the press corps' preference. "Gore elicited in us the childish urge to poke a stick in the eye of the smarty-pants," she writes. "Bush elicited self-recognition." Yes, those sentences actually appear in this book, and yes, they seem to be Carlson's explanation of Gore's lousy coverage. **"It's not hard to dislike Bush's policies, which favor the strong over the weak," she writes. "But it *is* hard to dislike Bush."**

Carlson's unintentional confession—that the press corps' attitude toward candidates is primarily the by-product of journalists' residual high school personality scars, which drives them to worship the cool popular kid and hate the overly serious geek— really does explain the crux of how our national presidential discourse is shaped.

Underscoring how much like "college life" our national journalists treat presidential elections, Carlson even cited the far better food served to journalists by the Bush campaign plane than the Gore plane as a metaphor for Bush's far cooler persona. On Bush's plane: "There were Dove bars and designer water on demand, and a bathroom stocked like Martha Stewart's guest suite. Dinner at seven featured lobster ravioli." But:

> Gore wanted the snacks to be environmentally and nutritionally correct, but somehow granola bars ended up giving way to Fruit Roll-Ups and the sandwiches came wrapped and looked long past their sell-by date. On a lucky day, someone would remember to buy supermarket doughnuts. By contrast, a typical day of food on Air Bush . . . consisted of five meals with access to a sixth, if you count grazing at a cocktail bar. Breakfast one was French toast, scrambled eggs, bacon.

In sum, as reporter Richard Wolffe—then of the *Financial Times,* now of *Newsweek*—admitted in a documentary produced by Alexandra Pelosi: "We were writing about trivial stuff, because [Bush] charmed the pants off us." The disparity in the Bush/Gore treatment by the press was so severe that even conservative Joe Scarborough acknowledged it on MSNBC in November 2002:

> I think, in the 2000 election, **I think [the media] were fairly brutal to Al Gore.** I think they hit him hard on a lot of things like inventing the Internet and some of those other things, and I think there was a generalization they bought into that. **If they had done that to a Republican candidate, I'd be going on your show saying, you know, that they were being biased.**

One would have assumed that the last seven years, which brought us Iraq and Katrina and chronic lawbreaking and pervasive corruption and torture and Abu Ghraib and all the rest, would have trained our vapid press corps to avoid the high school popularity mind-set when covering our presidential campaigns. But in 2008, one actually finds exactly the same dynamic—and the same verbatim themes—that caused our media stars to fall in love with George W. Bush driving their fawning, adoring coverage of John McCain.

Just as Bush was the honor-bound, though still likeably cool, high school jock who intimidated and thus inspired great respect in our media stars, so, too, does John McCain engender in them the feeling that they are privileged to be near him, lucky that he knows their names, honored that he is willing to spend time interacting with them. One need not speculate about any of this. The media stars seem bizarrely unashamed of copping to the swooning.

One highly representative sampling came in November 2007,

courtesy of *Time*'s new campaign reporter Michael Scherer, in which he cast the McCain v. Romney primary battle as *The GOP's High School Debate: The cool kid vs. the valedictorian:*

> Here's one thing you need to know about John McCain. He's always been the coolest kid in school. He was the brat who racked up demerits at the Naval Academy. He was the hot-dog pilot who went back to the skies weeks after almost dying in a fire on the U.S.S. *Forrestal.* His first wife was a model. His second wife was a rich girl, 17 years his junior.
>
> He kept himself together during years of North Vietnamese torture and solitary confinement. **When he sits in the back of his campaign bus, we reporters gather like kids in the cafeteria huddling around the star quarterback. We ask him tough questions, and we try to make him slip up, but almost inevitably we come around to admiring him.** He wants the challenge. He likes the give and take. He is, to put it simply, cooler than us.

Scherer underscored what is, in any event, self-evident from reading the reporting from our press corps—they view our presidential elections from the perspective of an insecure freshman seeking to recast their painful adolescent years and view even presidential candidates solely through the prism of vapid high school clichés. And just as George W. Bush did, the towel-snapping playboy John McCain is a unique beneficiary of this absurdity. Scherer continued,

> So here is the situation that Republicans in New Hampshire face on Tuesday: Do we elect the jock or the overachiever? Do we go with cool and confident, or cautious and competent? . . . So who won? It depends whom you liked in high school. Did you want to park with the jock?

Or did you admire the smart kid who volunteered Sundays at the foodbank? It's your call.

It is true that with regard to all presidential candidates—not just McCain—one effortlessly finds such stunted, high-school-based character analysis pervading the stories from our nation's most prestigious political reporters. Here, as but one example, is the 2007 analysis from *Newsweek*'s Howard Fineman of the two top contenders for the Democratic presidential nomination:

> You knew Hillary Clinton and Barack Obama in high school. At least I did. They were candidates in the student senate election. She was the worthy but puffed-up Miss Perfect, all poodle skirts and multicolored binders clutched to her chest. He was the lanky, mysterious transfer student—from Hawaii by way of Indonesia no less—who Knew Things and was way too cool to carry more than one book at a time. Who would be leader of the pack?
>
> **Presidential elections are high school writ large, of course,** and that is especially true when, as now, much of the early nomination race is based in the U.S. Capitol. It is even more the case when the party in question, and here we are talking about the Democrats, is not sharply divided ideologically. They have a good chance in '08 to oust the fading prep/jock/ROTC/Up With People alliance.

But just as was true for the rich, privileged, frat-boy persona of George Bush, the media's feeling of intimidation in the presence of McCain's bad-boy, fighter-pilot coolness produces almost uniformly favorable coverage. Even media critic Howard Kurtz, of the *Washington Post* and CNN, who normally loathes criticizing his journalistic colleagues for unduly favorable treatment of GOP politicians, acknowledged "McCain's ability to charm the press" and even admitted that such "charm" shapes the bountifully favorable, even uncritical, media coverage of McCain:

> Journalists tend to reward those who engage them and get testy when they are stiffed, concluding that such candidates are overly calculating and wary of unscripted exchanges.

Kurtz even quoted *Time*'s Ana Marie Cox as claiming that journalists are cognizant of their abundant affection for McCain:

> "The journalists who covered McCain in 2000 feel very self-conscious about the criticism that the press came under for apparently being so taken with John McCain," says Ana Marie Cox, the *Time* blogger who has been covering him. "There's a sense that the first time was so fun and exciting, but this time we're really going to be sober and critical and the dispassionate observers we're supposed to be."

The aspiration that Cox claims her colleagues share—to conduct themselves like actual professional reporters around McCain rather than giggling, swooning, grateful cheerleaders—is nowhere to be found in press coverage of McCain. Rather, the type of playful banter more appropriate for a loving couple, which Kurtz ended his column by recounting, continues to govern press behavior in McCain Land:

> As the Straight Talk Express rolled from Greenville to Spartanburg, McCain, sipping a Coke, was upbeat with a half-dozen reporters. . . . After he fielded questions on strategy, the economy, abortion, Iraq, Romney and Huckabee, **the assembled journalists seemed to run**

out of ammunition and the conversation grew more relaxed. . . .

"What did you do without us this morning?" asked *Chicago Tribune* reporter Jill Zuckman, since the senator had taken the unusual step of traveling separately from the press corps.

"It was terrible," McCain replied. "Withdrawal. Shaky. Had to have a couple of shots of vodka and calm myself down."

"Were you hanging out with other reporters?"

McCain acted horrified. "I was not unfaithful," he insisted.

It's as though adoring reporters deplaned from Bush 2000 and stepped right onto the equally playful 2008 McCain "Straight Talk Express" bus.

Time and again, watching reporters fawn over John McCain is redolent of the media's Cult of Personality that arose around George Bush in 2000. McCain's pronouncements are passed along uncritically, and every interview appears designed to bolster his character mythology. In January 2008, on the eve of the GOP's South Carolina primary, the primary election that likely decided the outcome of that party's nominating process, CNN political reporter John King had the opportunity to interview McCain while riding with him in the press bus, and these are all of the "questions" that were broadcast:

*JOHN KING, CNN CHIEF NATIONAL CORRESPONDENT: You were speaking yesterday on the one-year anniversary of the president calling for the troop surge about how, A, you think it was the right policy, and, B, you think, frankly, you deserve a little credit, because you stood up and pushed for it when it was unpopular.

It was interesting yesterday. I kept looking at my

BlackBerry e-mails all day long. I didn't hear the Democratic candidates talking much about that date. What does that tell you about the evolution of the politics of Iraq, if you will?

*KING: As you know, one of the issues you have had here in South Carolina in the past is either people don't understand your social conservative record or they're not willing to concede your social conservative record.

There's a mailing that hit South Carolina homes yesterday. It's a picture of you and Cindy on the front. It says, "Always pro-life, 24-year record." Why do you think you still, after all this time, have to convince these people "I have been with you from the beginning"?

*KING: The flip side of that mailing shows Cindy holding Bridget . . . tiny Bridget, at the Bangladesh orphanage. As you know, some heinous and horrible things were said in the campaign eight years ago about you and about your daughter. Is that mailing in any way meant to tell people, here's the truth?

*KING: You feel good about the state this time?

That was the whole interview as broadcasted by CNN—all four questions. To recap: (1) Democrats want to ignore your Glorious Surge; what does that tell you, huh? (2) Why are South Carolina voters failing to recognize what a stalwart rock-ribbed conservative you've always been? (3) Your baby daughter is absolutely beautiful, and it was reprehensible what was done to you and her in 2000. (4) How great do you feel? End of "interview."

One asks this question literally, not rhetorically: If McCain's actual Press Secretary had conducted this "interview," how would it have been any different? Maybe they would have at least tried to pretend the questions were a little more probing, less adulatory, just for the sake of appearances if not basic dignity. King's interview ended this way:

KING: You feel good about the state this time?
MCCAIN: Feel good. But I . . .
　　[*laughter*]
MCCAIN: . . . have felt good about this far out some years ago. We're not—but we're not revisiting the past.
　　Yes, I feel good, John.
KING: Senator, thank you very much.
MCCAIN: Thanks.

If one sought to parody the drooling vapidity of our media stars and their giggly collective crush on John McCain, it would be impossible to outdo John King's performance here. For reverent, propagandizing behavior from our Liberal Media comparable to this, one has to go all the way back to . . . the 2000–2005 lionization of the Great Warrior King, George W. Bush.

The media's adoring depiction of McCain's character is grounded in the same falsehood-drenched mythology that they used to build up Bush into the plain-spoken, honor-bound, swaggering cowboy-everyman. And no McCain mythology is as grounded in falsehoods as the media's relentless depiction of him as an independent-minded, unprecedentedly honorable trans-partisan maverick who is incapable of pandering or doing anything other than shooting "straight talk."

Indeed, the press's veneration of McCain as "a different type of Republican" has echoes of how George Bush was built into an iconic hero. In 2000, we were inundated with claims that Bush was a departure from the hard-core, Gingrichian right-wing Republican. Bush was no mere conservative, but a "compassionate conservative," someone who, exactly like McCain, combined the most admirable virtues of the conservative man with a streak of idiosyncratic independence that rendered him substantially different—better—than the standard right-wing Republican.

And exactly like the media's hero worship of McCain now, Bush in 2000 was presented as the sole figure capable of healing our partisan rift. He was a "uniter, not a divider," who venerated solutions above partisan bickering. Bush would reach across the aisle, recruit Democrats to his side, and just as he changed the tenor of politics in Texas, so, too, would he bridge the partisan divide in Washington after eight long years of Clintonian divisiveness.

Here is how then-RNC chairman Jim Nicholson put it during his 2000 Convention speech: "My friends, this is going to be a different kind of convention for a **different kind of Republican**." Bush spokesman Ray Sullivan mouthed a similar line during the campaign: "Gov. Bush has shown time and time again that he is **a different kind of Republican**."

Replace "McCain" in 2008 with "Bush" in 2000, and the cliché-ridden script has barely changed. Both then and now, the GOP nominee, despite a virtually unbroken record of standard conservative orthodoxy, is depicted as far too honorable and independent to be considered an ordinary politician, let alone a standard conservative partisan. Both the 2000 Bush and the 2008 McCain were mavericks—inspiring, honest figures who transcend partisan warfare and piously float far above the muck of traditional politics.

Indeed, the central praise typically heaped by journalists on McCain—that no matter what one thinks of his views, he always says what he thinks, because he is a man of real conviction—is exactly the marketing package in which George Bush was wrapped, particularly when he ran for reelection. Just compare McCain's media reputation as a plain-spoken, truth-telling maverick with the crown jewel of George Bush's 2004 GOP Convention acceptance speech:

> **THE PRESIDENT:** In the last four years, you and I have come to know each other. Even when we don't agree, **at least you know what I believe and where I stand.**
>
> [*applause*]

The depiction of McCain as a truth-telling, apolitical maverick is just about as accurate as previous similar depictions of Bush were. On virtually every policy issue of significance, McCain's positions—not his rhetoric but his actual positions—ultimately transform into those held by the dominant right-wing faction of the Republican Party and, even more so, are identical to the positions that shaped and defined the failed Bush presidency.

In every way that matters, this exotic, independent-minded maverick is nothing more than a carbon copy extension of the Bush worldview, nothing more than a George W. Bush third term. One sees this most clearly in McCain's view of America's role in the world, whereby he channels the central, and indescribably disastrous, Bush mentality almost verbatim.

The central animating principle of the two Bush/Cheney terms has been that Islamic radicalism is not merely a threat to be managed and rationally contained, like all the other threats and risks the United States faces. Rather, it is some sort of transcendent ideological struggle—a glorious War of Civilizations—comparable to the great ideological wars of the past. As such, it will engage all of America's military might and the bulk of its resources, as the United States navigates an endless stream of enemies and wars that subordinates all other national priorities and that assumes a paramount role in our political life. That was the central theme of George Bush's presidency, and it is the central theme of John McCain's worldview now.

In articulating a foreign policy at least as bellicose and war-seeking as that which defined the most radical and disastrous aspects of the Bush/Cheney years, McCain has even taken to using language almost identical to that repeatedly used by Bush. As the *Boston Globe* put it in September 2006:

McCain has nonetheless adopted Bush's sweeping language in defining the war on terrorism: "I think it's clear that this is now part of a titanic struggle between radical

Islamic extremism and Western standards and values,"
McCain said earlier this year.

McCain's unfettered willingness to commit U.S. troops to the
war in Iraq; his blithe acceptance of literally decades-long occupation of that country; and his extreme and often even joyous
vows to wage war on Iran, if he perceives that they are close to
acquiring the ability to develop nuclear weapons, are all part-
and-parcel of the same Bush/Cheney emphasis on Middle Eastern
wars and U.S. hegemony that has wreaked so much damage on
our country over the last seven years. Whatever else one might
want to call McCain's worldview, "independent" or "unorthodox"
or "a different type of Republicanism" is manifestly not it.

The preposterously simplistic and dangerously Manichean
approach common to both Bush/Cheney and McCain—United
States: Good; those who oppose us: Bad; therefore War Is
Needed—manifests in a virtually indistinguishable approach to
the world's most complex problems. In the middle of the raging
Israel-Hezbollah war of 2006, President Bush, unbeknownst to
him, was accidentally (and now infamously) recorded while
speaking privately to Tony Blair at a dinner of European leaders.
Bush, in between bites of food, made clear what the solution
was to the war: "What they need to do is get Syria to get Hezbollah to **stop doing this shit and it's over**." The Decider issues
orders. Everyone complies. And problems are solved for the
Good, regardless of complexities, obstacles, or realities.

Consider how identical—almost to the letter—was McCain's
prescription in the same year for how to solve raging sectarian
tension in Iraq, in remarks addressed to a gathering of GOP
donors, as reported by the *New York Observer*'s Jason Horowitz:

In a small, mirror-paneled room guarded by a Secret Service agent and packed with some of the city's wealthiest
and most influential political donors, Mr. McCain got
right to the point.

"One of the things I would do if I were President would be to sit the Shiites and the Sunnis down and say, 'Stop the bullshit,'" said Mr. McCain, according to Shirley Cloyes DioGuardi, an invitee, and two other guests.

That's the thoughtful, insightful view of the highly experienced, profoundly serious maverick for whom foreign policy is a mastered discipline. Apparently, all Iraq needed for the last five years was some profanity-laced commands issued by the American President to the frightened sectarian simpletons, and harmony would have reigned. This is precisely the same belligerent, narcissistic pretenses that rendered George Bush one of the most despised, destructive, and impotent American leaders in modern history. John McCain seems to believe that all that was needed was just a bit more belligerence and a more imperious tone when dictating to our subjects around the world.

Particularly when it comes to foreign policy and war, McCain has been following in the Bush/Cheney footsteps as steadfastly and loyally as any American politician. Prior to the invasion of Iraq, McCain was not only one of the most unyielding supporters of the invasion, but also propagated the most extreme and misguided claims in justifying it. He repeatedly affirmed the false Bush/Cheney link between the 9/11 attacks and the need to attack Saddam, pronouncing in an October 2, 2002, speech on the Senate floor:

America is at war with terrorists who murdered our people one year ago. **We now contemplate carrying the battle to a new front—Iraq**—where a tyrant who has the capabilities and the intentions to do us harm is plotting, biding his time until his capabilities give him the means to carry out his ambitions, perhaps through cooperation with terrorists—when confronting him will be much harder and impose a terrible cost.

Every myth and exaggeration used to justify the invasion of Iraq came pouring forth uncritically from the maverick's mouth. In mid-October 2002, McCain issued a statement on Iraq that began by quoting a think tank as follows:

> The retention of weapons of mass destruction capabilities is self-evidently the core objective of the [Iraqi] regime, for it has sacrificed all other domestic and foreign policy goals to this singular aim.

Thus, claimed McCain, Iraq was not merely developing weapons of mass destruction, but doing so was the "core objective of the regime"—its "singular aim"—and this fact was "self-evident." As George Bush and his neoconservative ideologues spun a tale filled with exaggerations and falsehoods in the parade to Baghdad, John McCain loyally marched in lock-step behind them, rarely deviating from a single step.

In those instances after the invasion where McCain ended up criticizing the prosecution of the Iraq War, the criticisms were based in mere differences over military *tactics*, never based upon the view that the invasion of Iraq was misguided or that it was achieved through a slew of false pretenses. If anything, McCain's complaint with the White House was that it was *insufficiently aggressive* when it came to the use of military force, using too few troops in too restrained a manner. Again, the sole differences between the Bush presidency and the one envisioned by John McCain is that McCain craves *more* of those aspects of the Bush tenure most responsible for the erosion of American power and credibility.

On the isolated issues where McCain did actually deviate in substantial ways from Republican orthodoxy, those deviations were largely confined to the 2001–2004 time-frame, when he was contemplating leaving the Republican Party because he believed, in the wake of his devastating 2000 primary loss, that it offered no path for him to the White House. But even with those deviations, the ones that earned him the drooling adoration of the press corps as a trans-partisan maverick, McCain ended up reversing himself completely after 2004, once he resolved to remain a Republican and concluded that he needed the support of the hard-core right-wing base if his presidential ambitions were to be realized.

In this regard, the media's mindless praise of McCain as a truth-bound maverick is, as usual, the opposite of reality. In February 2008, the *New Republic*'s Jonathan Chait examined a series of substantial policy reversals by McCain, compared those reversals to the "maverick" praise heaped on him by press consensus, and concluded,

> This assessment gets McCain almost totally backward. He has diverged wildly and repeatedly from conservative orthodoxy, but he has also reinvented himself so completely that it has become nearly impossible to figure out what he really believes.

Far from being the man who, like George W. Bush, always says what he believes no matter what the political cost, McCain has shifted positions so frequently—particularly in those areas where he once deviated from GOP dogma—that one can only engage in groundless speculation in order to determine what McCain's "real beliefs" are, if such a thing can be said to exist. As Chait put it: "Determining how McCain would act as president has thus become a highly sophisticated exercise in figuring out whom he's misleading and why." Thus, we once again find that the political press's personality-based hero worship of a GOP candidate is not only vapid, but the opposite of the candidate's reality.

The complete contradiction between McCain's media image and the reality of his behavior as a politician can be seen in virtually every area, *most egregiously* those cited by journalists as proof of his rock-ribbed integrity. McCain long opposed repeal of the estate tax, only to announce after 2004 that he would no longer block its repeal. He originally opposed the Bush tax cuts, only now to campaign on his pledge to make them permanent. He was long the symbol of pro-immigration policy proposals, only to abandon those views and claim that he "learned a lesson" that closed borders must come first—a lesson learned just in time to save his candidacy in the GOP primary.

These reversals of "conviction" were as naked an example of political hypocrisy and pandering as such flip-flopping gets—the exact attribute that McCain's adoring press fans claim he is incapable of exhibiting. With virtually every one of these reversals, Chait traced the cause to McCain's post-2004 realization that his only hope for winning the presidency lay in placating the right-wing Republican base and becoming more palatable to them. As Chait documented,

> After the Kerry flirtation ended, McCain obviously decided that his only plausible path to the presidency lay with the Republican Party in 2008. So he set about re-ingratiating himself with the GOP establishment while maintaining his reputation as an unwavering man of principle.

The mirage-like nature of McCain's alleged convictions can be seen most clearly, and most depressingly, with his public posturing over the issue of torture. Time and again, McCain has made a dramatic showing of standing firm against the use of torture by the United States only to reveal that his so-called principles are confined to the realm of rhetoric and theater, but never action that follows through on that rhetoric.

In 2005, McCain led the effort in the Senate to pass the Detainee Treatment Act (DTA), which made the use of torture illegal. While claiming that he had succeeded in passing a categorical ban on torture, however, McCain meekly accepted two White House maneuvers that diluted his legislation to the point of meaningless:

(1) the torture ban expressly applied only to the U.S. military, but not to the intelligence community, which was exempt, thus ensuring that the C.I.A.—the principal torture agent for the United States—could continue to torture legally; and (2) after signing the DTA into law, which passed the Senate by a vote of 90–9, President Bush issued one of his first controversial "signing statements" in which he, in essence, declared that, as President, he had the power to disregard even the limited prohibitions on torture imposed by McCain's law.

McCain never once objected to Bush's open, explicit defiance of his cherished anti-torture legislation, preferring to bask in the media's glory while choosing to ignore the fact that his legislative accomplishment would amount to nothing. Put another way, McCain opted for the political rewards of grandstanding on the issue while knowing that he had accomplished little, if anything, in the way of actually promoting his "principles."

A virtual repeat of that sleight-of-hand occurred in 2006, when McCain first pretended to lead opposition to the Military Commissions Act (MCA), only thereafter to endorse this most radical, torture-enabling legislation, almost single-handedly ensuring its passage. After insisting that compelled adherence to the anti-torture ban of the Geneva Conventions was a nonnegotiable item for him, McCain ultimately blessed the MCA despite the fact that it *left it to the President to determine, in his sole discretion, which interrogation methods did or did not comply with the Conventions' provisions.*

Thus, once again, McCain created a self-image as a principled torture opponent with one hand, and with the other, ensured a legal framework that would not merely fail to ban, but would *actively enable,* the President's ability to continue using interrogation methods widely considered to be torture. Indeed, by casting himself as the Supreme Arbiter of torture morality, McCain's support for this torture-enabling law became Bush and Cheney's most potent instrument for legalizing the very interrogation methods that McCain, for so long, flamboyantly claimed to oppose. Such duplicitous behavior is all the more appalling when one considers that McCain's status as Torture Arbiter was largely grounded in the fact that he himself was tortured while imprisoned, yet he is nonetheless willing to act as compliant dupe, if not active enabler, in legalizing torture by the United States.

The coup de grace in the exposure of McCain as a torture enabler came in February 2008. Senate Democrats—in the face of their knowledge that McCain's Military Commissions Act allowed the President to continue to use torture techniques, such as waterboarding, and motivated by the refusal of new Bush attorney general Michael Mukasey to declare such practices illegal—introduced legislation that would outlaw waterboarding by *all agencies* of the U.S. government, including the C.I.A., rather than merely outlawing its use by the U.S. military, as McCain's 2005 DTA had done.

Faced with the clearest test yet of the authenticity of his claimed anti-torture convictions, McCain, as he sought to placate the far-right base of his party, left no doubt that his anti-torture posturing was pure political theater. While the anti-waterboarding law passed the Senate 51–45, McCain voted *against* the waterboarding ban, notwithstanding years of dramatic protests over this interrogation technique. Worse, McCain's excuse for his vote—that there was no need for the law since waterboarding was already illegal—was a complete falsehood, since discretion for determining the legality of waterboarding continues to rest with the President under the very law, the MCA, that *McCain caused to be enacted in 2006.*

If one were to attempt to create a caricature of a Great American Hypocrite, one could do no better than describing John McCain's behavior on this torture issue, one of his signature maverick positions. After years of self-serving posturing as the moral leader on torture and after basking endlessly in the media reverence that accompanied it, McCain worked behind the scenes on one measure after the next that *enabled and legalized* torture. Then, when faced with as clear-cut a vote as could be imagined, he opposed a law that would have outlawed the very methods that the Bush administration had admitted using and that McCain long insisted constituted torture.

McCain's media reputation as the honor-bound, integrity-laden man of the people fares no better when one examines his rather turbulent personal life. In 2004, the right-wing slime machine made much of John Kerry's marriage to a wealthy second wife, Teresa Heinz Kerry. The hatemongering swamps on the Right routinely cited his second marriage to label Kerry a "gigolo," as illustrated by an article published on Free Republic by Taki Theodoracopulos, which spewed,

> If John Kerry wins in November, he will be the premiere president of this great country of ours to be also a gigolo. The dictionary defines "gigolo" as a man supported by a woman in return for his sexual attentions and companionship. It might sound rough for John Kerry, but it's right to the point. Let's face it. The 44th president (maybe) is as close to a gigolo as I can think of, and I have known many. . . .
>
> Both Kerry and Clinton learned to lie early and often, and have continued the practice because it has served both men very well. When Clinton was elected, I was the first to refer to him not by his name but as the draft-dodger. If Kerry wins the prize, he will be known in this space as the gigolo, or Mr. Flip-Flop. Better yet, the flip-flop gigolo.

World Net Daily's Joseph Farah echoed this smear with his article entitled "President Gigolo" that contained gems such as this:

> But if there is one characteristic of Kerry's life that should disqualify him absolutely as a candidate for president, it

is the fact that he has sought out millionaire wives to take care of him. Not to put too fine a point on it, he's a serial gigolo.

Ann Coulter wrote that Kerry "clearly has no experience dealing with problems of typical Americans since he is a cad and a gigolo living in the lap of other men's money." Rush Limbaugh repeatedly called Kerry a "gigolo" on his radio program, with comments such as this one: "He's basically a skirt-chaser, folks. He's a gigolo."

Indeed, entering "Kerry" and "gigolo" into Google unearths thousands upon thousands of items from right-wing pundits, blogs, and other assorted appendages of the right-wing edifice mocking Kerry for his second marriage to an extremely wealthy woman and suggesting that his marriage was a reflection of a lack of ethics and even a lack of manlihood.

When John McCain was in Vietnam, his then-wife Carol was raising the couple's three small children. In 1969, with her husband imprisoned in Vietnam, Carol was in a near-fatal car accident. P.O.W. advocate H. Ross Perot paid for her medical care, but—as the *New York Times*'s Nicholas Kristof described in a 2000 article—"the injuries left her four inches shorter and on crutches, and she had gained a good deal of weight."

McCain learned of the disfiguring effects of the accident only upon seeing his wife for the first time once he returned to the United States. Quite disabled himself, McCain undertook an intensive rehabilitation regimen, and Carol continued to raise their children and support her husband through his tribulations.

By 1979, it was clear that McCain's naval career had stalled, and he had no hope of becoming an admiral, as both his father and grandfather were able to achieve. He had considered a political career back in 1976, when he was asked by local party officials to run for Congress, which he almost accepted. With few prospects for future advancement in his military career, McCain in 1979 began seriously contemplating the switch to politics, and at that time, he made severe changes in his personal life.

Despite still being married to his first wife, the mother of his children, McCain began, to use Kristof's description, "aggressively courting a twenty-five-year-old woman who was as beautiful as she was rich." That woman, Cindy Hensley, was (and is) the heiress to an enormous beer fortune, is eighteen years younger than McCain (and much younger than McCain's first wife), and eventually became the second Mrs. John McCain. Kristof described the process by which McCain was able to rid himself of his aging, overweight, mildly disabled first wife in favor of the young, beautiful, and extremely rich new wife, as follows:

> Mr. McCain has acknowledged running around with women and accepted responsibility for the breakup of the marriage, without going into details. But his supporters and his biographer, Robert Timberg, all suggest that the marriage had already effectively ended and that the couple had separated by the time he met Cindy, his present wife.
>
> That might be the most soothing way of explaining a politician's divorce from a disabled wife and his remarriage to a wealthy heiress, but it does not jibe with accounts of family members and friends. . . .
>
> Late that year, the McCains finally separated, and Mrs. McCain accepted a divorce the next February. Mr. McCain promptly married Miss Hensley, his present wife. . . .
>
> Mr. McCain's three children in the first marriage were less forgiving at first, and none of them were in attendance when he married Cindy. No one blamed Cindy, however, for she seemed shy and it was clear that Mr. McCain had been the pursuer.
>
> "I was certainly disappointed and mad at Dad," remembered Andy, who said it took almost four years for

his anger to evaporate. He added: "I hold him responsible. I don't hold Cindy responsible a bit."

Because Cindy's family was based in Arizona, McCain chose to make that state his home. In 1981, McCain moved to Phoenix and was promptly given a job by Cindy's wealthy and well-connected father, in a public relations capacity that enabled McCain to travel around the state giving speeches. A year later, McCain announced that he was running for Congress, and his new connection to a well-known, highly-regarded, and lavishly funded Arizona family gave him instant credibility and cache as a candidate. That election launched John McCain's career as a politician, with Cindy, his second wife, at his side.

If one examines America's presidential elections beginning in 1980 to the present, what one finds is a consistent and unchanging pattern. The Republican Party dresses up its leaders in all sorts of virtuous personality costumes. The establishment press, driven by the vapid dynamics of high school personality complexes, digests and then promotes that iconography. National elections are dominated by personality imagery and smears and are almost completely bereft of consideration of substantive issues. Worst of all, the personality images that dictate our election outcomes are not just petty, but entirely false, grounded in pure myth.

In every one of these critical aspects, John McCain is perfectly illustrative of the same twisted process that has infected our political discourse and converted our national elections into, using the words of John Harris and Mark Halperin, a personality-based freak show. The media depicts McCain as a moderate despite his warmongering extremism. He is heralded as a "new kind of Republican" even though, as a candidate, he is the spitting image of George W. Bush and, on the issues, a more or less reliable supporter of the defining Bush/Cheney policies. He is relentlessly painted as an independent, apolitical maverick despite a willingness to change positions the minute that doing so is politically expedient. The press refuses to subject him to critical scrutiny because of their great personal affection for him. And he is held out as the honor-bound truth-teller despite both a public and private life that has long ceased to contain any actual acts of honor and truth-telling.

John McCain is a natural candidate, right at home in a political party led by Great American Hypocrites and with a press corps that reveres great American hypocrisy. The press adores him for the same vapid, personality-based reasons it adored George W. Bush. And McCain's media-built and media-sustained reputation as a trans-partisan man of principle and conviction is every bit as genuine as it was in the case of Bush. If the GOP-media machinery manages to elect him, he will undoubtedly produce extremely similar—if not worse—results.

ACKNOWLEDGMENTS

In the Acknowledgments section of my previous book, I noted that the collaborative nature of blogging, whereby one is endlessly interacting with readers, commenters, and other bloggers on a daily basis, renders it impossible to trace and thus acknowledge the exact genesis of every idea one has. That is still true. Where I was able to recall the original inspiration for a particular insight, I was as diligent as could be in crediting specific bloggers, but many of the unaccredited ideas in this book are undoubtedly the by-product of my being able to read the work of all sorts of political bloggers and comments from my readers. Constant exposure to new ideas, and having one's old ideas subjected to rigorous and immediate scrutiny, are among the principal benefits of the medium.

Numerous individuals provided invaluable assistance in the writing of this book. My agent, Dan Conaway, and my Crown editor, Sean Desmond, were both instrumental in shaping the theme of the book and helping to create its structure. Two students, Vincent Rossmeier of NYU's School of Journalism and Matthew Berman of George Washington University, provided superb, comprehensive research assistance with regard to virtually every topic covered here. And Mona Holland once again wielded a merciless editing pen in order to eliminate verbosity and keep the arguments tight and focused.

On a more personal level, several people are always due thanks for anything I produce, including Werner Achatz, Mark Greenwald, and my parents. And, as always, David Miranda is my eternal partner in everything, at the center of everything I do.

INDEX

ABOUT THE AUTHOR

Glenn Greenwald, a former constitutional lawyer, is author of the political blog Unclaimed Territory, at *Salon,* where he is also a contributing writer. His reporting and analysis have been cited by the *New York Times,* the *Washington Post,* the *Los Angeles Times,* and numerous publications. His first two books, *A Tragic Legacy* and *How Would a Patriot Act?,* were *New York Times* bestsellers.